MERTHYR
HISTORIAN

Cyfarthfa Park, Merthyr. 1912.

MERTHYR
HISTORIAN

— *Volume Seven* —

MERTHYR TYDFIL HISTORICAL SOCIETY
SOUTH WALES
1994

ISBN 0 9504845 8 X
1994
Printed and Bound in the UK by WBC
Book Manufacturers Bridgend
Mid Glamorgan
Typeset by Photosetting, Yeovil (01935) 23684

INTRODUCTION

The success which attended recent publications of the Merthyr Tydfil Historical Society has encouraged the Society to produce Volume Seven in the *Merthyr Historian* series.

The first offering is an account of the life and work of Robert and Lucy Thomas, researched and written by well-known Merthyr genealogist and television personality, Mrs. Eira Smith.

Next comes an essay by Edward Rhys-Price, recalling memories of Abercanaid, childhood, schooldays, going down the mine. He gives some account of his life in Canada, when he emigrated there. Experiences as a seaman are also related.

The third essay, written by retired teacher, and well known weather expert, Josh Powell, is an account of the history of the village of Cwmbargoed. Mr. Powell contribruted an essay "Winter, Nineteen- Forty Seven" to *Merthyr Historian*, Volume Five, and has written several books on local topics.

The fourth item, by long serving Honorary Secretary of Merthyr Tydfil Historical Society, Hugh Watkins, is a Diary of Mr. Watkins's personal involvement in the aftermath of the Aberfan Disaster. Hugh has many publications to his credit, including an essay "A Valley Comprehensive, Afon Taf High School, The First Twenty-Five Years, 1967-1992", which appeared in *Merthyr Historian*, Volume Five, 1992.

Item five recalls an old-time journey, on the Brecon and Merthyr Railway, and on other long-gone local railways.

The period 1893-1902 witnessed intense building activity in Merthyr Tydfil and district. Chapels, Churches, Libraries, Schools, a Town Hall, and Waterworks were constructed. Our sixth contribution contains accounts of Stone Laying Ceremonies and Opening Ceremonies for sixteen of these structures.

Veteran local historian and President of the Merthyr Tydfil Historical Society, Dr. Joseph Gross, contributed the seventh essay, an account of The Standing Conference of the History of the South Wales Valleys. Dr. Gross has long and very close links with The Standing Conference, and explains a link with the Aberfan Disaster. He contributed an essay "Merthyr Tydfil: The Development of an Urban Community" to *Merthyr Historian*, Volume Five, and has many other publications to his credit.

The eighth piece gives accounts, by Charles Wilkins, of the life and work of three Merthyr artists.

The ninth essay is an account of a Natural History Society which flourished in Merthyr about a hundred years ago.

In 1882 an Army engineer, Colonel Frederick Beaumont, cut a tunnel one mile long from Dover towards France, work was then stopped for political reasons. A second tunnel, begun in 1973, was abandoned in 1975, because of escalating costs. A Channel Tunnel was finally opened to goods traffic in 1994. The brief tenth contribution reproduces an account of an 1882 sermon, by the Rev. John Griffith, lively Rector of Merthyr, giving his views on the proposed 1882 Channel Tunnel.

Next we have an account of Pant Hospital by Mrs. Ann Lewis, who was co-author of an article on Morlais Morgan, Dowlais vocalist, in *Merthyr Historian*, Volume Five.

The twelfth offering is an account of the life and work of Merthyr-born artist, Penry Williams, by fellow-artist Thomas Henry Thomas, who visited Penry at his Rome studio. Examples of Penry Williams's work may be examined at Cyfarthfa Castle Museum, and postcards may be purchased.

The story of William Menelaus, Dowlais, a Giant in the world of Iron and Steel manufacture follows, related by Cardiff Librarian, J. Brynmor Jones and T. F. Holley. These authors contributed an essay "The Martin Family of Dowlais" to *Merthyr Historian*, Volume Six.

Finally, Dowlais-born Professor Glanmor Williams has provided reminiscences of his early schooldays at Pant School in the period 1924 to 1931.

The Editor wishes to thank the authors for placing their essays at the disposal of the Historical Society, for publication.

Thanks are tendered to the Committee, including Messrs. H. Watkins, J. Gross, J. Owen, R. Jenkins, J. Powell, Glyn Bowen, Keith Lewis, Mrs. A. Lewis and Mrs. Kate Williams, for advice and encouragement to the Editor.

The staff of Merthyr Central Library, including Mr. James, Mrs. Caroline Jacob and Mr. Downey, are thanked for their unfailing kindness and help, Mr. Derek Phillips, Cyfarthfa Castle Museum and Art Gallery, is thanked for providing photographs.

Those persons and institutions who have generously supported the Historical Society, by purchasing its publications, are accorded a hearty vote of thanks. The work of Mr. John Lloyd, *Daily Express*, in compiling reviews of the Society's publications, is greatly appreciated.

Finally, thanks are due to Colin Mawer, Commercial Director, W. B. C. Book Manufacturers Limited, Bridgend, for his invaluable help with Volume Seven and the two previous Volumes.

T. F. HOLLEY.
Chairman and Editor.
52, Chester Close, Heolgerrig,
Merthyr Tydfil. CF48 1SW.

CONTENTS

Robert and
Lucy Thomas

by Eira Smith

Life would never be the same for the residents of Lower High Street, Merthyr Tydfil, from the time a fountain with ornate canopy, and two horse troughs were erected in the middle of this part of the High Street.

Two inns, the "Carmarthen Arms" and the "Blue Bell" were demolished in 1904, to allow easier access along the main road into town. During the inquiry to the Incorporation Act in 1897, Mr. C. A. Cripps, Q.C., M.P., criticised the entrance to the town. When he questioned Mr. Thomas Fletcher Harvey, surveyor and engineer to the Merthyr Urban District Council, he referred to the buildings as a "throttle valve", as they stood at right angle from the shops, with a narrow foot-path between the shops and the "Carmarthen Arms". This inn together with the "Blue Bell" stood across the main road, leading to the entrance of Cross Keys Street, and so obstructed the flow of traffic.

In 1906, when the site was cleared the fountain and troughs were erected and became a landmark. In later years the annual carnival at Whitsun, organised for the Merthyr General Hospital, as part of the Fete and Gala, and ceremonial parades, e.g. Remembrance Day on November 11th, all assembled and commenced from this memorial, as recollected by the local residents.

Sir William Thomas Lewis and William Thomas Rees, of Aberdare, erected the fountain and troughs, and presented them to their native town, in commemoration of Robert and Lucy Thomas, of Waunwyllt, in this parish, the pioneers in 1828 of the South Wales coal trade. Both men were related to Robert and Lucy Thomas. Sir William Thomas Lewis was born in Plymouth Street at 3 a.m. on the 5th August 1837, and later married Miss Anne Rees, their grand-daughter, and William Thomas Rees was her brother.

Their ancestors, Job Williams and Ann James were married by licence at Neath

1

on the 27th February, 1780. Lucy their daughter was baptised at Llansamlet on the 11th March, 1781. Lucy Williams married Robert Thomas on the 13th June, 1802, at Llansamlet. Nothing is known of them until 1816, when they occupied CWMCANAID, in the hamlet of Gellideg, Merthyr Tydfil.

It has been difficult to trace the site of Cwmcanaid, but it was probably south of Cwm Pit colliery, in the Canaid Brook valley, and so covered by the refuse of the mine in later years. Coal was obtained from a level at this site as early as 1768, for the Cyfarthfa Ironworks. Both the poor law rate for 1816 and the land tax assessments revealed that Robert Thomas occupied Cwmcanaid, and that it was owned by Lord Dynevor and Richards. The land was valued at £4. In 1821, Robert Thomas together with Richard Morgan was an assessor of the land tax, and his bold signature can be seen on the document.

In 1824, he wrote to John Maughan, an agent of the Earl of Plymouth. He replied on the 29th December, 1824, and gave permission for Robert to "Work coal and iron-stone on the estate of the Right Honourable, the Earl of Plymouth called Wayn Wyllt in the parish of Merthyr Tydfil, paying a shilling a ton Royalty for each, reserving to the said Earl or any one who may hold under him the power of letting Mine and Coal for the establishment of Iron Works upon the said property leaving to yourself a *Sale* Colliery to the extent of 4,000 tons annually on such lease." The letter was badly mutilated and some lines are missing, but John Maughan wished, "The concern may prove of benefit to you, and that you will experience no interruption in the forming and using your intended Railway to the Wharf and Canal."

Robert wasted no time and on the 28th January, 1825, he wrote from Cwmcanaid, to the committee of the Glamorganshire Canal, and the letter read, "Having taken a Colliery from Lord Plymouth under Wayn Wyllt and Penlan in the parish of Merthyr Tydfil, at the distance of 320 yards from the line of your Canal, it is my intention to make a communication with your Canal by means of a Tram Road under the Powers of your Act." He continued to ask, "That you will grant me permission to make a small wharf in the side of your Canal adjoining the Farm of Clyndyris." We can tell from this information that the level was south east from the farm we call Waun Wyllt. This farm lies on the Merthyr end of the Aberdare tunnel, on the left hand side, and Cwm Pit lay on the right.

Further information about this site was revealed by Robert Fletcher's report on the coal and iron mines belonging to the Earl of Plymouth, in Merthyr Tydfil, when he wrote to Mr. Henry H. Oddie, another agent of the Earl. He said, "In an estate called WHINE WHILT near the western bank of the river Taf, a coal vein 6ft in thickness has lately been opened by Robert Thomas, who is now oc-

2

cupier of a part of the said estate. From this vein a supply of coal for the neighbourhood, and a conveyance for the same to the canal by means of a Railway might be easily obtained under the power of the Canal Act. In this estate within the depth of about 100 yards from the surface are 8 several veins of coal, the aggregate thickness of which is about 14 yards, and within the depth of 120 yards from the surface, and principally within the last 20 yards there are mines of Iron Stone averaging in the aggregate about 2 yards in thickness. The working of the coal so opened by Robert Thomas, has been suspended, but if it were to be continued it might produce to his Lordship from £100 to £200 per annum."

No reason was given for the suspension, but in the meantime Robert was employed by the estate agents to bore for coal at Llanfabon, Glamorgan. Obviously his knowledge of coal levels had been recognised by them, and in the Plymouth Estate accounts we read that he was paid on the 17th December, 1825 "£100 towards expenses incurred in searching for coal at Lanvabon." On the 4th January, 1827 he was paid a further £60, and there was another payment on the 22nd December, 1829 of £25.0s.6d, the balance of the account, "For boring at Lanvabon and for sundry matters connected with Wain Wyllt Tramroad."

The accounts give details of payments for improving the housing and general maintenance of the Earl's properties, as well as any mining operations. There are several of these accounts for Waun Wyllt and the one for the 15th May, 1826, reads as follows:

Repairing at Wain Wyllt, Merthyr:

Paid					
Wm Snelling	blacksmith			18.	11
Dd Morgan	mason		13.	3.	8
T. B.. Evans	ironmonger		2.	15.	7 ½
Rd Lewis	tiler		2.	2.	0 ½
Rd Lewis	for labour and tiles		1.	17.	7 ½
Wm Richards	carpenter		8.	0.	5
Wm Richards	carpenter		3.	13.	5
H. Miles	for nails		1.	4.	9
T. B. Evans	ironmonger			7.	9
T. Prothero	sawyer		4.	3.	0
Dd Isaac	for flagstones			17.	0
			£39.	4.	2 ½

On the 17th June, 1825, Robert Thomas received £100 from the estate towards the monies he had expended on the Waun Wyllt colliery. Later a further £23.5s for a drain he cut, measuring 92 perches 5 yards and yet another £12.19s for the carriage of lime and stones. The earl's estate even paid the £1 poor levy, on land planted at Waun Wyllt and Penlan.

By December 1826, Robert Thomas was purchasing wood from the estate which cost him £19.4s.6d. He started paying royalties on the coal raised between the 23rd June and the 31st October, 1828, and this amounted to:

882 tons of coal @ 1/-	£44.1.0
409 tons of small coal @ 4d	6.16.4
	£50.17.4

and this was the commencement of the Waun Wyllt colliery.

From the 1st November, 1828 to the 2nd May, 1829, 2,434 tons of coal were raised, and a total amount in royalties of £247.15.6d was paid during the rest of the year. Now the colliery at Waun Wyllt was repaying the Earl of Plymouth for the outlay, and the faith the agents had in Robert Thomas as each year the royalties rose. There was a price increase on the small coal royalty from 4d to 6d per ton. Pitwood was purchased from Dan y derri, Pant Glaes, Coedcae Bont as well as Pontygwaith, and so the surrounding areas were being denuded of trees on behalf of the growth of the coal trade. Beech and oak were also sold, but the woodlands were planted to replenish these trees.

Robert sold his coal to the house holders of Merthyr Tydfil, and its reputation for its intense heat and smokeless quality interested Mr. George Insole, a coal dealer in domestic coal. He came to Cardiff in 1827 and became a coal shipper as well as a coal owner. The quality of the "Waun Wyllt" four foot seam coal, as it was now called, encouraged him to buy two boat loads from Robert Thomas, for which he paid him £14, on the 10th February, 1829. It was fortunate for Robert that he had overcome the opposition of the ironmaster, William Crawshay, thus enabling him to use the Canal. He had opened an account with the Glamorganshire Canal Coy. in July 1828, and the first entry of his coal to Cardiff was in February, 1829.

George Insole as an independent coal shipper, acted as an agent for Robert, and he sent small cargoes of the coal to Devon, Cornwall and Ireland. In November, 1830, a small cargo was sent to London on the ship *Mars*. The profit for Insole was £19.11s, hardly warranting sending it so far. The smokeless quality and the steam-raising power of the coal attracted attention at the London Coal Exchange. In 1831, Insole contracted to supply 3,000 tons of Waun Wyllt coal to Edward Wood & Co., London. He also sent a small cargo to Malta in the same year.

Robert's coal was considered to be the most superior of all sent from the valleys to London, and Insole urged him to send more. However, on the 19th

February, 1833, Robert Thomas died, aged 58 years. His estate was valued as being under £1,000, and his wife Lucy was granted probate. At the court were George Insole, now termed gentleman of Cardiff, and Lucy's eldest son William, a farmer of Waun Wyllt. On the 13th March, 1833, all three were sworn that the information given by them was correct, as Robert did not leave a will. On the same day William Thomas received a cheque from George Insole for the balance of £41.10s, he owed to Robert for coal. From that time, George Insole paid Lucy Thomas for the coal dispatched to him by her. They vary from month to month, from nearly £200 to above that amount.

In October, 1833, Lucy had headed paper printed (as illustrated). This was an aid for her on the accounts as she could not write, and signed her name with the mark "X". During Robert's busy years of extracting coal there had been no mention of Lucy, until the accounts were changed to her name, after his death. She had been busy raising a family of two girls and six boys. It has been difficult to ascertain the births of these children, because they were Unitarian non-conformists. The deaths of this family are also not recorded, in the records available for the Hen Dy Cwrdd Chapel, Cefn Coed y Cymmer, Breconshire, where the family are buried. However, from the monumental inscriptions and death certificates I have ascertained the following births.

| William | 1805, | Margaret | 1806, | Robert | 1810, | David | 1812, |
| Catherine | 1814, | Thomas | 1817, | Francis | 1820, | John | 1825. |

and there will be more on these children.

Lucy together with her eldest son William, continued to extract coal from Waun Wyllt, and George Insole begged them to transport more coal to him. On the 1st May, 1838, a lease was signed by them with the Morgan family of the Graig estate for 59 acres. The rental for these acres was £1,000 per annum and the royalties were 1s.3d. for large coal and 6d per ton for the small coal.

In 1836, Insole supplied the Cardiff & Bristol Steam Packet Co. with 21½ tons of coal weekly for use on their two cross-Channel steamers, *The Prince of Wales* and the *Lady Charlotte*. The Glamorganshire Canal Co. returns ending 31st December, 1839, show that Lucy Thomas sent 17,097 tons of coal to Cardiff but only 9,771 tons were sent to London.

The royalties Lucy paid between 1st May, 1837 to 31st October, 1837, show what she paid per ton, and where the coal was sent:

6100	tons of large coal		@ 1/6 per ton	£457.	10.	0
54	tons of large coal	to Landaff	@ 1/7 per ton	5.	8.	0
3314	tons of large coal	to Merthyr	@ 1/- per ton	165.	14.	0
360	tons of large coal	to Pontyrun	@ 1/6 per ton	27.	0.	0

300	tons of small coal	to Cardiff	@ 1/- per ton	15.	0.	0
860	tons of sundries		@ 1/- per ton	43.	0.	0
				£713.	12.	0

Iron ore was also extracted from the estate for which 1s.0d per ton royalty was paid. Each year the royalties grew and a William Williams was paid £65 per annum, by the Plymouth estate to weigh the coal extracted by Lucy.

Nothing is known of the men and boys employed at both collieries, but it is said to be about 50. The 1841 census reveals that her sons were employed in the coal industry, and some lived in Upper Abercanaid. Only her son John resided with her, possibly at the property now called Abercanaid House. Next door the Baptists built a chapel called Shiloh, on ground leased by Lucy. When the congregation became too large, the members built another chapel, once used as a schoolroom in lower Abercanaid, called "Deml".

Lucy and William are named on another lease granted to the Welsh Calvanistic Methodists on Graig land. This chapel subsided because of the coal mining beneath the building, and a new chapel called the "Graig" was built near "Deml". The grave-yard of the old Graig still exists and is of special interest to local historians for the monumental inscriptions.

At one time there were 46 properties in Upper Abercanaid. The 1841 and 1851 census do not name the streets. However, the 1861 census names them as being:

    9   properties in Chapel Square
   15   properties in Lewis Square
   13   properties in Roberts Square
    8   properties in Quay Row
    1   property uninhabited which is possibly Abercanaid House
  46

No documentation seems to exist on any of these prior to the beginning of this century and, so it is possible Abercanaid House was built in 1835. If so, Lucy as a coal merchant and her son John, together with a female servant, lived there in 1841. Her son William lived with his sister Margaret at the "White Hart" inn nearby. In 1843, he opened a coal mine in Aberdare called the "Lletty Shenkin". When he died in Swansea in 1850 his will revealed he had made a Deed of Settlement on the 18th September, 1849, in which the collieries called the Graig and Lletty Shenkin, had been entrusted to Lewis Lewis, David Sims and his brother-in-law William Rees. His estate was valued under £2,000 when he died.

Lucy suffered with typhoid fever for 14 days before her death on the 27th September, 1847, at Abercanaid, aged 66 years. She had made a Will in January that year, which is quite revealing. Her son William already held a half share in the Graig colliery, so she left her half share between the remainder of her children. However, she did leave William her house and garden valued at £180, four cottages and a stable; these would be in the grounds of Abercanaid House, valued at £150. He also inherited all the household furniture, plate, plated articles, linens, china, household effects, double barrel gun and pouch valued together at £57.11s. The inventory of the Graig colliery was more revealing: horses, plant, trams, colliers' tools, engine, crab winder, rope, carpenter's shop, blacksmith shop, two dwelling houses, coal, all valued at £4,576.15s.0d and William's half share amounted to £2,288.7s.6d, so this amount was also her half share.

Her interest at the Waun Wyllt colliery consisted of horses, plant, trams, colliers' tools, boats, coal, valued at £817. Together with mortgages, notes and cash valued at £6,035.5s, her estate was valued at £11,448.3s.6d.

The bequest to her daughter Margaret Jenkins was the "White Hart" inn valued at £200, £20 more than Lucy's house, and three houses adjoining valued at £150. Her son Robert, a collier, had gone to live in Caedraw and became a grocer. He died of tuberculosis on the 31st May, 1847, so Lucy left to his children eight leasehold houses in Upper Abercanaid, valued at £320. Another son, David, also died of tuberculosis, from which he suffered eight months until his death on the 1st April, 1850. Lucy left him four leasehold houses valued at £160 and a further four leasehold properties valued at £120, also 13 houses at Cethin Farm valued at £520.

To her daughter Catherine Rees, Lucy left six leasehold houses valued at £210. Catherine had married William Rees, a grocer of Aberdare, and they lived near the Iron Bridge. They were to inherit from the estate of her brother William Thomas. Catherine and William were the parents of Anne, who married William Thomas Lewis, later to become Lord Merthyr of Senghennydd.

Lucy did not forget her two brothers. William Williams, a victualler, of Swansea was to manage the Waun Wyllt colliery, and her brother John was to receive 8 shillings a week. Nothing is further known of these two brothers. The trustees of her estate were Lewis Lewis, clerk to the magistrates of Merthyr Tydfil, and William Williams, a victualler of Troedyrhiw, who between them inherited five houses valued at £240. They were responsible for monies to be invested for her grand children. From the administration granted by the courts to her sons' widows and children, descendants can be traced of this woman with the "indefatigable spirit".

It is difficult to obtain a true picture of Lucy as her Will tells of no jewellery or clothing, i.e. personal items. It gives locations of her properties surrounding her house, so she still gathered her family around her in these properties. It was not a healthy family, as only her daughter Margaret Jenkins of the "White Hart" inn lived to 71 years of age. Interred with Lucy and Robert Thomas at Hen dy Cwrdd are her sons:

Thomas	died 22nd December,	1835	aged 18 years
Francis	died 28th May,	1843	aged 23 years of a fever
John	died 14th June,	1843	aged 18 years
William	died 5th June,	1850	aged 45 suddenly at Swansea.

Behind this grave is that of the Rees family and from that we know Catherine died on the 20th November, 1860, aged 46 years. The Jenkins' family grave is to the right hand side, a tall monument. The inscriptions have been obliterated from the headstone at the foot of Lucy and Robert's grave, which is the grave of Robert and his family, their son.

Possibly the only description we have of Lucy was from the memoirs of John Nixon, who travelled to Merthyr to purchase coal from her, to no avail. He found her at the Graig colliery carrying on a very good business, "She sat in her office, a wooden hut near the pit's mouth and traded for cash, placing in a basket over her head the moneys which she received for her coal. Her cleverness, her witty tongue, her pleasant manner were known to all the countryside. At her pit's mouth it may be said that the poetry of the Arcadian world joined hands with the prose of a busier time to come. 'Laughing girls' like those who trod the wine-press of old (save that they were grimy with coal-dust), handled the coal, sorting it by hand and picking out the lumps, which were afterwards placed on boats, "as carefully as if each lump was an egg; and Mrs. Thomas was then raising the amount, considerable in those days of 150 tons by the day." This was the lady who came to be called, "The mother of the Welsh Steam Coal Trade".

When the fountain and troughs were erected in Lower High Street, by Sir William Thomas Lewis and his brother-in-law, they must have admired the Thomas family greatly. Several of the properties have been demolished at Upper Abercanaid, but Abercanaid House still dominates the surroundings. The Rees family went to live there after the deaths of Lucy and William to whom she willed it. In 1871, Thomas William Lewis with some of his children went to live there, since his son had married Anne Rees. We again find him living there in 1891 until his death, aged 81 years, on the 10th February 1900. He was a civil and mechanical engineer for the Plymouth Works. Sir William Thomas Lewis purchased the property on the 4th November, 1908.

For those of us who grew up in the Merthyr area the name "Lucy" is synonymous with the drift mines opened by the Thomas Merthyr Colliery Company between 1906 and 1946, until the National Coal Board was established.

In 1995, the canopy of the old fountain together with a new fountain is to be erected again on a suitable site. Reminder of Robert and Lucy Thomas pioneers of the Welsh Steam Coal Trade, in 1828, and visitors should have a more appreciative view when it is moved from its present site, against St. Tydfil's church yard, to wherever its new site will be.

Acknowledgements

I wish to thank the staff of the National Library of Wales, Aberystwyth; the Glamorgan Records Office, Cardiff; the Central Library, Merthyr Tydfil, especially Mrs. Carolyn Jacob; the Registrar Merthyr Tydfil; the staff of Merthyr Tydfil Borough Council, especially Mrs. Muriel Davies and Mr. Peter Coughlin; Dr. and Mrs. T. F. Holley; the residents of Upper Abercanaid; Mr. Eddie Thomas and Mr. Clive Thomas; all my old neighbours of Cross Keys Street and Lower High Street; and a special thank you to the men of NACRO, Mid. Glamorgan, without whose help Hen dy Cwrdd cemetery would not have been cleared. Apologies to anyone I have omitted.

Abercanaid, Some Remembered Yesterdays

by EDWARD RHYS-PRICE

The Death of my Father

My father was a coal miner. He was a good man, strict but very fair. If he told us children to do anything we did it. If we boys stayed out late or created a disturbance in the street this sometimes resulted in a visit from the local policeman. He would have a few words with my father and on leaving he would always say, "I'll leave the matter in your hands." That meant a firm warning from Father and early bedtime without any supper. If our father left the house for only a short time our mother called us and we scampered downstairs for a quick snack, then back to bed. We never boasted that we had got the better of him and we took heed of his warning because we did not want a repeat performance. He was a strong man who shrugged off all illnesses, but after an accident at the mine in July 1911 he developed pneumonia due to the heat and damp of the mine and that is what killed him. He was ill for about a week at home and my mother nursed him to the best of her ability. I was nine years old when he died at the age of forty-four.

There was a hospital at Merthyr, but when he died the post-mortem was carried out at our house on the kitchen table and my mother could hear the saw going through his bones. She was grief-stricken after his death. We came into the kitchen on the morning of the funeral to find her sitting by the fire where she had stayed all night. After we had washed and dressed ourselves we children made only a pretence of eating breakfast. We were content to drink our tea and leave the table one by one. We were allowed to spend the morning as we wished

10

in a quiet and orderly manner until the time came for us to be dressed in our black suits and stiff white collars.

When all the mourners had assembled in our house and the pastor had commenced his prayers, my brothers and myself were comforted by our uncles who placed their hands on our shoulders, the better to sustain us in our grief. Taking our example from them we too were brave and did not burst into tears when the plain oak coffin was lifted from the trestles in our tiny front parlour. When the pastor ended his prayers with the words, "Father in Heaven, comfort this widow and her children now..." my mother's sobs broke out anew. She was still crying as the family and other mourners followed the coffin outside and it was placed on the hearse drawn by horses.

Four or five of us got into a horse-drawn cab but the floor was so rotten we were almost afraid to put our feet down in case they went through the boards. The horses were equally decrepit and the three miles to Cefn Coed Cemetery seemed a very long way. It was a very hot day and the sun shimmered on the red earth of my father's grave on its hillside overlooking the river that hurried to the sea. During the graveside service I was aware of a farmer attending to his sheep in a field above the cemetery. Their bleating mingled with the pastor's last words, "Ashes to ashes, dust to dust..." For the earth which sustains us also receives us.

We journeyed home in the same dismal black cab drawn by the now tired horses. As we neared the village school the children streamed through the school gates, some to hurry home, some to linger at roadside games. When the period of mourning had passed I would join them in their games again. There would be swimming in the old canal and other games which changed with the seasons. But today their laughter contrasted strongly with my depressed state after burying a good and loving father and for many days afterwards we children would comfort our mother in her heavy sorrow.

When we got back to the house the first thing we noticed was the strong smell of mothballs which were used to fumigate the room where the coffin had been. Food was waiting, prepared by my mother and the other women. They were in mourning, of course, but in Wales at that time no woman ever attended a funeral, not even of her own husband or child.

When another long night had passed we found that again our mother had not slept. She had passed the night crying to herself by the fireside which had grown cold.

But time and work mercifully make us face our duties. There were meals to prepare and household duties to be taken up again. So our mother released her hold on our dead father and prepared to sustain her children. The long night had passed and morning had come again. Many years later when I was a grown man living in America I woke up one morning with the events of that day so vividly in my mind that it was as though I was a child again and had just come back from burying my father.

It was at such times of trouble and misfortune that the spirit of help and togetherness was so evident in these mining villages of Wales. Before the funeral, neighbours would take the youngest children of a bereaved family to their own homes out of the way. If a man was injured in an accident in the mine a prize draw would be got up, and anyone who could, donated small items such as cigarettes or a small bottle of whisky. The tickets were sold for sixpence each. It was very rare for anyone in the village to refuse to buy one because they never knew when it might be their turn to need such help.

There was a strange sequel to my father's death. Not long afterwards my uncle Hugh died. He lived in the house opposite ours in Nightingale Street so the window blinds in our house were drawn for quite a while as was the custom in those days. I was in bed with my brother in one of the two upstairs rooms and my two brothers were in the bed alongside us. My three brothers were asleep, but I was still awake and suddenly I saw standing by my bed a white form with arms outstretched. I knew it was my father because I recognised his features, but I was so afraid I hid under the bedclothes until I eventually fell asleep. I have been told that I must have been thinking of my father at the time, but in fact I was thinking, as boys do, that when I was grown up I would be able to buy a motorcycle, so I was not thinking about my father at all. The next night the same thing happened and again I hid under the bedclothes, but this time it was a long time before I fell asleep. I was very scared.

Next day I did everything I could to try to tire myself out so that I would fall asleep as soon as I got into bed. I ran up the mountain, swam in the canal and tried to make myself really exhausted, but I still stayed awake and my father appeared to me again. This went on for a few days until my Uncle Hugh's funeral.

A few days later I was invited to a seance in the village. These were quite regular occurrences and some of us young people would gather in someone's house. Perhaps this seems a strange thing to do, but you must remember there was no radio and television in people's homes so we all had to make our own amusements and this is one of the things we did. On this occasion we sat round a heavy oak table and as we sang a hymn the table moved in time with our singing.

When our hostess asked if anyone wanted to say anything I mentioned what had happened the previous week when I had seen my father in my bedroom for several nights running while my uncle lay dead in the house across the street from ours. She asked if I wished to speak to my father. When I said I did she started a series of knocks and after a few minutes announced that the spirit of my father was near and his message to me was, "I have been with you in your bedroom for five nights and why did you not speak to me?" In my reply I said I had been terribly afraid and would he refrain from coming to see me again. The reply was "Yes" and I never saw him again.

Because my father had died of pneumonia and not as a direct result of the accident the coal company refused to pay any compensation whatsoever to my mother. She did receive a small payment from an insurance company. It was enough to pay for the funeral and the headstone, that is all. There were several stone-masons in Cefn Coed so the headstones were not too expensive. Because she had a large family to bring up my mother was forced to apply for parish relief. This was administered by a Board of Guardians made up of prominent businessmen in Merthyr. They each gave a small sum each week and this was distributed to the people who needed it.

Each Monday the relieving officer would come to our house and those of us who were still at home had to stand against the wall in the kitchen with my mother and all had to look suitably contrite as though we had committed some awful crime. The relief my mother got was around nine shillings a week. This went on for some time until a school master, Mr. T. T. Jenkins, was elected to the Board of Guardians. He came round to see us and asked if we were satisfied with the way everything was done. My mother described how we had to stand in a row and told of the others who were made to do the same. This school master at the next meeting made such a fuss about this that the Board of Guardians was afraid the row would be printed in the *Merthyr Express*, so they asked the offending man to mend his ways. On the next Monday my mother was astonished when he bade her good morning and of course there was no more lining up against the kitchen wall for us children.

My mother could never afford to buy any of us children new clothes. When anyone in the village died their clothes were passed on to the poorer families and then the travelling dressmaker altered them to fit. I can remember going to school in a mourning suit with black braid on the front. If any of my friends at school thought fit to make any rude remarks about this they were taken into a quiet corner and given a couple of thumps and that was the end of it.

I was very pleased when at the age of ten I got a job collecting the bundles of newspapers from the railway station and taking them to the news agents. For this I received sixpence a week which at least was a help to my mother. I have often thought what a very remarkable woman she was. Not only did she cook and garden for her large family, but she had remarkable powers of healing. If a child in the village was screaming and could not sleep my mother was sent for. I have seen her stroke the child's head and face with her hands until it very quickly quietened and fell asleep. I am sure that if she had been born into different circumstances she could have been a doctor.

Our grandmother, Mary Griffiths, Mam's mother, lived with us until she died in 1921 at the age of 84 after falling down in the garden. The doctor said she had broken a bone in her leg and at her age there was no hope of it knitting together again. So for one and a half weeks we had to watch her die. She had never worn glasses and could see to sew without them. We younger children used to share her bed when we were little, so she was like a second mother to us.

She barely understood English and preferred to converse in Welsh. I believe that as a young woman she had worked in the coal mines, never earning more than 4s 6d a week, but she would not discuss her past life with anyone.

My father was descended from a Brecon sheep farmer who had a small acreage high on the mountains. As a grown man I searched for my father's birthplace and found the farmhouse in ruins, but the canopied bed was still in place in the kitchen. My great grandfather, who was born around 1780, lies buried in the village churchyard not far away.

My grandmother on my father's side was a very thrifty woman, born on a farm in Breconshire. When I remember her she was living in a little house near Castle Pit about a mile from Abercanaid on the side of the mountains. Some people called Castle Pit the slaughter house because so many miners were killed there. Some coal mines are favoured by nature with big seams and strong roofs, but Castle Pit was presumably in unstable ground. My grandmother kept hens and a vegetable garden and pigs. In those days five terraced houses could be bought for £100. She wanted to buy a house for my father, but the price could not be agreed upon so no house was bought, but such was her thrift that when she died in her early fifties 800 golden sovereigns were found in the house and her second husband got rid of it all in about a twelve month through drink and other pleasures.

When my mother died in the 1940s we thought she was seventy-six, but on checking at Somerset House some years later I found she had actually been seventy-eight. She died in Nightingale Street where she had spent all her married life, at number 21, a house which my brother Tom had bought for about £100, looked after by her three daughters. As she lay dying she said that if she had been worth a million pounds she could not have been looked after better. The doctor who attended her said she was suffering from no illness, her body was simply worn out by her hard life. I tried to find out something at Somerset House at the same time about Mary Griffiths, my grandmother, but could find no record of her there.

School Days

Before I'd barely finished my breakfast the Abercanaid Mixed School bell would be calling me to lessons.

It was nothing to see a young lad arrive at school clad in his sister's shoes and wearing a full grown man's funeral suit, cut down to size by the travelling dressmaker, who spent at least one week a year, every year, in my village. If an idiot boy was daft enough to pass any rude remarks about another's clothing it was soon remedied. A few well placed thumps was known to have a marvellous stilling effect upon hurtful tongues.

The school at Abercanaid was run by Merthyr District Council and was divided into Infant and Junior in two separate buildings. After two years in the Infants we were moved up to the Juniors. I started school between the ages of five and six, and left at thirteen. How I ever achieved grade 7 I shall never know as, apart from English, History and Geography, I was a complete dunce, but I still love all those things today.

Our school day began with a religious service and then the hall would be partitioned off into classrooms. We sat at individual wooden desks, each with his own china inkwell, ready for you to blot your page. I did plenty of blotting because other than for History I was a complete dummy. Our teacher sat out in front, near the fire in Winter and in Summer he would spend time chasing the blackboard around the room out of the way of the sunlight's glare.

We had one Welsh language lesson a week but no-one seemed to care whether we learned anything or not, it seemed simply a formality. I did learn enough from it to understand the meanings of Welsh place-names but that is about all. Funny that a Welsh-speaking North Walian should once a week badly teach us Welsh-speaking children grammatical Welsh. Seventy per cent of my class spoke Welsh at home but at school it was passively discouraged. It was the same in some homes too. Quite a lot of our elders believed our mother-tongue was dying and were mostly resigned to letting it go. At lunch-time we would all rush home, since neither school milk nor school meals were available. The welfare state was not yet born.

Poetry was my favourite lesson and I can still remember many of the poems I learned nearly eighty years ago. I can even date my love of poetry to the time I was introduced to two particular poems - *Elegy in a Country Churchyard* by Thomas Gray and *The Rubaiyat of Omar Khayyam*. These were music to my ears and still are.

One poem I learned at school was about the Welsh prince Owen Glyndywr:

> When Owen Glyndywr walked through the land,
> He came to the gate of a castle grand;
> "May I and my man come in," said he,
> "And share a night's lodging with ye?"
> "Come in, come in!" the Baron cried,
> "And take your seat by my fireside..."

It is a long poem and at the end Owen is supposed to have told the Baron,

> " 'Ere I go, I say to thee
> That Owen Glyndywr shakes the hand
> Of Sir Lawrence Burcloss where he stands."
> Dumb with surprise did the Baron stand...

Owen Glyndywr was being hunted by Sir Lawrence Burcloss who was partially blind, which explains how he came to entertain the outlaw in his own castle without recognising him.

A song we sang was *The Rowan Tree*:

> O Rowan tree, O Rowan tree
> Thou art so dear to me;
> Entwine thy heart with merry glee
> For home and infancy.
> Thy leaves they are the first in Spring,
> Thy flowers the Summer's brightest.
> There was no' such a bonny tree
> In all the countryside.

16

Another song was:

Before our lands in East and West
I love my native land the best
No gold or silver here is found,
Yet men of noble souls abound,
And eyes of joy are gleaming.

I can still recall a poem I saw on a calendar during my schooldays. There was a picture of a pheasant and the following poem:

Clad in a thousand gorgeous dyes
The swift cock-pheasant springs
Like a bursting rocket to the skies,
And with a flash of whirring wings.
But high o'er the spinney's tallest trees
He looks his last at the sun,
For there's death in the slant of the Autumn breeze,
And his glorious days are done.

Someone lent me a book of poems written by Leslie Coulson, a British officer killed in the First World War. This was called *From an Outpost and Other Poems*. I copied out the following poem and learned it by heart. It made a deep impression on me.

When I come home, dear folk of mine,
I'll drink a cup of olden wine;
And yet however rich it be
No wine will taste as good to me
As English air.

How I shall thrill to drink it in
On Hampstead Hill, when I come home;
When I come home and leave behind
Dark things I would not call to mind.

I'll taste good ale and home-made bread,
And see white sheets and pillows spread,

17

And there is one who'll softly creep
And kiss me ere I fall asleep;
And tuck me 'neath the counterpane
And I shall be a boy again,
When I come home.

When I come home from dark to light,
And tramp the lanes I tramped of yore,
And see the village greens once more,
And hear the lark beneath the sun,
'Twill be good pay for what I've done,
When I come home.

Here is another fragment of a war poem.

Where war has left its wake of whitened bone,
Soft stems of Summer grass shall wave again;
And all the blood that war has ever strewn
Is but a passing stain.

In lighter vein I used to enjoy reading boys' papers such as *Gem* and *The Magnet*, with their stories of boys' school adventures so different from my own life. These papers showed me a new world. I had to walk to Merthyr each week to buy them as they were not stocked by the newsagent in the village. I never waited until I got home before I started reading them but would stand for ten or fifteen minutes at a time, lost in the stories. Fortunately I never walked along the road to get to Merthyr but always along the railway line as this was both safer and more direct. It was used by trains only in the morning and at night, taking miners to and from work at Merthyr. For the rest of the day it was used by pedestrians. When we children went with my mother to tidy my father's grave each Springtime, this is the way we went. Once or twice a day horse-brakes operated between Abercanaid and Merthyr but because the road was uphill most of the way it was no quicker. At one time a man in our village decided he was going to set up in opposition to the horse-brakes. He bought a horse called Bugler and every day he used to complain how much the horse ate and how expensive it was to keep him, so he gave up his plan and sold him again.

There was a Carnegie Library in the village and it was here that I discovered the novels of Sir Walter Scott. Again I was transported into another world as I read all that I could get hold of. Another of my favourites was *Flamebearers of Welsh History*, about the bygone heroes of Wales. The library was supposed to contain a selection of magazines on the reading desks but they were usually missing, although there was a selection of daily newspapers. Rumour had it that the librarian used to let her friends take the magazines home to read.

Another magazine which I bought for myself when I could afford it was *Wide World*, with its stories of true-life adventure in many lands.

The teachers at school were all very dedicated and discipline was strict but fair. All punishments were meted out by the Headmaster. I can't remember how the girls were punished, but we boys were punished with the cane on our hands. For that purpose we carried a bunch of hairs from a horse's tail or mane in readiness. These we twisted around the base of our fingers to make a kind of pad or cushion to deaden the strokes of the cane. Sometimes the Headmaster spotted it, sometimes he didn't.

There was one boy in our class who, when sent for punishment, created a great disturbance in our classroom when he came back, by kicking the floor with his heavy nailed boots. But after being sent off for punishment for doing this he quietened down and peace reigned again.

Around the class were drawing boards on the wall and when we had our once a week drawing lesson we stood at those to draw with chalk. We young artists were able to choose our own subject to draw and we signed it with our initials. This led to some nicknames, for one boy Lewis Oswald Morgan was known as Lom. Lewis Owen Davies was known as Lod and myself, Edward Rhys-Price was known as Erp. This weekly lesson did produce one really good artist, Felix Francis Samuels. He painted a picture of St. David and another of the Welsh dragon which were kept in school for many years, but sadly he died soon after leaving school. His father was a coal miner and was anxious to be on the Town Council, so after work he would come around the streets with a bell to advertise his meetings, but somehow he never got elected.

At school all our books, chalks and pencils were provided free of charge. We certainly couldn't have gone to school if it had been necessary for us to buy our own materials. At playtime boys and girls played in separate yards, although we had lessons together. First thing in the morning the one long classroom was open and we all had a short religious service to start the day. Then the wood and glass partitions were slid across and the room was divided into two or three classes.

In the Summer we were taken out to the countryside for nature study one afternoon a week and it was in this way I learned to appreciate the beauties of nature.

At one end of the village was Gethin Farm and here it was that the first coal mine in Abercanaid, as opposed to the drift mines, was opened about forty years before I was born. Translated this name means "the dark place" but it was anything but dark to me, it was a place of joy where I liked to spend as much of my free time as I could, and lots of time that I shouldn't as well. If I knew the shepherd was going somewhere in the pony and trap I used to try to go with him, but if we passed any of the teachers who were cycling to school I had to lie down on the floor of the trap so they couldn't see me, because the note I took to school next day would read "Please excuse Edward as he was not feeling well". I was called Eddie at home and at school, but of course in a formal letter I was known as Edward.

My greatest happiness was to be among horses, cattle and sheep on the Gethin Farm which I suppose was only natural since my father came from farming stock in the County of Brecon. I ran errands for the bailiff and his wife, Mr. and Mrs. Ferguson, and for the shepherds who were hired at the Brecon Fair each year. Sometimes as a treat I was allowed to accompany the shepherds when they were sent to different farms on business, and in the evening I enjoyed listening to the farm workers discussing their experiences around a blazing coal fire. I remember also Jack, the bailiff's son, who used to charge us a packet of sweets before we were allowed to follow the hay-wagon during haymaking. I can still smell the sickly sweet smell as the hay was loaded onto the wagon and then the strong sweet tea that was brought out to us in the hay field in a small milk churn, not to mention a basket of various sandwiches and cakes.

One of the visitors to the farm, a shepherd, walked from Aberdare which was in the next valley across the mountain. Many times when he appeared the worse for drink after a visit to the Gethin Arms, Mrs. Ferguson would implore him to stay the night at the farm, for the journey across the mountains was hazardous on a dark night. He always refused, saying that his dog would see him safely home, and it always did. Before becoming Lord Aberdare's shepherd he had worked for some years as a deputy at the Senghenydd coal mine but had left because he felt unable to sign the daily reports that his area of the mine was free of noxious gases. This was the coal mine which suffered the explosion in 1911, resulting in the deaths of hundreds of miners, the worst mining accident in South Wales.

I was quite a hero to my friends at school when I took a coconut to share with them. My friends at the farm had gone to a Fair at Brecon and while they were away I had fed the livestock for them. They brought the coconut back for me as a reward - not that I needed any reward, for some of the happiest days of my life were spent at Gethin Farm.

One of my favourite jobs was to take the dirty washing from the farm to the steam-laundry at Merthyr, on horseback. I had to cling on to the horse's mane until I got clear of the village because as soon as my school mates saw me coming they would take a piece of wood to urge the horse into a gallop in the hope of unseating me, but I always held on safely until I was out of their reach.

Every year as soon as the weather improved in the Spring my mother would take us younger children to the cemetery at Cefn Coed, about three miles from the village to tidy up my father's grave. We carried buckets and scrubbing brushes along with bunches of any fresh flowers we could find. There was a cold water tap in the cemetery so we got water from there in our buckets and scrubbed the headstone with its verse in Welsh, and painted the railings around the grave. Then we placed our flowers on it. My mother always insisted on fresh flowers for the grave, she would never have artificial ones. Then we would sit in the sunshine and eat the sandwiches we had brought with us before walking back to Abercanaid.

I had only two really frightening experiences when I was a boy. One, of course, was when my father appeared in my bedroom after his death. The second was during a very severe Winter when a man was found frozen to death on a piece of common land. Many people were asked if they could identify him but no-one knew who he was so he was buried in a pauper's grave. Unwept, unhonoured and unsung.

But the things which come back to me most clearly are the long, hot Summers we enjoyed in those Edwardian days, and the attractive dresses worn by the girls, and the parasols they carried to protect their complexions from the sun. Not all the young women could afford such things, of course, but the girls who had left the village to work elsewhere seemed to enjoy coming back to let us see how well they had done for themselves.

Going Down the Mine

I left school at the age of thirteen and became an errand boy at five shillings a week delivering bread on a bread wagon. Then when I was fourteen years old and a day I went down the coal mine at a wage of sixteen shillings a week, rising to a maximum of two pounds a week at twenty-one. I had always said I would never become a miner. I had heard my father and my brothers and the other miners go along the streets in the dark of a Winter's morning and return home after

21

dark in the evenings, so that the only time they saw the light of day in the Winter was at weekends. But what could I do when the money was needed at home?

However, I knew we had an aunt in Philadelphia, one of my father's relatives, and when I was small she had paid us a visit. She had told my mother that if any of us ever went to America she would look after us, so I was determined to save hard so that one day I would be the one to go.

The first time I went down the pit my heart was in my mouth. As the cage neared the bottom a bell rang in the winding house on the surface and the man responsible for lowering us would slow down. The same when the cage was coming up at the end of the shift. The winder was so experienced that he never made a mistake. The lives of those men depended on him and he was aware of it. At the top of the shaft an official gave each of us a safety lamp. This was done in the lamp room. Each lamp bore a number and the miners were each given their own lamp every time they went down. At the end of the shift the lamps were handed back in and if one was missing it was checked against a list and it was then easy to see which miner had not come in so that a search could at once be started for him. Of course it was a very serious offence to take someone else's lamp because then if someone was missing he could not be identified.

Each lamp ran on oil and was basically unchanged since its invention by Sir Humphrey Davy, who was born in 1778, except that it was lit by electricity. No naked flames were ever allowed in the mines for fear of gas. In some mines electric lamps were in use. These were worn on the front of the miner's helmet and worked from a battery carried on his back, but I never came across any of these in the mines I worked in. If anyone had the misfortune to drop his lamp so that it went out he often had a walk of several miles back to the lamp room so that it could be relit. The only method of finding the way was to walk with one foot on the tram rail or hold on to the wires above.

These wires were up there so that when about a dozen trams had been pulled from the side workings by the horses and shackled together in the main gallery, the man in charge could make a signal by holding the two wires together and knocking on them. Then the man in charge of the hauling engine would start the electric motor and the trams would be pulled along and put two at a time into the cage to go to the surface to be emptied and then be sent down again empty. I was making my way back in the dark to the lamp-room one day when I heard someone talking. "Well, Godfrey," the voice was saying, "we're behind with our work, so we shall have to work hard to catch up." I expected to meet some miners, although I didn't know anyone called Godfrey, but instead I met a driver coming along with a horse. It was the horse he was talking to, just as though it

22

was a human being. The drivers became very fond of their horses and usually brought a carrot or a piece of apple for them each day. If a miner was away sick and heard that someone had ill-treated his horse there was usually a fight over it.

Life was not easy for the horses in the mines. Unlike horses on the surface their shoes had to be put on cold instead of being heated by the blacksmith and hammered into shape, because of the danger of gas. This meant that the fitting of the shoes was rather a hit or miss affair, with subsequent discomfort for the horses. If the horses had hairy legs and the mud and wet was not cleaned out thoroughly they could develop sores which would fester.

The horses were all given the same initial letter to their name depending on the year they came down the mine. In this way it was easy to know how long they had been there. I don't know what the average life of a pit pony is but I do know that when they were no longer fit for work they were taken to the surface and shot. After the nationalisation of the mines they were at least retired to farms where they lived out their last days in peace. I love horses and if I had the money I would create a refuge for worn-out horses where they could end their days in peace.

During the First World War officials from the army used to go around the mines collecting ponies to go to the front, so the miners used to hide them in old workings and crossed poles would be placed across the entrance to indicate that it was unsafe. On one occasion the man who had the job of buying the hay for the horses was dishonest enough to buy poor hay which horses would not eat. The money he saved was put into his wife's business. Fortunately he was found out and dismissed.

For every £1 a miner earned, twopence was deducted by the mining company and paid direct to the doctor. This money also covered the miner's family if they needed treatment. Sometimes the cuts and gashes sustained while working took a long time to heal. Because of the coal dust and dirty water in the mines there was a constant danger of gangrene or Weil's disease from the rats. There was no sick pay in those days so everyone tried to get better again as soon as possible. If the doctor's treatment did not bring about a cure he would throw up his hands and say, "I can't do any more for you. You will have to go to Mrs. Lewis." She was a partially blind woman who mixed her own ointments from herbs and other things. She would warn that her treatment would hurt for the first few days while the poisons were being drawn out. After that she would put on a different ointment and the cuts healed quickly. She charged a fee of a few shillings but the miners didn't mind as they wanted to get back to work as soon as possible.

Before the miners were allowed down the mine they were always searched for matches, and before they could begin work either in the morning or at night, the fireman, or deputy as they are called in England, had to examine the stall where each miner was working. He would lower the flame on his lamp to test for "noxious or harmful gases" and then chalk his initials and the date on the roof. He also filled in a book which he carried to say that the working place was safe. Sometimes I had to carry this book back to the lamp room and I would read it as I walked along. "Noxious or inflammable gases none" was the entry after entry, but sometimes I had my own thoughts on that. I could test for gases as well as the fireman, even though he had passed an examination on fire safety and I had not.

Sometimes on a Sunday I would help him out by testing for gas in one part of the mine while he did another part. He had shown me what to do, but I knew at once if there was gas present as I could smell it and I felt a headache start. When I chalked the initials on the roof to say whether it was safe or not I always put his, TLP, so that he would not get into trouble for designating part of his work to me.

The gas was always a danger in the mines as it was explosive and could be set off even by a spark struck from stone by a pickaxe. It was not poisonous to man, but the afterdamp which followed an explosion was. To counteract this, all mines had to be provided with an escape route for foul air. A second shaft was sunk some distance from the first and at the top of this fans could be used to keep the current of fresh air moving.

Of course there were hundreds of sidings leading off from the main one and these were provided with a door consisting of a wooden framework on which was hung a coarse linen-like material called brattice. These could be kept open or closed to control the movement of the fresh air.

One of the other dangers in the mine apart from the gas was the rats. The bacon and cheese sandwiches we took down for out bait-time had to be carried in a tin box and our water or cold tea carried in metal bottles called jacks. I remember once I took an apple in the pocket of my jacket. I hung the jacket up and when I came to it again the apple had gone. While we were working we hung our coats on a spike, a metal rod with a knob on one end, which could be driven into a pit prop. While we ate our bait we hung our lamps on the spike to give us light.

Some mines had rats and some had mice, but never both. How did they get down the mines? My guess is they got down there in the horse feed. One female rat can produce eight litters in a year with anything up to twenty little ones in each litter, and at about three months of age those young ones can start breeding, so it will be seen that the numbers of rats in the mine soon became a problem. Then the mine would be emptied of men, the horses were brought to the surface and all the canvas doors would be fixed open, but the door at the end would be closed. Sulphur would be burned in the main tunnel and this would send all the rats to the closed door where they were overcome by the fumes and died. Their bodies were then shovelled into trams and either burned or buried, and for a little while we would have peace again.

The main hazard of the rats, apart from their nuisance value, was in the pools of water which often lay about in the mine, because some of these were quite deep and the rats had to swim across them. The miners were told never to get this water on their skin if they had a cut, but one miner who either forgot or was careless, washed his hands in this water. He died and his organs were sent to London for analysis to find the cause of death. The answer was Weil's disease, caused by the urine of rats getting in a cut on his hands.

The other health hazard was dust which got on the lungs and clogged them up, eventually causing pneumoconiosis. If the dust was very bad hoses were used to water the coal face and of course this helped to add to the water which was often lying about the mines.

The boys who worked in the mines were helpers to the older miners until they became twenty-one. Each year they got, or were supposed to anyway, a small increase in their pay whatever they were doing. I worked with Idris Skym, my brother-in-law, who was married to my eldest sister. As he hacked the coal from the coal-face he would push it behind him for me to scoop up with a metal, box-like structure with two handles, which was then dragged backwards. This coal was then tipped into the tram, or trolley, which had our number chalked on the side. Later, in the 1920s, coal-cutting machinery was brought into use in some of the mines, but in my day it was all hard work by hand. In a particularly difficult seam a small charge of gunpowder was sometimes used. A hole would be drilled by hand, then the gunpowder was inserted and clay packed into the hole. The area was cleared of miners and only one man was allowed to handle the explosives or set off the charge, he was called the shotsman. Every miner had impressed upon him the golden rule - "If it doesn't explode, leave it alone." An uncle of mine who was in charge of a drift mine had a miner under him who disregarded this rule and was blown to pieces. It was the gruesome task of my uncle to pick up as many pieces as he could find and put them in a sack for burial.

Another job the boys had to do was to drag away any rubbish after a fall of rock as the mining progressed, or to steady the pit props as new ones were put in to support the roof. As we went along the sidings it became necessary for new rails to be laid for the trams to run on, and the miner was paid a small amount extra for this and also for the work he had to do sometimes to make the tunnel higher, to give him more room to work properly. Each week an official would come around and measure the length of rail which had been put in, or the height of the roof, or the number of pit props which had been used.

We worked in measured stalls, thus ensuring that each miner was treated the same. These were passages cut out from the side of the main seam. When a tram was full the boy would shout and a man with a pit pony would come to haul it away and bring an empty one. At the top the trams were weighed by a representative of the mine managers and a miner. The miner was chosen by the others as a man they could trust because at one time a lot of cheating went on and the miners didn't always get their due amount for the coal they had dug out. Each miner was expected to send up ten hundredweight or more of coal a day, not counting any small coal or slag. If he sent up less than this it sometimes meant the mine would not make a profit for the owners.

It was not only the mine owners who sometimes cheated; at one mine where I worked the accountants in Cardiff were puzzled because it always showed a loss. They sent someone to investigate and it was found that the names of men who had been dead for years were still on the books, and the money was disappearing into someone else's pocket. Once this was discovered the mine soon began to show a profit.

At the top of each mine was the ambulance shed where the horse-drawn ambulances were kept. Here canaries were kept in cages and every so often these would be carried down the mines to test for gas. If they died it was obvious it was a build-up of gas, so this was quickly cleared by opening and closing doors rapidly to get a through draught of fresh air. If a miner was injured in the mines it was a chancy business whether he would get compensation or not. It cost the union sixty pounds for every case they had to take to court and often they lost because the mine owners could afford top lawyers and very often the County Court judge was biased in favour of the owners anyway. Then again if the mine company had taken out insurance with a shaky insurance company, which went bankrupt, there would be no money to pay the compensation.

One rule which was strictly adhered to in the mines was that there must be no fighting underground. There were enough natural hazards in the mines without adding to them. On rare occasions when men did come to blows they were given the choice of being taken to court or donating a sum of money to charity. I never witnessed a fight in the mines in my years as a miner. Quarrels yes, but the men exercised common sense and waited to fight until they got to the surface.

One of the worst aspects of mining was working in wet clothes all day. We had one-and-a-half miles to walk to the mine in all weathers, so if it was raining we were soon soaked through. Then there was often an hour's walk underground to reach the coal face with no way of getting dry. When I got home I would have to strip off and my clothes were hung on the brass rail in front of the fire to get dry. Then I had a bath in front of the fire; the bath was like a wooden barrel cut in half with carrying handles. We young men would strip off to wash our chest and arms then the women folk would go into another room and we would undress our lower half and sit in the bath. If any of us were planning to go out in the evening we ran home from work to try to be first in the bath, otherwise we would have to wait for more kettles to be heated on the fire.

Many of the miners did all they could to discourage their sons from going down the mines. If a boy went down against his father's wishes the father used to find out which man the boy was working with and say, "Treat him as badly as you can. Tell him he's no good and break his spirit." In that way he hoped the boy would leave mining of his own accord and do something better for himself.

One miner I used to walk to work with was so determined his son would not become a miner, that he gave up smoking to be able to afford private coaching in mathematics for the boy. When the son applied for a position in the bank in Merthyr he passed the written examination and then had to be interviewed by the bank inspector. Everything went well until the man asked the boy what his father did for a living. when the boy said his father was a coal miner, the inspector shook his head and said, "I am sorry, my boy, we cannot employ a miner's son in the bank."

Men who had worked down the mines themselves often found it difficult to get other employment, because the miners had a reputation for militancy, but very often if they were given a job they rapidly rose in their new profession. I remember one man who was taken on by an insurance firm and quickly rose to be superintendent. Anyone who wanted to get out of the mines used to study the *Western Mail* or the *South Wales Echo* in the hope of finding a job but when they went for an interview one thing often gave them away as miners, for if anyone got a cut on his hands while working in the mine the coal dust got beneath the skin so the scars which were left were blue. For this reason the men always tried to hide their hands during interviews.

All the time I worked in the mine I was saving as much as I could because I was still determined to go to America. In fact like a true Celt I never spent more than half my wages. But in 1921 when I had saved enough for my passage the miners were locked out because they refused to take a substantial cut in their wages. We didn't know it then but a twenty-year depression, or slump, had begun. Some of Britain's pre-war customers no longer needed the products they had always bought from her. India now had her own factories and during the war other countries had begun buying from the U.S.A. and Japan. So fewer goods meant fewer jobs in cotton mills, ship yards and coal mines. At the beginning of this century Cardiff alone used to export 90,000,000 tons of coal each year. It was extremely good coal. Admiralty Number 1 was the name much of it went under as it was used greatly in ships. The empty Coal Exchange in Cardiff is a reminder of those days.

In Merthyr by 1934 seven out of ten men would be unemployed. In 1913 the mines gave jobs country-wide to 1,505,000 men. By 1932 only 319,000 were needed. The world had too much coal chasing too few customers. The mine owners cut the price of coal in an effort to win them back. In 1920 coal was £4 a ton, by 1923 it was to be £2.10s. Export prices dropped even more, from £5 a ton in 1920 to just over £1 a ton a year later. Miners' jobs and wages of course depended on these world prices. The cheaper the coal the fewer the jobs and the lower the wages.

In March 1921 the mine owners had said that miners must work for less money and they refused. The miners asked the railway and transport workers for support, but were turned down. They called this day, April 15th, 1921, "Black Friday" and were forced to go back on the mine owners' conditions. To avoid more trouble the Government agreed to pay a subsidy of £10,000,000 a year until 1925, in the hope that prices would rise. Prices didn't and the owners told the miners that when the subsidy ended they would have to work an extra hour a day for less pay. They refused and began to prepare for another strike.

As it looked as though the rail men and other big unions would also strike, the Government gave another subsidy until May 1st, 1926, and in the meantime set up a commission to look into mining. This commission said that the subsidy should end after May 1st, 1926 and miners' wages should be reduced. So on April 13th, 1926, the owners said the miners would have to work longer hours for less money. Arthur Cook, Secretary of the Mine Workers' Federation said, "Not a penny off the pay, not a minute on the day." The owners replied by shutting down the pits. By the first of May, 1926, the T.U.C. called 3,000,000 other key workers out on strike to support the miners.

This came to be known as the "General Strike" though T.U.C. leaders like

28

Ernest Bevin of the Transport Workers, denied this and said it was a "National Strike". The strike collapsed after nine days. The miners struggled on alone for another six months, when cold and hunger finally drove them back down the pits in Winter on the mine owners' terms. A few miners managed to get other jobs but those who were known as trouble-makers were black-balled. The mine bosses would warn other employers and these men could not get another job. One such was Aneurin Bevan, who fought for the rights of the miners. His sister supported him in his fight until he eventually entered Parliament. A miners' agent was appointed by the miners to negotiate on their behalf. After the lock-out not all miners wanted to join the union again because they knew the funds were depleted and the union would not be able to fight their case. If a miner was injured it cost the union £60 to take the case to court, as I have mentioned earlier. Mine owners promised the miners work, but then kept turning them away when they reported to the mine. They wanted the miners to beg to go back.

But there was a lighter side to all this. Noah Ablett, the miners' agent for Merthyr and District, used to organise a brass band made up of miners and other supporters. He took this around to the homes of those who refused to join the union. The men would see them coming and lock the front door and run upstairs. Then the band would strike up a popular song of the day, *Old Pal, why don't you answer me*. If the man didn't come down, Noah Ablett would say, "Strike up again." And after that the man would be so ashamed of his neighbours knowing that he hadn't joined the union and so fed up with the noise that he would come down and join just to get rid of them. The bandsmen were all shapes and sizes. The man who beat the big drum was very short, so the drum was above his head when he was carrying it. Sometimes he went down one street when the band had gone down another, much to the delight of the small boys who were following.

Nature was kind to us during the lock-out of 1921. It was the most glorious Summer I ever remember. Everyone was sun-burned and there was a minor population explosion some months later.

That Summer of '21 also saw the death of my grandmother. I was at home when I heard a cry from the garden and ran out to find my grandmother had fallen off the large stone she stood on to reach the washing line. I carried her in and laid her on her bed and then ran to find my mother who was out visiting a neighbour. She had broken her leg but the doctor could do nothing for her because of her age. It was a sad day for me because she had been part of our family ever since I could remember.

While I was working I had saved up for a cheap violin. It may seem a strange thing for a coal miner to buy, but I have always loved music and my brother-in-law, Idris Skym, who was a gifted musician, encouraged me. He could play the piano, the organ, the harp and the violin. But as for me my enthusiasm was greater than my talent. And when I practised upstairs in the bedroom the family downstairs used to emit terrible groans. Of course they were teasing me like families do, but I became discouraged and sold the violin.

One day I walked across the mountain to Aberdare to see the famous boxer Jimmy Wild in the ring, but he was held up in London so I was disappointed. South Wales has produced several world champion boxers. Jimmy Wild was a coal miner in the Rhondda and it is said he got his strong back and arm muscles from crouching at the coal face using a pick. He was not a big man and always had to box above his own weight.

Another boxer, Jimmy Driscoll, was of Irish descent and came from Cardiff, but his great weakness was drink. As soon as he had any money he would go off and spend it all. When his boxing career was over a Welsh evening paper opened a fund for him and paid him a small amount from this every week, so that he had enough to live on but not to drink. Freddie Welsh, or to give him his correct name, Freddie Hall Thomas, was a very clever boxer, but not a heavy puncher. He emigrated to America and opened a health farm. Tommy Farr was born in a mining village and started as an exhibition fighter, taking on all-comers at fair grounds. He fought Joe Louis and at first it was thought he had won but the points decision was given against him. This was many years later when I was living in Chepstow, I was walking down a long street and heard a radio commentary at the top. I thought to myself that by the time I reached the bottom the fight would be over, with Tommy Farr knocked out, but he was still going strong. Another boxer, Billy Eynon, from Merthyr, boxed mostly in London because he could get more money. He lost most of his fights but always put up a good show. Howard Winston was trained by another famous boxer, Eddie Thomas.

After some time I managed to get a job working the hand-pump in the mine, seven nights a week, eight hours at a time, a job that no-one else wanted because there were no Saturdays and Sundays off. This hand-pump kept the water at an acceptable level in the mine for the miners who had gone back to work. It was hard, boring work but I thought of the money I was saving and put up with it, as I was more than ever determined to go to America.

I was usually working about three-quarters of a mile from the coal face, where the other miners were working and I had some very frightening experiences. At 3 a.m. one morning I was sitting having my bait when I heard slow footsteps approaching, echoing from the walls of the mine. I had heard of people's hair standing on end and now I felt my own doing it, because I was so frightened. I shouted but got no reply and the footsteps came steadily nearer. Then in the light from my lamp I saw that my visitor was one of the horses. He had somehow got loose from the stable and when I had finished my food I took him back.

Other visitors were the rats. On many occasions I would see their red eyes gleaming as I sat eating and would hear them squealing when I threw a stone to scare them away. My job was certainly not one for the faint-hearted. One visitor I should have had but didn't always see him, was the fireman. He was supposed to come down twice at weekends when the other miners were not working during the night, to make sure I was alright, because then, of course, I was completely on my own underground. Sometimes he didn't bother to come. I met him after one of these occasions when I had been on my own for eight hours, just as I was hurrying home. "Thank goodness you're alright," he said to me. "I couldn't sleep for thinking about you." I thought to myself, "Maybe you couldn't sleep, but you didn't get out of your comfortable bed to make sure I was alright." Of course if anything had happened to me the fireman would have been out of a job because it was his responsibility to make sure I was safe. The other men used to see me going to work when they were on their way home and shout to me, wanting to know what I was going to spend all my money on.

My Family and My Best Friend

When I had my horoscope cast many years ago I found that I was born under the sign of Virgo and I learned that Virgoans make few close friends but like to keep the ones they have, and this has certainly been true of my life.

At about the age of fifteen I met a young man eighteen months older than myself, Charles Lionel Alexander Ward, and we remained good friends until his death on September 3rd, 1976, a sad loss for me. We met when we were both fishing in the canal which ran at the back of our house in Nightingale Street. He was having no luck so I went and got a handful of my mother's bread dough which she had left to rise. I threw bits in the water and put some on his hook and soon he had a good catch of roach. He told me he had been born in Monmouth and was now working as a porter on the Rhymney Railway, having started work as a porter in Monmouth and then being transferred to Abercanaid.

One day we were walking down the canal embankment and he looked down into a garden and saw an empty shed. He asked me who it belonged to and when I told him he went to see the person and proceeded to rent the shed and turned it into a shop. When he filled the slot machines on the station platforms with pen-

31

ny chocolate bars he would purchase some for himself and sell them a penny-ha'penny in his shop. He was a born business man. Seeing an empty glasshouse he rented this as well and used it for drying the rabbit skins which he bought.

He took me to stay with his family in Watery Lane, Monmouth. There were eight children, the same as in my family. As well as Charles, who was always called Lionel, there was Cyril, Melvyn, Eric, Violet, Phyllis, Muriel and Dorothy. Violet had a lovely voice and used to sing in concerts. To make the accommodation easier Lionel and I used to sleep in a caravan in the orchard. If we were hungry in the night we could put our hands out of the window and pull apples out of a nearby haystack where they had been put to ripen. I cannot express what a joy these visits were to me for I was working in the mine all week and the fresh air and smell of growing things in the market garden was a real tonic for me.

Lionel's father was a big man who was a wonderful gardener, but he was not a good businessman, though two of his sons turned out to be. He used to send fruit and vegetables to Abercanaid by train and Lionel used to sell it to the shops in Merthyr. Some of the baskets of fruit had been picked from the big gardens which still existed at that time behind the shops in Monnow Street.

One very hot day we were working in the market garden, stopping every so often to wipe the sweat out of our eyes, when one of Lionel's sisters passed by on the other side of the hedge, dressed in white and carrying a white parasol. Her father was angry, I suppose because she looked so cool and fresh while we were all working hard, but his wife, who was only a little woman, sprang to her defence.

I can never remember a time when we didn't have a dog at home as part of the family, usually a spaniel. These were not pets but working dogs, for they went hunting with my brother David John on the mountain. The most famous of our dogs was Nora, a spaniel bitch who bred many puppies who grew up to be champions. One day when David John was out hunting he mistook her for an otter and shot her. When he realised what he'd done he carried her home in tears to a friend's house. There on the kitchen table they got out as many of the pellets as they could and put her in a basket by the fire to recover, hoping she would stay there until she was well again. But every time the door was opened she came back to our house, so she was allowed to stay. She always had a limp afterwards but was still able to go on having puppies. She was a wonderful dog.

David John had two other hobbies besides shooting. When he shot a fox he would skin it and send the skin away to be made into a fashionable neckpiece for a woman. These he would give away to anyone who wanted one. His other hobby was rather unusual. He always carried a sharp knife and a skein of knitting wool in his pocket. He would cut pieces from his favourites among the rose bushes which Mam grew on our vegetable garden and he would graft these on to wild roses, binding them around with wool. If they were not broken off or eaten by the sheep they usually continued to grow. These sheep occasionally raided the gardens if we had a hard Winter and grazing was sparse, but of course no-one complained, they were simply a fact of our life in the valleys.

My brother Thomas, always known as Tommy, was secretary of the cricket club at Pentrebach, although he didn't play cricket. During the First World War my mother saved his life. This is how it happened. He had joined the army without telling anyone. The first my mother knew of it was when she received a letter from him to say he was being sent overseas. She mentioned this to a neighbour who asked how old he was. Learning that he was under eighteen, the neighbour told her to write and tell the commanding officer. My mother did and Thomas was withdrawn from the draft. The men he should have gone with were never heard of again, they were all wiped out.

As soon as he was old enough he enlisted again and was sent to France. There he had a very gruesome job - he had to tie together the bodies which were buried in flooded ground so that they would stay beneath the soil. All the time he was away my mother sent him a parcel every week, putting in home-made cakes, knitted socks, candles and anything else she thought he might need. She wrapped each parcel in strong material and sewed it up, then she painted his name and regiment on it and he got every one of them safely. Thomas never married. During the Second World War he organised concerts to raise money for soldiers from the village. A little girl called Petula Clark used to sing to help with the fundraising, for she was evacuated to Abercanaid to stay with her grandfather William John Phillips.

In the 1930s my youngest brother Glyndwr, worked as a miner but although he was twenty he was only paid a boy's wage. So he left and went to Chiswick in London in the hope of finding a job. But when he tried to register for employment he was told the mine manager had written to say there was work waiting for him in the mines. He refused to go back, saying that he had been doing a man's job for a boy's wage and demanded to go before a tribunal. While enquiries were being made he was without money for six weeks but the case against the mine-manager was proved and so he received six weeks' back pay, and from then on he never looked back. He got a job with Chiswick Borough Council on the roads, and one day the surveyor came and asked if he would like to work with him. My brother jumped at the chance and as his work took him around inspecting houses he was able to buy them cheaply and ended up with twelve, always borrowing money from the bank to buy them. He also bought a small factory producing toys, and the Do-It-Yourself shop. He was a diabetic, whose only hobby was fishing and sad to say he died of overwork at the age of about sixty-six. He had a son and daughter, Jeff and Marion. David John remained a bachelor, like my brother Thomas, and was a coal miner all his life until he retired.

My eldest brother, William, was a lay-preacher. He and his wife used to conduct open-air meetings in the streets of Merthyr Tydfil. They had two boys and two girls but the eldest boy died.

My eldest sister, Jemima, who took me to chapel, went out to service at the age of fourteen, at the house of the coal manager. She received five shillings a month and one half-day off per fortnight. Each Tuesday we would go to the house to collect any scraps of cakes or pies which were left over. Mr. and Mrs. Green and their family used to come into the kitchen and tell Jemima, "Make sure they take it all."

My sister, Mary Anne stayed at home helping my mother until she got married. Olwen, when she left school, obtained a job at Woolworths in Merthyr and stayed there until she got married. She was a Junior Supervisor.

We were a happy, united family and I knew it would be a terrible wrench to leave home, but I was still determined to do it.

I go to Canada

By the time I had saved enough for my passage the American Congress had brought in a law limiting the numbers of immigrants they were willing to take. But I was still determined to get out of coal mining, so knowing that a family in the village had relatives in Toronto I asked them for the address. Then I did a foolish thing. I went to Canada in the depths of Winter, without a trade. Fortunately everything turned out alright. I am convinced there is a guardian angel who looks after us in such circumstances.

I went by ship from Southampton and then by train to Toronto. I soon learned that in the Canadian Winter it is necessary to protect the ears from the intense cold because they freeze easily, also that one must wear overshoes of rubber which slip over one's normal shoes, and are taken off before one enters a house. I was not so much aware of the cold in my first Winter. I felt it much more in the second.

34

The Williams' family to whom I went first had no room for me, but they took me to some of their friends, called Oakley, and I stayed there for the two years I was in Canada, at 26, St. Clair Gardens. My board cost eight dollars a week. My fellow boarder, Roy Lazier, a French Canadian barber, thought he could find me a job in a laundry. He took me to the West End Laundry at Queen Street West, Toronto, and introduced me to Mr. Pridham the owner. He said he would give me a trial for six weeks as one of his employees wanted to go back to visit England. The man who took me round was amazed when I took out a pencil and paper to make notes of what he told me, but I was a long way from home and needed the job.

I learned to wash clothes and put in the right amounts of soap powder and bleach. The clothes were washed first in cold water, then with hot, in big drums. A card was propped up on each one to say when it would be ready. Then the hot water was run off and it was washed again, then finally rinsed and put through wringers. The only things that had to be hand-washed were fragile materials. The washing was dried in huge hot rooms, but I was only in the washing part. My job was completed when I had put the clothes in big trucks ready to be moved on.

For the first six weeks my wages just covered the cost of my board and lodging. Afterwards I received an increase but they were never princely. However, you don't complain when you are 3,000 miles away from home! At least the work in the laundry had its good side - it enabled me to save money regularly because I was so tired after the day's work that I never felt like going out anywhere to spend it.

After living with the Oakleys for some months I asked Mrs. Oakley why they did not buy a house. They were not a very enterprising couple and she seemed surprised at the idea. Her husband was a woodworker who could neither read nor write. I offered her two months' board in advance and she eventually saw the sense in my idea. As the Oakleys became more prosperous they bought a secondhand car and we used to go for drives into the countryside at weekends.

In the Spring we liked to watch the collection of maple syrup going on. A hole would be made in the bark of the trees by the farmers who owned them and a tin was hung below to catch the sap which flowed out. This collection of the sap never seemed to affect the trees. The sap was collected each day and boiled up over a fire. The scum would be taken off and what was left set hard like toffee, and was sold in slabs to be broken up into maple sugar, which was delicious.

Some weekends were spent with a friend on his father's farm and there we had griddle cakes for breakfast, made of buckwheat flour and served with maple syrup. As I remember the mixture was made in a milk churn from buckwheat flour, sour milk, sugar and a small quantity of snow. They were so light and delicious that we used to eat around fifteen for breakfast.

Every Spring a well-known bakery company used to insert the following verse as part of its advertisement in the papers:

Robin down the logging road
Whistles, "Come to me!"
Spring has found the maple grove,
Sap is running free.

After I had been in Canada for some time my aunt came from Philadelphia by train to take me back with her. We got as far as the border at Niagara Falls and I was questioned by an American immigration officer. I had no visa to enter so I tried to bluff my way in. But nothing I said did any good, so I had to go back to Toronto while my aunt returned to Philadelphia.

I went back to the Oakleys and resumed my job again, because fortunately I had not given in my notice. All this time I had kept in touch with my mother, of course, and even sent her small amounts of money from time to time. I had gone to Canada with the aim of getting to America and going to live with my aunt, but this time I had to write to my mother to tell her I had not been successful but I was going to try again.

We used to eat our lunch at the laundry in the basement and after I had told the staff about what had happened at the frontier one of them said to me, "Don't worry, I'll find a way of getting you over the border." Some time later she took me aside and told me that her husband, Earl, was travelling to Detroit by car, leaving Toronto at eleven that night. If I wanted to risk it, he would take me. I agreed, and after travelling most of the night we got to Niagara Falls again and he told me to get into the back seat and pretend to be asleep. I think the immigration official must have been half asleep as well because, of course, he should have woken me to look at my visa, but he waved us through and that is how I got to America.

When we got to Detroit, Earl took me to a friend's house and I slept until the evening. Then I took a train to Philadelphia and after a few days' rest at my aunt's I began looking for work. This was easier said than done. My uncle was also looking for work. However, he and my aunt were able to live in their house rent-free provided they kept a fire going in the central heating boiler in the basement. It only had to burn for a few hours each day, just to keep the water pipes from freezing. I used to help them collect newspapers and cardboard boxes as fuel. Sometimes we would find a wooden packing crate which we could break up. The agents knew it was better to let the house rent-free than to leave it empty and have the pipes freeze. This was the only way many people got a roof over their heads because there was simply no money available to pay rent.

One day I was stopped in the street by a recruiting sergeant of the American Army who asked if I wanted to join up. I told him I was no good to him as I was a Johnny Bull, but he said that didn't matter. However, I walked away as I was afraid he would ask too many questions and find out that I was an illegal immigrant.

Eventually I found work as a steam-fitter's mate, what we would call in England a central-heating plumber's mate. The pay was thirty-seven and a half cents an hour, the lowest paid work there was, but at least I could now pay my aunt something for my board and even have a little something left over.

After working at this for some time, my cousin Catherine's husband Joe found me a a job at the Philadelphia and Reading Railroads Depot, watering the engines. They were all steam engines in those days, of course, with massive tanks to be filled with water. I was always eager for something to read and used to collect the newspapers and magazines from the engine cabs when the drivers had finished with them. Reading about New York I decided I would like to see it, so I went there for a day by Greyhound bus. It was 94 miles but the buses were very cheap. I liked New York so much that I decided I would go there and look for a job.

One of my happiest memories of Philadelphia is of going to church at Christmas, and as I walked home afterwards in the snow I heard music coming from the basement of a church I was passing. It was a choir singing that lovely hymn, "Be still, my soul..." to music by Sibelius. I have never forgotten that beautiful sound in the snowy, lamplit street with everyone going home from church. I don't know much about music but there are five composers whose work I admire very much. Sibelius is one of them. The others are Tchaikovsky, for his symphonies five and six, and the *1812 Overture*; Granados for his *Andalusian Suite*; Vaughan Williams for *The Lark Ascending* and practically all of Edward Elgar's music.

If anyone in Philadelphia was planning to move house they used this as an opportunity to get even with their neighbours if there had been any bad feeling between them. They did this by selling their house to a Negro family because such was the feeling against coloured people at that time, their action brought down house prices all along the street.

I go to Sea

Before leaving Philadelphia I had learned that a fellow Welshman, John Morgan, kept a small hotel on West 14th Street, New York City. I went straight there as soon as I reached New York and was able to book a room. A man called Edmund Roberts helped me find work on a building site for a few months. After this John Morgan gave me a letter to take to the port steward of the United Fruit Company, or the Banana Navy as it was called, at Pier Nine, North River. In this way I got a a job on the S.S. *Zacapa*, running from New York to Jamaica, the Canal Zone and Central America.

My job had a high-sounding title, the Silver King, but in fact it was the lowest in the steward's department. I had to wash the silver serving dishes used for the meals, polish them and stack them in the little cubbyhole next to the kitchen. I also had to help the pantryman.

I was called at 5.30 a.m. when I helped to bring up food for the cooks. Then I went back to our cramped quarters to wash and shave, eat a quick breakfast and then go back to help serve the passengers' breakfasts. The meals for the lower orders of the stewards' department were very poor. The cook was very generous with the rice and this was filled out with any scraps left over, including what the passengers left on their plates.

The other members of the stewards' department would have turned up their noses at this sort of thing. They made their own arrangements about meals. For example a waiter would order not just one chicken dinner but two. One was for himself and he would contrive to hide it somewhere and pick it up when he could. One day the chef was worried because although there were only forty passengers, sixty chicken dinners had been ordered. He spoke to the steward who promised to investigate. When he went to our quarters he found the food hidden under pillows and everywhere else.

The chef was in charge of the kitchen. Then there was the second chef, the roast cook, the sauce cook, the bakers and the vegetable preparers, about ten in all. The number of waiters depended on the number of passengers.

These passengers could be of all kinds - honeymoon couples, business people, or South Americans going back home from New York. Some of them were very critical of their homeland, especially if they had been to school in America. They told us that in one town a certain man had the concession to supply electricity. The town had grown but the electricity supply had not kept pace with it, with the result that there were frequent power failures. However, the man was a personal friend of the President so no-one dared to set up in opposition to him. Meanwhile he lived in Paris on the profits.

The experienced waiter could sum up the passengers at a glance and knew how much he was likely to get in tips. Sometimes we would hear the waiters mutter under their breath, "I shall have to teach this lot how to eat!" or "I'll sell this lot for a dollar." If passengers looked like being good for a large tip the waiter made sure to make himself indispensable to them while humbler people just got the minimum of service. Sometimes the waiter would have to show them which of the array of cutlery to use.

Most of the food was taken on in New York and plenty of ice-cream was always included, the most popular being a yellow one in the shape of a banana. Each day the baker used to make two kinds of sorbet, only ever the two kinds, but he used to give them all kinds of names, presumably in the hope that no-one would know. Any dessert left over was put out so that the crew could help themselves.

The voyage took nineteen to twenty-one days and apart from the passengers the only cargo was the bananas, about 60,000 stems for a ship the size of the *Zecapa*. These were brought on board green and kept in the hold at low temperature so that they would not ripen. They were checked several times a day and if any did ripen they were hung around the ship for the passengers to help themselves. Or they would be roasted lightly in the oven and then a small quantity of rum would be poured over them which was set alight at the table. But going out from New York the holds were empty.

As the ship went along the coast the captain would radio ahead to the United Fruit Company agents in each port to let the man know what fruit we needed. Then the fresh oranges, limes and pineapples would be ready for us to take on board. When I became a pantryman it was my job to squeeze this fruit to make drinks. The oranges and limes were easy as the squeezer was worked by electricity but I had to squeeze the pineapples by hand. This was a long, slow process. We also took on board a special kind of melon with very red flesh and black pips. We would cut slices of this and put it on any meat which was a bit tough and the juices would tenderise it. This same melon was used for any passengers who had stomach upsets.

In addition to the passengers who came on board in New York we also picked up passengers at other ports of call. Apart from those in the cabins there were also deck passengers who were mostly picked up at Colon on the Panama Canal. These people had to provide their own beds on deck and their own food which they cooked themselves. Once in a while they might pay for a hot meal to be brought out to them.

These were natives of all colours and many of them were expert smugglers, who would buy things cheaply in Colon before they came on board and sell them in the ports we visited. At each port there was a commandant who expected to take a cut of all goods brought in. When the President of the country was elected for his term of five years he got rid of all the old officials and put his friends in their place so they all knew it was up to them to make as much money as they could while they had the chance. This is why smuggling was so rife. I remember one commandant was a tall, red-headed man. He was of Scots descent but could not speak a word of English.

It was possible to buy a great many things very cheaply in Colon - perfumes, genuine Panama hats, silks, watches, jewellery - even shrunken heads at sixty dollars each if you wanted them. It used to nauseate me to look at them, for there would often be a whole window full of these horrors, all staring at the passers-by.

Many of these smugglers became familiar faces to us. Sometimes members of the ship's crew would smuggle something back to New York to sell at a profit. The stewardess would often take bottles of perfume ashore strapped to her legs and hidden by her skirt. On one of these occasions I was going ashore with her when the customs' man stared long and hard at her. With great presence of mind she asked him calmly, "Do you want to search me?" But he waved her through, to my great relief.

Living conditions aboard ship were very crowded for the workers in the stewards' department. About twenty men lived and slept in a place measuring about twelve feet by eight feet in the forward end of the ship. This was known as the "glory hole",. There was nowhere to sit down, the only thing to do was to lie on one's bunk. We had nowhere to eat our meals, they had to be eaten standing up. Sanitary conditions were very primitive, but the night watchman would change our bed linen, put clean towels and generally clean up after us, and for this we all gave him something at the end of the voyage. This was in addition to his wages.

The bunks were arranged one above the other to save space and during a storm those sleeping in the top bunks had to pass a rope around themselves and fasten it to something, to save being thrown out as the ship pitched and tossed.

As we went further into the tropics the heat down there became unbearable. Sometimes men would find it too much to bear and go berserk. I have known them to run out on deck with the silver serving dishes and fling them into the sea. I remember hearing that on another ship a piano had somehow been man-handled to the side and tipped overboard.

It was far too hot to wear pyjamas or even put as much as a sheet across ourselves, and as the heat increased so tempers frayed and quarrels and fights became commonplace, with the men snarling at one another over the least thing. The whole voyage took about nineteen or twenty days and as soon as we landed in a foreign port we all got ashore as quickly as we could. After a glass or two of rum and a visit to the local brothel we were all as quiet as lambs.

If this seems a coarse subject to mention you must remember that I am trying to tell you the truth about my life as I remember it. You must also remember that the tropics have a very different effect on a man than the temperate zones we are used to. On board all the ships of the United Fruit Company there were condoms and prophylactic ointments freely available for the crew, from the chief steward's cabin, and armed with these we were pretty sure to escape any of the diseases we laid ourselves open to.

In Panama the Americans had a prophylactic station for the use of their own personnel stationed there so that after a visit to a brothel they could go and disinfect themselves. There were no attendants but everyone knew what to do and any visiting seamen were able to go in and make use of the same faculties. If an American soldier caught a disease and did not report it he was given medical treatment but his pay was stopped until he was well again. If he did report it his pay was not stopped. This was a very sensible arrangement.

When the pantryman was unfortunate enough to contract gonorrhoea and had to leave the ship, I took his job. This meant I had to bring up the fruit and vegetables from the hold for use in the kitchen, make the tea and coffee, and cut cheese into small portions. The cheese then had to be placed on a cream cracker, on a plate prepared with a paper doily. The favourite combination was cream cheese, with guava jelly on another cracker. The guava grew in the tropics and made a very refreshing and pleasant jelly which we bought in jars from the natives who came on board at ports of call. These natives would also take away our dirty washing and bring it back clean next day. We paid them either in money, or in clothes we didn't want, or in hot, spicy foods which they enjoyed.

It was the job of the chief steward to write out the menu and he then gave it to the chef in the kitchen. I would study the menu and draw what was needed from the stores, making a note of what I'd taken. Everything possible was done to please the passengers. If anyone asked for something which was not on the menu or needed a special diet the second steward, who was in charge of the dining room, would give me a chit authorising this and I would bring whatever was required.

Standard pay on the ships of the Banana Navy was:

the chief steward	150 dollars a month
the chief cook	140 dollars a month
the second steward	90 dollars a month
the pantryman	60 dollars a month
waiters, assistant stewards	40 dollars a month.

The deck crew got more than this, but they were supposed to be trained able seamen and they only worked six days a week as opposed to our seven.

The deck stewards' job was to look after the passengers on deck and in consequence they got a lot in tips. No man could live on the lowest rate of 40 dollars a month, so it is not surprising that the waiters tried to ingratiate themselves with the people whose tables they served in the hope of receiving tips to boost their pay. They could not have managed otherwise. The meaning of the word "tips" is, after all, "To Improve Personal Service".

A few days before we arrived back in New York a Gala Evening was held on board ship. A four- or five-piece orchestra played, and the leaflets with the words of popular songs on them were distributed among the passengers. Some of these songs were music hall songs and I can still remember some of them today. One was about "Frivolous Sal":

They call her Frivolous Sal,
A peculiar sort of a gal,
With a heart that was mellow,
A real good fellow,
Was my pal Sal.
Your troubles, sorrows and care
She was always willing to share:
A wild sort of devil,
But dead on the level,
Was my pal Sal.

Another was:

Goodbye little yellow bird,
I cannot mate with you.
I love you, little yellow bird,
But I love my freedom too.
So goodbye little yellow bird,

I'd rather face the cold
On a leafless tree,
Than a prisoner be,
In a cage of gold.

Then there was:

The boy I love is up in the gallery,
The boy I love is looking down at me,
Can't you see, he's waving his handkerchief at me,
Merry as a robin on a Christmas tree.

In New York when the ship berthed we were given an allowance of $1.50 per day, and a meal at that time could be had for 50 cents. Pay day was the next day after berthing. The pantryman, night watchman and anyone else from the stewards' department who had helped the waiters in any way used to line up waiting for a hand-out, because the waiters were the men with the money after collecting all the tips during the voyage. The men from Head Office would come at the same time and go through the books. $1.10 was allowed for each passenger's keep per day, so Head Office didn't want the meal allowance to be scrimped. On the other hand neither did they want to overspend. They had got it down to a fine art.

There was also a representative of the Seaman's Bank present on pay day, and the crew could deposit all or part of their wages so they would not spend it all on drink or get robbed. But some of them used to ask me to look after their money for them. I suppose I had an honest face.

The first place we all went when the ship docked was to the Seaman's Mission to collect our mail, but we couldn't have it before sitting through a religious service. Never have rough seamen been more eager for a service to start, and we used to ask them to hurry up. Afterwards we had to find a room for the night. We used to buy a copy of the *New York Herald Tribune* between us to look at the rooms to let. These rooms were supposed to have been inspected, but whoever did it must have been blind. If it was getting late and there was no time to find somewhere else we just had to put up with what we got. We could have gone back to the ship, of course, to sleep, but no-one ever did. A very small proportion of the crew were married so they went home.

I used to keep a small notebook and in this I wrote down the addresses where I stayed. If it was a good place I marked a "g" by it, if it was very good "vg", others were marked "nbg". It was a real lucky dip, but sometimes if I found a really bad place I would be too tired to look for somewhere else. All I wanted to do was sleep, with the knowledge that next day I could look forward to walking the streets of New York - a free man again!

In New York I always tried to stay at Welshman John Morgan's hotel at West 145th Street, because that is where I had gone first on coming to the city, as he often heard where there were jobs for me, but very often he was full up. He told me once about a sailor who went there with a woman whom he said was his wife. John Morgan knew the woman of old so he decided not to go to bed that night. In the small hours of the morning he heard her creep downstairs so he locked the front door to prevent her getting out. Then he marched her back upstairs to confront her "husband". As John Morgan had guessed, the man's pockets had been emptied and he only just managed to stop the sailor beating her up. He sent her off and told her not to come back.

On one occasion while wandering through the New York Jewellery Exchange, an arcade of little shops run by Jews, selling secondhand jewellery and watches, I fell in love with a gold watch and chain which I bought for myself. I took care never to take it to sea with me, for there is a saying, "There is a thief on every ship" and it is quite true. I always took it to the pawnbroker before we sailed and for a fee of a dollar or so, I knew it would be safe until I came back. I had it until quite recently when I gave it to my niece's son. There was a belief that these Jews would never turn down the first offer which was made to them on a Monday morning. I tried once or twice but I found it wasn't true.

Thanks are offered to Mrs. I. Stevens, Miss C. Gibbon, and Mrs. M. Hopson for access to Mr. E. Rhys-Price's manuscripts and permission to publish.

THE RISE AND FALL OF A MOUNTAIN COMMUNITY

by JOSH POWELL

Part One - The Area Before 1830

Cwmbargoed means "Bargoed Valley" and on old maps it referred to the entire valley of the Taff Bargoed River which flowed through the villages of Cwmfelin and Bontnewydd before joining the River Taff at Quakers Yard. However in more recent times Cwmbargoed was the large saucer-shaped area where the mountain streams converge to form the Taff Bargoed River - From Twynywaun in the north to Nantyffin in the south. The whole area was more than one thousand feet above sea level and formed part of the old hamlets of Heol Wermod and Forest.

Nantyffin was two miles above Cwmfelin and a further two miles from Bontnewydd. Here at the mouth of the valley there were five farms and a few farmworkers' cottages. It was rumoured that Charles the first visited Nantyffin when he was staying with his friend Colonel Pritchard at Llancaiach in 1645. The Church bought Brynceira Farm in 1742 and its tenants became responsible to Nantddu Church, Cwmtaff. John Wesley, the founder of Methodism, preached at Blaen Cwmbargoed Farm in the eighteenth century. The other two farms were called Pwll Glas and Blaencwm. Twynywaun, two miles to the north, was more than thirteen hundred feet above sea level. Its proud history dated back to the twelfth century and Waun Fair was known far and wide. Four times a year farmers from all parts of Wales and the Border Counties, gathered at this elevated spot. It was a hiring fair but generally they were concerned with the buying and selling of animals especially sheep and mountain ponies. The Full Moon Inn welcomed weary travellers - Hywel Harris the Welsh evangelist stayed there in 1766.

There was a Courthouse to punish wrong doers.

The small settlement near Twynywaun was called Trefhir (Longtown) and the cottages were occupied by miners working along the northern edge of the South Wales Coalfield. Iron making had started in Dowlais in 1759 and the raw materials of coal and iron were obtained by tunnelling into the seams that came to the surface in this area. Ponds were constructed on the mountainside to provide the constant supply of water needed to manufacture iron. Rhaslas Pond was the largest.

On the hill near Trefhir, there were three houses called Trecatty - "Tai Nos". The houses were reputed to have been built during the hours of darkness with smoke ascending from the chimneys at dawn. This was in accordance with the Laws of Twm Sion Catty.

The Rev. Rhys Jones, the third minister of Zion Welsh Baptist Church, Twynyrodyn, preached at Trefhir in 1810. Ieuan Dyfed (E. T. John) described the scene. "Apart from Trefhir, there were only a few cottages here and there on the mountainside. Long before a service commenced the people would pour in from every direction - women carrying babes in arms and men walking hand in hand with the children or carrying them on their shoulders". It was in this way that Rhys Jones filled the area with the Word of the Gospel. Twenty years later in 1830 Zion released fourteen members to establish Salem Welsh Baptist Church in Cwmfelin.

Part Two - Industrial Growth

It was in 1830 that Isaac Morgan sank the first deep mine in the area and he chose a spot half way between Nantyffin and Twynywaun near the road to Penrheolferthyr. It seems to have had a short active life. The following year there was industrial unrest and the Merthyr Riots leading to the execution of Richard Lewis (Dic Penderyn). More importantly the Cwmbargoed Balancing Pits were opened in 1839. Water was used to raise the coal in this kind of pit so dry spells caused problems. When the deeper mines of Nantwen in 1870 and Bedlinog, South and North Tunnel in 1874 began to operate, steam power was in use. There were four pits within a radius of a mile and there were smaller mines at Tyla Dowlais and Pantywaun - on the northern edge of the area.

The colliers, who worked in these mines, lived in the neighbouring towns and either walked or were carried to work. However it was important for the officials to be on hand so the owners built rows of stone cottages to house these

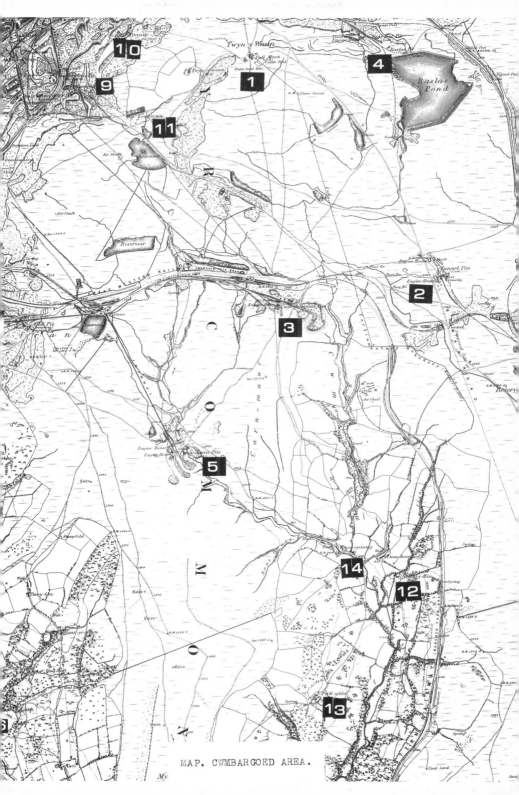

MAP. CWMBARGOED AREA.

MAP. CWMBARGOED AREA. 1885

KEY

1. Twyn y Waun and Full Moon.
2. Tunnel Pits. Coal.
3. Cwmbargoed Pits. Coal.
4. Four feet Pit and Raslas Pit. Coal.
5. Penydarren Pits. Coal.
6. Taibach Pit. Coal.
7. Pit No. Six. Ironstone.
8. Pit No. Seven. Ironstone.
9. Tyle Dowlais Pit. Ironstone.
10. Trecatty.
11. Longtown (Trefhir).
12. Nant-y-ffin. Farm.
13. Pwll-glas. Farm.
14. Brynceira. Farm.

men and their families. The sinking of the mines led to the rapid growth of local villages. Just as Pantywaun and Fochriw owed their birth to the coal mines, so the sinking of Nantwen and Bedlinog collieries changed the small hamlet of Cwmfelin into the closely-knit community of miners and their families that took its name from the latter mine. Public houses and places of worship were built - Salem was enlarged in 1876 and four more chapels were erected - Moriah in 1876; Sardis in 1877; Gosen in 1885 and Soar in 1899. Further down the Valley, the hamlet of Bontnewydd grew into the village of Trelewis when the Deep Navigation Colliery was sunk in Treharris in 1879. St Mary's Church was built in 1886 and Ebenezer in 1889.

However on the bleak moorland which formed the upper reaches of the Taff Bargoed Valley, development was confined to the scattered rows of cottages near the mines - South Tunnel Cottages; Cwmbargoed Pit Row; Penydarren Pit Houses and Isaac Morgan Pit Cottages. Most of the occupants had come from other parts of Wales - Tom Jones the pitman at Penydarren pit was a North Walian; 'Farmer' Jones, the engine man at Cwmbargoed came from Beulah; Joshua Owens the farrier at South Tunnel, was a native of Radnorshire while Llewellyn Nicholas, the winder in the same pit, came from Carmarthen - on one occasion he wound up the body of one of his sons who had been killed underground. There were frequent fatal accidents like that of young William Jenkins who was buried by a roof fall at Longwork Pit, Cwmbargoed in November 1885. With so few 'tied' cottages the population was always changing. The stone cottages were small and functional but the occupants converted them into snug homes. Coal was cheap and plentiful so the warm glow of the fire illuminated the kitchen. Most of the miners kept pigs and poultry in the back gardens and many grazed a pony on the mountainside. Although economic circumstances had persuaded them to leave the areas where they were born, the miners had brought with them the rural way of life.

During the early days coal was carried along railroads and inclines to Dowlais and Merthyr. One of these from Penydarren pits was laid along the road to Penrheolferthyr; another, from Fochriw, Cwmbargoed and South Tunnel wound round the mountain to Dowlais Top.

In 1865 the Colly Line was laid from Dowlais to Fochriw and Bedlinog. The coal from these pits was conveyed along this railway to the insatiable furnaces of Dowlais Iron Works. The demand for iron ore to be imported and the need to export coal lead to the most revolutionary change in the history of Cwmbargoed. The old Colly Line was inadequate so in January 1876, after years of discussion the Joint Great Western & Rhymney Railway was opened between Dowlais

Caeharris and Nelson / Llancaiach with connections to Cardiff and Pontypool Road. From Nelson to Cwmbargoed the line followed the contours of the lovely Taff Bargoed Valley but from Cwmbargoed to Dowlais there were problems that required great engineering skill. These were solved by excavating a deep cutting between Colly Box and Penydarren Platform and building a high mineral platform between Penydarren Platform and Dowlais Junction. The tracks rested on this high table, jutting out above the mountain slope and formed a gentle curve. At Dowlais Junction the line divided - straight into the Upper Works and Coke Ovens; via the Zig Zag Branch to the Lower Works; or along the passenger line into Dowlais Caeharris Yard. The Yard was a hive of industry with a large loco shed and a giant turntable. Dowlais was the terminus of the Branch line where the engines - Class 56 - were loaded with coal and water. The station, made of stone, contained a booking office, two large waiting rooms and a lamp room while close by there was a very high goods shed and a coal yard at the end of Cwmcanol Street.

There is no doubt that the Railway made Cwmbargoed. The Dowlais Iron Company built a large marshalling yard on the open mountain and the coal from their pits was carried down the Valley to the markets at Home and Overseas.

Cwmbargoed was a busy centre and before the First World War, it was not unusual to see more than a dozen engines pulling, pushing or banking the heavy journeys along the very steep gradients. There was a spectacular crash at Llancaiach in August 1899 when a train, consisting of 24 trucks of steel rails from Dowlais, got out of hand, gained speed and crashed into a coal train from Aberdare, thus blocking all tracks. Fortunately no one was killed. In 1905 a deputation of M.P.s, railway officials and members of the Board of Trade witnessed the new Either Way Brakes being tested at Dowlais Junction and Ffaldcaiach.

In addition to the goods traffic, there were six passenger trains in both directions daily and the journey to Dowlais Caeharris was only eight minutes. It needed three signal boxes to control this traffic - Nantyffin, Cwmbargoed and the Colly Box near Isaac Morgan's old pit.

Cwmbargoed Station had a commanding view of the Taff Bargoed Valley and trains could be seen soon after they left Bedlinog. The Station was a stone building with Booking Office and two waiting rooms. On the 'Down' platform there was a high wooden shelter and near the end of the platform was the lamproom - a small hut made of corrugated iron sheets where the smell of paraffin was overpowering. The Station signal box and Yard were lit by Tilley lamps. The Guards, porters and shunters used hand lamps while the small signal lamps burned for a week without refilling. Near the Station there were cattle pens and on Waun Fair days, ponies were loaded into trucks and sent to all parts of the British Isles.

The Company built fine houses for their officials. The Stationmaster has a palatial house in a large garden. The two houses at Nantyffin and the six houses in Railway Terrace accommodated the signalmen and platelayers. Railway houses were nothing like the miners' cottages - they were brick built with large rooms; wooden stairs and rows of water closets with drains leading to cesspools. Again the occupants were different. At a time when Welsh was the language of the surrounding area, Cwmbargoed was English. The reason was easy to understand. The miners had come from parts of Mid and North Wales but many of the railway men came from the west of England and the Border Counties. Mr Parker the Stationmaster was a Londoner while Charlie Probert the signalman and Bert Jones, the ganger came from the west of England. Harry Goddard, the ganger and Ted Etheridge, the wheeltapper were from the Swindon area while Alf Wyatt, another signalman came from the Forest of Dean.

When the railway came to Cwmbargoed there was no place of worship - some of the people walked to the Church in Fochriw or the chapels in Dowlais or Merthyr while others held cottage meetings in their own homes. Some employees had started a Railway Mission in Dowlais Caeharris Station but they had no building. Eight years later in September 1892, the Mission Hall was erected near Railway Terrace. It was built from two old signal boxes with a large coal fireplace on the one side and four large windows on the other. It had a slate roof and was lit by paraffin lamps hanging from the ceiling. Its first secretary was Mr Arthur Lucas, a railway guard and a plate layer, Mr John Holland, was treasurer. The Mission Hall became the centre of the religious and social life of the village. The railwaymen belonged to every denomination - Church of England; Methodist; Baptist; Salvationist; etc. - so the Railway Mission was Interdenominational. Although there were Missions in all the big railway centres of Great Britain and Overseas, the only other one in Wales was at Builth Road.

The Hall provided Sunday Services; Sunday School; Band of Hope; Bible Study; Penny Readings; Lantern Slide Lectures; Concerts and Parties to which all the villagers, not only the railway families, were cordially invited.

On 22nd January 1905 Evan Roberts, the famous evangelist preached in Dowlais and the Revival led to the Mission Hall being packed half an hour before a service commenced. Mid week services were often drowned by the noise of trains.

Cwmbargoed was a very busy centre during the Pre War years and the incessant noise penetrated the rooms of the old houses - the hooters of the various pits; wagons crashing as they were being shunted in the network of sidings; and the engines groaning as the they pushed or pulled the heavy trains up the steep gradients. There were iron ore trains from Cardiff which needed four engines to bring them up the steep bank from Bedlinog. They consisted of forty four, 21 ton hoppers. Then there were coal trains from Nantwen and other collieries; coke trains from Bargoed via Fochriw; and tarmac and steel trains from Dowlais. The rails manufactured in Dowlais were seventy five feet long and were carried on special low Bogey wagons. The collier trains, called CWBS, were cattle trucks with wooden seats - they spewed out wave after wave of dirty miners at Penydarren Platform for the quick dash down the Bogey Road to their homes in Merthyr. When his father obtained a job in Dowlais Iron Works, Elisio Cuesta left their home in Billbao, Spain. He started as a cleaner in Dowlais Engine Shed and later became a noted driver on the Branch line. Every Sunday the noise and bustle ceased and peace reigned.

Nantyffin was a peaceful haven in the busy cauldron and life had changed little - cows from the five farms provided milk for the community while sheep and horses were there in great numbers. Eddie Slimmonds, of Pwll Glas Farm, carried the fresh milk in a metal jack and a half-pint ladle was used to transfer it to the jugs in the cottages. The Kinseys occupied Nantyffin and Brynceira Farms. One of their grandfathers had been a farm labourer in Radnorshire but when he moved into the area, he took out contract work building mountain walls. The other grandfather lived in Blanche House, Dowlais - he hired horses to most of the small mines and grazed them at Brynceira. Knackers' carts were always seen picking up the carcasses of dead animals - at the end of their useful lives they usually ended up in Boultons.

James Boulton built a slaughter house in Penrheolferthyr in 1907. The four large iron boilers were fired with cheap coal and each one could hold half a dozen animals. Boultons was a valued customer of the Great Western Railway and the boiled meat was sent in metal containers to zoos and pet shops in the big cities.

The children of Nantyffin went to Penybanc School in the Fochriw Valley while those of South Tunnel Cottages went to Fochriw School. The children of Penydarren Pit Houses went to Twynrodyn School but the majority in Cwmbargoed attended the famous Dowlais Central School, designed by Sir Charles Barry and opened by Lady Charlotte Guest in 1855. Some were fortunate enough to progress to the Higher Grade School in Caedraw. Every child had a long walk in all kinds of weather and with no canteens, they had to carry a packed lunch and drink. Although the cottages were scattered the children met each other at every opportunity. The Mission Hall was a favourite meeting place but there were also the ponds - for swimming in summer and skating in winter.

When King George the Fifth and Queen Mary visited Dowlais Works on 27th June 1912, the Royal Train passed through Cwmbargoed.

A few years before the Great War, electric pylons were erected on the mountain and brought tragedy. Local boys had great fun sliding down the wires using bucket handles until the current was switched on. Charlie Weaver's arms were burnt away but when his body hit the ground, his heart started to beat again.

The Great War started on 4th August 1914 and it affected the lives of the mountain folk just as much as those in the Valley towns. Although railwaymen and miners were in reserved occupations, many were caught up in the euphoria and answered Kitchener's Call. Harold Allen, the porter signalman, was lucky enough to survive and he described how most of his comrades were wiped out before they could fire a shot.

Part Three - Industrial Decline

The First Great War ended on 11th November 1918 and the lucky ones returned home. Will Evans was demobbed before being posted to the Western Front and his War bride, Lillian returned after working on the 'Shell' ships in Newport Docks. They arrived home with high hopes but they soon discovered that it was not 'a land fit for heroes'. The First Great Strike took place in the hot summer of 1921. The demand for coal decreased and in 1924 the deep mines closed - Cwmbargoed and South Tunnel shared the fate of Fochriw, Nantwen and Bedlinog. Some of the Miners found work in Nantyffin Drift or Taff Merthyr Colliery near Trelewis, opened by Powell Duffryn in 1926. This colliery had pit head baths so they didn't use the CWBS. However some moved to mines outside the area - to Ogilvie or Groesfaen collieries in the Fochriw Valley and Tower or Aberpergwm mines in the Neath Valley. It was bed to work and work to bed. Obviously the closure of the pits affected the Railway and the Nantyffin and Colly signalboxes closed in 1924. Worse followed when the iron and steel making stopped in Dowlais in 1930 and the Works moved to Cardiff. The marshalling yards were no longer needed - the sidings fell into disrepair and were lifted. The railwaymen's wages were low but they had security - yet natural wastage had the same effect as redundancies. Cwmbargoed lost its stationmaster in 1934 and so many of the railway houses, which had been 'tied' cottages were occupied by families not connected with Great Western Railway. The Ivor Works still used the line to Nelson / Llancaiach but traffic did not buck up until 1939 when the I.C.I. opened a Works in Pant and a number of small factories used the Zig Zag as an outlet.

During the Inter War years, Morgan Kinsey of Nantyffin Farm bought Blaen Cwmbargoed and Pwll Glas while his brother, Evan, farmed Brynceira. So there were two farms where there had been five. Morgan Kinsey was a progressive farmer and in 1930 he became a pioneer in silage making. Bryn and Bert Howells worked as shepherds and farm labourers but they also employed John Morris and his sons at shearing and harvest time. In Autumn Morgan and Evan drove their sheep to South Glamorgan in search of Winter tack and collected them the following Spring. Twynywaun Fair was still held four times a year and dealers gathered from all parts of the country. Horses were in good supply and they grazed on the bleak moorland. Boultons was thriving having bought ex Army lorries to replace old knackers carts.

If the life of the mountain man was hard, that of his wife was much harder. She carried out the normal household chores - cooking, washing, cleaning and raising her family - without the benefit of electricity and modern appliances, and she had to replenish the pantry. There were no shops in Cwmbargoed so pantries had to be well stocked. For most people Saturday was 'Shopping Day'. As ten o'clock approached, small groups of women and children made their ways to Cwmbargoed Station where they exchanged the weekly gossip. Three hours later, having purchased the weekly goods in Dowlais, they returned weighed down by their heavy shopping and facing a long walk to their homes.

Many of the villagers kept poultry and pigs while others had well cultivated gardens. Although the soil was poor there was plenty of manure as a fertiliser. The weekly goods were supplemented by tradesmen who called regularly - Billy Davies of Mountain Hare, who still delivered the fresh milk from a metal jack with a half-pint ladle; Fred Showers the Costerer; Mrs. Weaver the Fishwoman ; and Mrs Sherman the Packwoman. In an area where there was no electricity none was more welcome than Mr. Jenkins the Oilman. His horse drawn covered wagon contained paraffin, mats and brushes. All worked hard to earn a living in difficult times. Callers were always welcome - they brought news of the outside world as well as essential wares. Cwmbargoed was served by the Dowlais Post Office. Every morning the postman picked up his bag at six thirty from the Sorting Office in North Street but the villagers didn't receive their mail before lunch. The reason was simple - he began his delivery in Dowlais Top and Penywern before proceeding to Pengarnddu, Gypsy Castle, Pantywaun, South Tunnel, Cwmbargoed, Penydarren Pits, and Penmaen fawr - a six hour walk. No wonder Les Pound and Stan Fisher joined the Guards in the Second World War.

During the Inter War Years the Mission Hall played an important role in the lives of the villagers and their children. There was no resident minister but the Sunday Services were conducted by lay preachers who walked across the mountain from Dowlais, Merthyr or Fochriw. Charlie Probert worked hard among the young people until he retired to Exeter in 1928. Then two young teachers - Miss Thomas and Miss Hughes - took over the Wednesday Band of Hope and they continued to do so during the dark days of the Depression. Summer and Christmas parties were always part of the Church calendar. The Annual Outing to Barry Island began in 1925 and only stopped when World War Two was declared.

Apart from the concerts and magic lantern shows in the Mission Hall, there was little entertainment. The men might visit the public houses in Mountain Hare, Dowlais or Fochriw while the rest of the family went to see films in the two cinemas in Dowlais or the five in Merthyr Tydfil.

Wireless became a reality in the twenties and soon the men on the mountain were making their own sets. These sets required a 120 volt High Tension Battery and a 1½ volt wet accumulator that needed recharging every week. When the programmes improved, the radio became more popular than the clockwork gramophones.

In 1935 there was a major reorganisation of education in Merthyr Tydfil. The children of Nantyffin and South Tunnel still attended Fochriw School but the rest were provided with a bus (The Flying Pig) from the top of the Bogey Road to the schools in Twynyrodyn or on Queen's Road. No longer would Cwmbargoed children pick their way among the Patches on their way to and from Dowlais Central Schools. As the Depression grew worse, many people could not afford to buy coal. So little groups of men spent their days digging for coal in the Patches near Black Vein. Of course it was illegal so they had to watch out for the police. There was also trouble in the mines and in 1938 there was a bitter dispute in Taff Merthyr Colliery. There was enmity between those who worked and those on strike and families were split.

The Second World War was declared on 3rd September 1939. During the previous year there was an increase in the traffic on the Branch line due to the building of the I.C.I. Works in Pant and the extension of factories along the Goat Mill Road. There was a R.A.F. Observation Station above Bedlinog and an Army Camp in Fochriw. Now the Government built twenty Nissen huts equipped with electric lights and cooking facilities, near Cwmbargoed Station. A party of Royal Marines were posted there but they left after a few months and it remained empty until August 1943 when it was opened as the East Glam. Sector Weekend Training Camp for the Home Guard. In July 1944 the Camp was visited by General Sir Harold Franklyn, Commander in Chief of Home Forces.

For the people of Cwmbargoed the night of 30/31 July 1940 was the most frightening of the War. Thirteen German Bombs fell in a line from Boultons in Mountain Hare to South Tunnel. Fortunately none of the cottages was hit and no one was hurt. Yet there was deep sorrow at the news that Will Tom Lewis had been killed in Crete in May 1941.

The War in Europe ended on 8th May 1945 and the War against Japan three months later. Horace Morgan returned to his job on the Branch line and Tom Kinsey went back to Nantyffin Farm but others were less fortunate and joined the long queue in the Dole Office.

V. E. Day was a time for rejoicing and the villagers celebrated with a party in the Mission Hall. For the children it was a new experience. Rationing had been introduced in January 1940 and it continued for many years after the War. The villagers deposited their food coupons in the shops in Dowlais. Those who kept poultry and pigs, surrendered their meat and eggs coupons in exchange for corn and meal. In 1946 the Labour Government nationalised the mines and railways but the Branch line still served the I.C.I., Ivor Works and factories on the Zig Zag. Trains were used to remove the petrol dump in Fochriw and the large vans containing shells and ammunition while Bren Gun Carriers were taken to be scrapped in Dowlais Works. The passenger trains still provided a vital link with the Outside World but there had been changes. A Co-op Lorry from Pant delivered bottles of milk to the scattered houses; a little red Post Office van worked the old round in ninety minutes; and a Baker provided bread and cakes. However with no electricity in the homes Jenkins the Oil was of vital importance. The inhabitants still depended on wet accumulators to work their wireless sets. The cinemas in Dowlais and Merthyr Tydfil still attracted some and the public houses offered hospitality and companionship provided people were prepared to leave the warmth of their homes and walk across the bleak moorland.

It started to snow on 27th January 1947 and it stuck. There were further snowfalls causing disruptions along the Branch line and there was no respite. Low temperatures and strong easterly winds prevailed throughout February and the railwaymen worked day and nigh clearing the drifting snow from the points. The villagers were accustomed to hard winters but not even the oldest inhabitant could remember anything like the frightening north easterly blizzard that swept in on the 4th March. It entombed the Newport to Brecon passenger train in the deep Pantywaun cutting and blotted out the lines from Cwmbargoed under an avalanche of snow. The power stations needed coal but the miners couldn't reach the collieries. R.A.F. jet engines and ex Army flame throwers attempted to clear the drifts but eventually it was a gang of volunteers from the Dole Queue in

The Carmarthen Arms and the Blue Bell inns before demolition in 1904.
Cross Keys St. on right hand side.

The Fountain taken from Cross Keys Street, 1907.

Hen dy Cwrdd chapel and graveyard, 1994
l to r. William & Catherine Rees & family   Robert & Lucy Thomas & sons
Daniel & Margaret Jenkins & family   Robert & Abigail Thomas & family.

*n account of the tonnage of coal sent to George Insole in October 1833, by
ucy Thomas. The names of the boatmen are given and what she was paid for
ach boatload.*

eproduced courtesy of Mid Glamorgan Record Office/Mrs. A. Burton.

A bust of Lady Charlotte Guest, sculpted by Joseph Edwards. Cyfarthfa Cast
Museum and Art Gallery.

Evan Roberts preached in Dowlais on 22.1.1905. See J. Powell.

t. Mary's Church, Fochriw, 1920. Now demolished. See J. Powell.

Brynceira Farm, Cwmbargoed, about 1970.

*Tunnel Tavern, 1985, formerly four cottages known as South Tunnel Cottages.
Demolished in 1992 to make way for King Coal.*

The Gordon Lenox Constitutional Club, Aberfan. See Hugh Watkins's Diary. 1994.

Bethania Chapel, Aberfan, an older Bethania once stood on the site. 1994.

The royal train which carried the Queen and the Duke of Edinburgh to Merthyr Vale, at High St. Station, Merthyr Tydfil, 29th October, 1966. A Western Class diesel-hydraulic D 1054, Western Governor.
Photo, Keith Lewis.

Disaster Children. Afan Lido, Aberavon. December 1966.

Pant Glas Secondary Modern School. December 1966. See H. Watkins's Diary.

Last Day Before Demolition. Pant Glas Secondary Modern School, December 1966.

Form 3B, Pant Glas Secondary Modern School, 1966.
Back Row
Edward Watkins, John Garland, Andrew Rees,* Kathleen Clayton, Yvonne Williams, Linda Samuel, Robert Coffey.*
Middle Row
Allen Morgan, David Price, Howard Rees, Gerald James, Malcolm Manfield, Paul Lovis, Brenic Parker, Raymond Collins.*
Yvonne Brown, Alison John, John Nash, Denis Holder, Tony Minney, Terry Morris, Phillip Timbrell, Marilyn Sims,

Teachers, Pant Glas Secondary Modern School, 1965-66.
Back Row, L to R

Mr. Reg Chandler, Art; Mr. Lyn Thomas, Science (deceased); Mr. Eric Jenkins, English; Mr. Cyril Vaughan, Remedial;
Mr. Hugh Watkins, History, Geography and R.E.
Front Row

Mrs. May Howells, Domestic Science; Miss Gwynneth Evans, Deputy Head; Mr. Ken J. Davies, Acting Head;
Mr. Geoff Davies, Maths, P.E.; Mrs. Anne Hickey-Jones, Needlework (deceased); Mrs. Pat Hanks, Girls' P.E. and
Games.

Calfaria Chapel, Heolgerrig, Merthyr, 1994. Twelve memorial stones can be seen. See "Foundations".

Smyrna Chapel, Aberfan, 1994. An interesting building disfigured by badly sited lamp posts, toilets and no-parking signs. See "Foundations".

Heolgerrig Action Song Choir. Conductor - Mr. E. R. Abraham. Winners of 2nd Prize, Pontypool National Eisteddfod, 1924.

Photo courtesy of Merthyr Central Library.

Sisterhood, Calfalria Chapel, Heolgerrig. Presentation to Mrs. Lydia Osborne, Mayoress of Merthyr Tydfil, 1954-55. Photo courtesy of Mrs. Jen Jones.

Eighty years old. Mrs. Hannah Jane Meyrick's party in the vestry, Calfaria Chapel, Heolgerrig.
Photo courtesy of Mrs. Jen Jones.
Left to right
Mrs. Doris Morgan, Rachel Richards, Sister Margaret, Mary Jane Childs, Gwladys Morgan, Maggie Price,
Lydia Osborne, Harriet Osborne, Hannah Jane Meyrick, Ruth Thomas, Valerie Salmon, Nellie Coleman, Jen Jones,
Jennie Meyrick. The lady in the back row behind Mrs. H. J. Meyrick has not been identified.

Hope Chapel, Merthyr, 1994. See "Foundations".

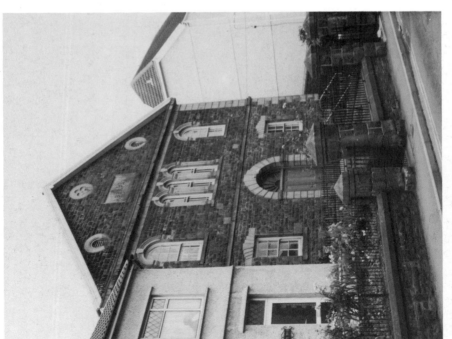

Aberfan Chapel, Aberfan, 1994.

Dowlais that opened the line. Cwmbargoed men undertook many dangerous journeys across the mountain to purchase food and fuel for their families.

During the glorious Summer of 1947 a pipeline was laid through the village connecting the gas works in Merthyr to that in Bargoed. The inhabitants were not amused - they already had electricity overhead now they had gas beneath their feet.

Nantyffin and Brynceira were still sheep farms but now lorries were hired to send the sheep away for winter tack. When Morgan Kinsey's younger son got married, he built a bungalow in the farm yard. It was the first house erected on the mountain this century. Nantyffin was in Gelligaer and the children had gone to Fochriw School but now Gelligaer paid for them to be educated in Merthyr Tydfil. When Hoovers opened their factory in Pentrebach in 1948, many railwaymen left the Branch line to work in the washing machine giant. The vacancies were filled by men glad to leave the mines for a safer job. In 1948 twenty four years after its closure, Cwmbargoed pit claimed its last victim. Fourteen year old Derek Jones of Pant was birdnesting when his foot slipped and he plunged down the nine hundred feet shaft. His body was never recovered and the following month two hundred people assembled at the pit head for a memorial service conducted by the Rector of Dowlais.

Trelewis Drift Mine, near Taff Merthyr Colliery, was opened in 1954. The Nantyffin miners, who had alighted from the CWBS at Bedlinog Junction Box, were transferred to the new drift. They travelled on the Taff Merthyr train. When the two railway houses at Nantyffin became vacant, they were demolished. So was the Stationmaster's house.

At last in 1958, electricity came to Cwmbargoed and villagers took full advantage with lights, heaters, cookers, vacuum cleaners and of course television.

Part Four - Depopulation

In 1958 the old Mission Hall was demolished and was replaced by a small wooden building only half its size. It had electric lights and heating but it was never filled.

The mountain community had longed to have electricity in the village. Little did they realise that it would lead to the eventual destruction of the area as they knew it. In 1958 Taylor Woodrow started opencast mining on the Rhymney Common - The Royal Arms Site - and they were able to build screens in the Cwmbargoed Railway Sidings. Coal reclamation from the old tips had been carried out for many years. Now Larry Ryan was able to build a large washery in the village. Not only did the reclamation scar the scenery but the noise and dust made the people's lives a misery. Furthermore a fleet of lorries carried waste from all the tips from miles around. They turned the Bogey Road into a quagmire.

In 1961 the occupants of Penydarren Pit Cottages were rehoused in the new Gurnos Estate and the houses were demolished. Those, who remained in the village, threatened to keep their children home from school.

Tom Kinsey claimed that in some ways the early months of 1963 were worse than 1947. It started to snow on the previous Boxing Day and lay on the ground until Easter. Once again the lines from Cwmbargoed were buried under the snow and three engines coupled together failed to break through the drifts in the Nantyffin Cutting. During the height of the January blizzard, an ambulance took Mrs. Nancy Powell to Gwaunfarren Maternity Hospital. It was a perilous journey and the request for the return trip was declined. It illustrated the problems of living in an isolated community with no telephone. Some of the families in Cwmbargoed Pit Row and Railway Terrace gave up the fight against the noise, dust and severe winters and moved to Dowlais.

On the 13th June 1964 Dr. Beeching closed the passenger service between Dowlais Caeharris and Nelson / Llancaiach. The last train, driven by Crad Lewis and Mel Davies with Terry Strange as guard, was packed as it passed through Bedlinog at one o'clock the next morning, there were men, women and children lining the platform. The closure of the passenger service was the last straw! Villagers were forced to use private transport or walk.

There had been no deaths in the village during the severe winters of 1947 & 1963 but a blizzard on Ash Wednesday, 3rd March 1965 caused the death of John Parry of the Merthyr Express near Isaac Morgan Cottages. The tragedy led to the opening of Cwmbargoed Weather Station. Later that year Cwmbargoed Railway Mission closed.

In 1973 the tenants of South Tunnel were rehoused in Fochriw and the landlord, Billy Gardner, converted the old miners' cottages into the fashionable Tunnel Tavern. It was opened in 1977 but when he left, it was vandalised and demolished in 1992. Mrs Lillian Evans came to the area long before the First World War and she had lived in Cwmbargoed Pit Row for more than half a century when she died in 1992. Derek, her youngest son, had built a bungalow and repair garage near Pit Row in 1981 but shortly after his mother's death the Opencast bought him out. Two years later in 1994 they bought out the last occupier in Railway Terrace. All the houses were to be demolished.

Although the passenger service ended in 1964, the goods traffic from Dowlais continued with diesel locomotives replacing steam. When Dowlais Caeharris Yard closed, a single track ran from Dowlais Junction to the Ivor Works. However in 1984 the rails below Colly Box were lifted. Yet Cwmbargoed is still an important coal centre. Taylor Woodrow removed coal from the Royal Arms/Trecatty site untill May 1984. Then after a lull, they erected larger screens in Cwmbargoed Railway Sidings before opening the East Merthyr Reclamation site in 1991. Fleets of lorries carry the reclaimed coal along the old railway embankment below Penydarren Platform to be blended. Then powerful diesel locomotives pull the long trains of loaded trucks to Aberthaw Power Station. There is little doubt that opencast mining contributed to the closures of Trelewis Drift Mine (1989); Deep Navigation (1991) and Taff Merthyr (1993). With the present scheme extending into the next century, it will become increasingly more difficult to discover traces of Cwmbargoed's colourful past.

See also Alun Morgan, Bedlinog: Glimpses of a Pre-War Society. Glamorgan Historian Volume Eleven.

"From Chaos to Calm"

The Diary of the Gordon-Lennox Education Centre, Nixonville, Aberfan

from Thursday, November 3rd, 1966 to Thursday, December 1st, 1966

by Hugh Watkins, Deputy Head, Lower School, Afon Täf High School, June 1994

It was less than a year since the most tragic event in the history of British schools took place in Aberfan, namely the Disaster of Friday October 21st, 1966, and the opening of Afon Täf High School, Merthyr's first Comprehensive, on 31st August 1967. How had the children adjusted during that short period of less than a year? Would or could they cope with another dramatic upheaval, namely moving to a large Comprehensive School?

A great deal had happened during that short period. How could 200 children adjust once again to lead normal lives? While the planning of the children's education was an urgent matter, the rehabilitation of the children was the immediate task in the early days after the disaster. It was left to the surviving teachers of the Pantglas schools to bring some assurance, warmth and stability.

The then Director of Education for Merthyr Tydfil, Mr. John Beale, M.A., set up on Monday October 31st, 1966, an educational centre in Aberfan Park, namely, two caravans, manned by the then Acting Head of Pantglas Secondary Modern School, Mr. Ken J. Davies. It was to act as a Supply base where a wide range of school material was stored and which children could call for and take

58

away to their homes: a Communication base where parents could keep in touch with all the recent developments; an interviewing base where there would be space and time for private and confidential interviews; a friendship base where it was hoped the education committee could build up a close relationship with parents in order to restore them to a happy, normal routine. During that Monday, 60 - 70 senior pupils and 20 junior pupils reported to the trailer.

With just two caravans at our disposal, Mr. Ken Davies thought that these arrangements were too unsatisfactory. With very inclement weather, one caravan was proving to be unsuitable so children had to amuse themselves as best they could. Toys, books, equipment, like pencils, crayons, coloured pencils, colouring books, etc., were distributed to parents and children.

At the time, I said to Mr. Ken Davies, "What about getting the use of the Gordon-Lennox Constitutional Club in the village, as an Educational Centre?" I negotiated with the then Secretary, Mr. R. Colston, with regard to rental or hire of the Gordon-Lennox Club. Mr. Colston arranged for me to meet the President and the Committee, who were meeting on Tuesday, November 1st, 1966.

Meanwhile, more pupils were reporting to the trailer: 75 seniors and 34 juniors. With extreme kindness, the Ebbw Vale Council placed their magnificent modern swimming baths at the children's disposal. The visits were frequent and as time went on, clearly therapeutic. Forty-five pupils were taken by P.E. Master Mr. G. E. C. Davies and Mrs. E. Hanks, P.E. Mistress, accompanied by Miss J. Morgan, to the baths.

On Tuesday evening, accompanied by my wife, Thelma, we met the then President of the Gordon-Lennox Club, Mr. R. Richards, Secretary, Mr. R. Colston, Mr. D. S. Evans, Treasurer, and fellow committee members, from 7.30 to 8.30 p.m. It is surprising what a few cigarettes, offered by my wife, could do to ease a situation.

My proposal was "On behalf of the Education Authority, my Headmaster, Mr. Ken J. Davies, we would like to hire the use of the Hall for educational purposes, not as a school, but as a recreational centre on a temporary basis, duration one month, for recreational work, painting, drawing, games, filmshows, reading, etc." I agreed that we would keep the premises as clean as possible, keeping damage to a minimum. Having made many inquiries in the village, finding halls, chapel vestries, etc., unsatisfactory, many of *them* still acting as mortuaries, rest centres for relief workers, army personnel. I was extremely pleased when the Committee unanimously agreed to let us have the Hall. They would not consider the question of monies. I promised to abide by their wishes and agreed that damages (if any) would be met by the Education Committee.

59

My wife and I were then shown around the Club - a large hall, well-ventilated, heated by eight electric ceiling heaters, a large stage, points for films, recorder, etc., toilet facilities. Cleaners would prepare the place, as the Centre had been used as a W.V.S. Rest Centre. Girls from Pantglas Senior School would help with the dusting, etc. I reported my findings to Mr. K. J. Davies.

Wednesday November 2nd, 1966

I reported to Mr. J. Beale, M.A., then Director of Education for Merthyr Tydfil, acting on my Headmaster's behalf, concerning the Gordon-Lennox Club. The Club was inspected by the Director of Education, Assistant Director, Mr. Eddie Roberts, Alderman Tal Lloyd, Chairman of the Education Committee and Committee members. I stressed that it was only a temporary measure, the two caravans in the Park proving to be inadequate.

Activities continued in the Park: Five-aside football with Mr. G. E. C. Davies and netball with Mrs. E. Hanks.

Mr. Roberts, H.M.I., visited the Centre to see for himself what arrangements had been made.

Thursday, November 3rd, 1966

The rehabilitation of children into an educational environment is one that had not yet been experienced in the Merthyr District so, in the hope that it might one day be of interest to future educationalists, I kept a detailed diary of the day-to-day activities undertaken by the staff involved in the Gordon-Lennox Club, and it reads as follows.

First day at the Centre opened at 9.30 a.m. until 12 noon. Afternoon 2 p.m. until 4 p.m. During the morning 40 - 50 children assembled; as the day progressed we had up to 120 children of all ranges. One could see the grief and shock written on many faces: no-one smiled. The movement of a table made a rumbling sound, which resulted in an unhealthy silence in the hall, as this was immediately associated with the rumble of descending slurry.

All children were given painting books, drawing books, crayons, pencils, etc. Mr. Ken Davies stated that he would remain at the Caravan Centre to deal with parents and the innumerable problems that had arisen, assisted by Miss K. Wood, the Borough Education Department Psychologist.

The job of Mr. Ken Davies and his staff, using the utmost humility, was trying to restore the children to a normal way of life, also to let parents gain confidence in letting their children be out of sight once again after such a traumatic experience.

Our policy was, in almost insurmountable circumstances, to attempt to ascertain the children's return to both self and team assertion. The only way to accomplish our goal was by the extreme human kindness of the staff and boundless energy and enterprise in organising PLAY with a capital P.; the elixir of mental absorption and youthful abandonment - the cure for nightmares.

With typical Nonconformist suspicion, would the children come to the Centre? The children heartily accepted the place, finding it both spacious and friendly. The steward and stewardess, Mr. and Mrs. Jones, now took on a new role as host and hostess, which they did with an abundance of kindness.

The Staff organised and set up activities, according to their professional ability and interests. Mr. Eric Jenkins set up a Reading Section and Library; Mr. Reg Chandler set up an Art Section with painting and drawing facilities; Mrs. Joan Williams and Miss Mair Morgan ably assisted with the Juniors and Infants. Miss Jane Morgan assisted with the films and projector. I had a History and Geography Section, where pupils could read about the past, draw and illustrate, read Geography books about different parts of the world, anything to get their minds off what they could see every day: the desolation of their schools, the black mass of slurry, their village in turmoil. Mrs. Ann Hickey set up a Needlework Section.

Miss Gwyneth Evans, Music teacher at Pantglas Secondary School, together with Mr. Cyril Vaughan, had been requested by the Merthyr Tydfil Education Authority to visit every parent in order to enable them to talk about their lost children, arrange school photographs, and to try to comfort them. It proved to be a very heart-rending task.

Following the disaster, many children wanted to hide at home. School had become a place of terror. But the appearance of "Teacher", Mr. Cyril Vaughan, well known in the village, at the door had now become a matter of joy. A bond had grown between teachers and parents that had never quite existed before. "Aw, Miss," said a little girl to Miss Evans, "My mother said you've been working hard."

Friday, November 4th, 1966

The weather was not on our side. In very wet conditions, the Centre opened as promised on time, 9.30 a.m. We were glad to welcome 120 children, 100 Seniors and 20 Juniors. They dispersed to the activities according to individual interests.

Three reporters visited the Centre to take many photographs. I gave them the required information as to why we had this Centre. I listed all members of staff with the various functions for which they were responsible. No-one was in charge, but all responsible to Mr. K. J. Davies, to whom I reported every day.

At 11 a.m., 80 pupils were taken by Mr. G. E. C. Davies, Mrs. E. Banks, Mr. Cyril Vaughan and Miss J. Morgan in Merthyr Tydfil Borough Transport to Ebbw Vale Baths.

Mr. Eddie Roberts, Assistant Director of Education for Merthyr Tydfil, visited to view the proceedings at first hand.

Miss Gwyneth Evans, Deputy Head, accompanied by Mr. Melville Thomas, County Drama Adviser for Monmouthshire (Gwent) arrived to make arrangements for a visiting Touring Drama Group. Various notices were displayed: Firework Display, Aberfan Park, Saturday 5th November 1966 at 6 p.m.; Swimming, Ebbw Vale Baths, Monday, 11 a.m.

Monday, 7th November, 1966

Centre opened at 9.30 a.m. Eighty-one pupils went swimming to Ebbw Vale Baths, accompanied by Mr. G. E. C. Davies, Mr. C. Vaughan, Miss J. Morgan, Mrs. E. Hanks and Mr. E. Jenkins. Remaining pupils carried on with recreational activities.

Visit of Mr. Len Rees, father of Andrew Rees. Mr. Rees expressed a wish for a memorial to Andrew who lost his life tragically. Mr. Rees's niece, Miss Mary Lenanton of 3, Fox Covert Lane, Misterton, Doncaster, Yorks., wished to present a memorial shield for football. The boy's father wished it to be called the PANTGLAS MEMORIAL SHIELD, to be played for each year by the various Secondary schools in memory of the seven pupils of the Secondary School who died so tragically: ANDREW REES, RAYMOND COLLINS, ROBERT COFFEY, MICHAEL JONES, VINCENT PARFITT, PATRICIA PROBERT and SHEILA FITZPATRICK.

I informed the father that I would pursue the idea further, putting the proposal to Mr. G. E. C. Davies, the P.E. Master, who in turn would contact the Merthyr Schools' Football Association. It is a shame nothing came of it, as we were soon involved in the throes of Comprehensive Education.

Monday 2 p.m. Films shown to approximately 200 pupils.

Tuesday, 8th November, 1966

Centre opened at 9.30 a.m. Numbers of pupils arriving each morning increased. Visit of newspaper reporters for the *Evening Standard*. During the morning Mr. Ivor Duncerton of B.B.C. *Twenty-Four Hours* Programme arrived to negotiate arrangements for filming at the Centre. On the 4th November I received a letter from Mr. W. A. C. Hall, Town Manager, Capitol Theatre, Cardiff, of the Rank Organisation, Theatre Division, extending the hospitality of the Capitol Theatre for the children to see the then famous film *The Sound of Music* with Julie Andrews.

Telephoned Capitol Theatre, Cardiff, and made arrangements with Mr. W. A. C. Hall, Town Manager, to accommodate 190 pupils and staff to see the film *Sound of Music* for the 2.30 matinee, Thursday, 10th November, 1966.

Tuesday 2 p.m.

Visit of London Drama Group in Charge of Mr. Melville Thomas, Drama Organiser for Monmouthshire. Mr. Emyr Jones, H.M.I., promised to make arrangements for some form of entertainment if not yet accommodated at Troedyrhiw and Merthyr Vale Schools.

Mr. Ronald Chenery and his team of players: Jenny Moody, Claire James, David Gilpin and John Griffiths (formerly of Troedyrhiw) performed an excellent play which was thoroughly enjoyed by all present, and held the children enthralled by its audience participation. It was a pleasure to see the young audience appreciate live entertainment, for some their first experience of the theatre. After the performance I expressed my profound thanks to the group on behalf of the Education Authority, the parents and the children of Aberfan. Other arrangements completed that day: the transportation of children from the Gordon-Lennox Centre to the Grove, made through Mr. Rafferty, of Merthyr Tydfil Omnibus Department; arranged for swimming activities the next day. Today 240 children were present at both the morning and afternoon sessions.

Wednesday, November 9th, 1966

Usual morning activities. Mr. Roberts, H.M.I., paid a visit to the Centre. He was surprised to see that numbers were increasing, both Juniors and Seniors.

At 10 a.m., Mr. Fyfe Robinson of the B.B.C. visited the Centre to make arrangements for filming.

11 a.m. Eighty-eight pupils taken by Merthyr Transport with staff to Ebbw Vale Baths. Mrs. Ann Hickey and Mrs. E. Hanks proceeded to Cardiff to collect a new batch of films from Sound Film Services, 27, Charles Street, Cardiff.

Wednesday, 2 p.m.

B.B.C. team of six began filming in the Centre. Over 200 pupils were present. Visit of a *Merthyr Express* reporter and photographer; I informed him that we were not a school but a recreational centre; no lessons were taking place, only senior pupils reading in the Club Lounge, which I had acquired that day with the consent of the Steward, Mr. Jones, as a quiet reading room.

Senior pupils present, 160; Juniors and Infants 90, total 250.

Thursday, 10th November, 1966

The majority of children reported at 9.30 a.m. All children were allowed home at 11 a.m. for lunch. They had to report back at 12.15 p.m. for instructions regarding the afternoon procedure.

12.35 p.m., 190 children and six staff proceeded to Cardiff in two double-decker buses, provided by Merthyr Tydfil Borough Corporation, to see the film *The Sound of Music*. We arrived in Cardiff at 1.45 p.m.; Cardiff Constabulary ably assisted in traffic control, allowing the buses to pull up in front of the Capitol Theatre. We were met by Mr. W. A. C. Hall, the Town Manager of the Capitol Theatre, Cardiff. Children were televised by both B.B.C. and T.W.W. cameras. The Management excelled themselves in giving the children a great welcome. Each child received a bag of sweets; during the interval, free ice-cream, drinks, etc., were distributed. At the end of the performance, the children were televised by 20th Century Fox, for distribution in America.

I thanked the Management on behalf of the Education Authority for their extreme kindness to the Aberfan children. Three hearty cheers were given to Mr. Hall. The party returned safely to Aberfan by 6.45 p.m. A letter of thanks was later forwarded to Mr. Hall for his kindness.

Notice

Mr. Stan Rees, Manager of the Concrete Block Factory, Aberfan, arranged free transportation for the Saturday Football Match, Merthyr Town playing Kettering (a Top of the League) team. Anyone wishing to attend this match, adults and children, would be allowed free transportation and free entry into the match.

Numbers of pupils in the Centre, 260.

Friday, 11th November, 1966

The Centre opened at 9.30 a.m. with roll call and the usual activities. *Daily Express* photographer arrived to photograph the pupils. The Centre was visited by Mr. W. Lawrence, Teachers' Secretary at the Merthyr Teachers' Centre, with a French visitor; also a visit from Mr. J. Lambert, Headmaster of Troedyrhiw Secondary Modern School, with Mr. Josh Powell, Maths and Science Teacher.

Friday 11 a.m., 80 pupils proceeded to the Ebbw Vale Swimming Baths. I received a telephone message from Mr. Eddie Roberts, Deputy Director of Education. To quote, "I was to proceed to Crescent Street, Taff Street and Nixonville

64

to find out how many senior pupils lived in this area, informing them that School would be available for them at Troedyrhiw from Monday next, arrange with parents about transport, School dinners, etc ." Also spoke with Mr. John Beale, Director of Education in respect of one pupil, William Kenneth Williams.

After lunch, proceeded to Nixonville at 2 p.m. - half-way through my interviews. Met Mr. J. Beale, informed him where the boy, Williams, lived.

Met the parents of the following pupils who unanimously agreed to send their children to Troedyrhiw. Parents were only too glad for their children to go back to school. I informed them that a bus would pick up their children at 8.55 a.m. at Crescent Street, near the Square, and that Troedyrhiw School started at 9.20 a.m. Pupils' homes visited: Carol Jones, age 11; David Williams, age 11; Christopher O'Brien, age 11; Terence Misselbrook, age 11; Michael Timbrell, age 13; Gaynor Sullivan, age 13; Susan Davies, age 11; Lorraine Williams, age 11; Edwina Williams, age 11; William Kenneth Williams, age 12. I reported to Mr. K. J. Davies at the Caravan Centre in the Park, in due course notified Mr. J. Lambert, Head of Troedyrhiw School and Mr. Ingham, Bus Manager, Merthyr Corporation.

Notices

Mr. Cyril Vaughan would be in charge of the arrangements for the Saturday Football Match. Mr. S. Rees had arranged drinks for the children in the Club Board Room, squash, cordials, lemonade, etc. Mr. Vaughan would then proceed before half-time to Thomas's Pies Ltd., to pick up 15 dozen pies, pasties, etc., for the Aberfan children.

Monday, 14th November, 1966

A party of 80 pupils proceeded to Aberavon to the AVAN LIDO where they were officially received by the Mayor and Mayoress of PORT TALBOT. They were entertained at the SPORTS CENTRE where the senior boys chatted with Jeff Jones (4 for 93 for England against the Aussies) and Alan Rees, former Welsh rugby international and still a Glamorgan cricketer, and then with ex-Empire welter-weight champion Eddie Thomas, a great hero still revered in Merthyr by every boy of five upwards. An excellent free lunch was provided and the afternoon was spent in the Lido.

Teachers accompanying the party were: Mr. G. E. C. Davies, Mr. E. Jenkins, Mrs. E. Hanks and Miss J. Morgan. Mr. H. Williams was in charge of the Juniors.

The remaining pupils carried on with recreational activities at the Centre.

During the morning we had a visit from a team from Italian State Television. The production was to be called *ABERFAN ONE MONTH AFTER*, under the Director F. BIANCACCI. The team took many photographs and interviewed the three Infant and Junior teachers.

The Rev. Pemberthy, who had proved to be a "light in this period of darkness", for whom nothing was too much trouble, visited the Centre with a guest, Mr. Samuel Ngala. He was a Methodist Minister from MOMBASSA, KENYA, a liaison officer between the Church and the State Education Authorities.

Tuesday, 15th November, 1966

At the Centre we had films in the morning. The afternoon was spent in taking school photographs.

Wednesday, 16th November, 1966

Mr. Duncerton of the B.B.C.. visited the Centre in the morning with a television team, filmed the children at the Centre, interviewed the Junior teachers and took recordings.

Mr. Roberts, H.M.I., looked in to see if everything was running smoothly. Seventy-six pupils proceeded with staff to Ebbw Vale Baths.

Wednesday, 2 p.m., Visit of Mr. Melville Thomas, Head of Drama for Monmouthshire, who entertained the children at the Centre.

Mr. Brian Way, director of Theatre Centre, entertained the children with a delightful performance of *The Clown*. This was thoroughly enjoyed by all pupils present. As Miss Gwyneth Evans commented, "The smiles are coming back," "Even the Seniors are smiling".

Thursday, 17th November, 1966

Centre opened at 9.30 a.m. Recreational Activities. Afternoon - films.

Friday, 18th November, 1966

Party went with Mr. G. E. C. Davies and staff to Ebbw Vale Baths. Afternoon, films.

Monday, 21st November, 1966

The Centre opened at 9.30 a.m. with recreational activities. Mr. G. E. C. Davies took 76 pupils accompanied by staff to Ebbw Vale Baths.

Mr. Hugh Watkins and Mr. Reg Chandler proceeded to Cardiff to obtain films from SOUND FILM SERVICES. I thanked them personally as all films during our month's stay at the Centre were given free of charge. During the morning Acting-Head Mr. Ken J. Davies visited the Centre to talk to Junior Staff. Mr. J. Beale, M.A., Director of Education, visited the Centre.

Monday 2 p.m. Films shown in the afternoon. Visit of Miss Evans, a teacher from SWINDON, WILTSHIRE, to have a first-hand impression of the Centre.

Tuesday, 22nd November, 1966

Centre opened at 9.30 a.m. for Infants and Juniors, closed to Seniors. Eighty-eight pupils and staff proceeded by Merthyr Transport to Aberavon to the Avan Lido. There they were met by Mr. Graham Jenkins, brother of the actor, the late Richard Burton, organiser and in charge of the Avan Lido. Children also met Mr. Bryn Thomas, Sports Officer and Welsh sports celebrities employed at the Centre, namely: Allan Rees, Jeff Jones and Philip Robinson, weight lifter.

The morning was spent swimming in the pool, the afternoon spent in the Sports Centre Gymnasium. After a free lunch, sweets and chocolates were given freely to the children by the kind courtesy of the Port Talbot Round Table.

I thanked Mr. Graham Jenkins and his staff for their kind hospitality shown to the Aberfan children. A day thoroughly enjoyed by all. At the Centre the Drama Group from Monmouthshire entertained the remaining pupils at the Centre.

Wednesday, 23rd November, 1966

Centre opened at 9.30 a.m., recreational activities. Seventy pupils to Ebbw Vale Baths with Mr. G. E. C. Davies. Mr. John Kelly, photographer for the *Daily Sketch*, arrived at the Centre and photographed groups of children. Mr. Kelly photographed all children in the Centre at 2.30 p.m., on the bank next to the Gordon-Lennox Club.

Films at 3 p.m. - *Ivanhoe* and *Comedies*.

Thursday, 24th November, 1966

Centre opened at 9.30 a.m. Preparations were now being formulated for the closure of the Gordon-Lennox Club, for senior pupils. Mr. Michael Moynihan of the *Sunday Times* visited the Centre to report on its activities for his newspaper.

Afternoon - film show.

Friday, 25th November, 1966

Centre opened at 9.30 a.m. Party of children left for Ebbw Vale Baths.

2 p.m. Drama Group from Monmouthshire under the leadership of a Miss

Flowers entertained Infants and Juniors.

All pupils in the Centre were given a copy of the Director of Education's letter.

The Centre was to carry on for another week for Seniors and for another fortnight for Infants and Juniors until they moved to Merthyr Vale Junior School. The senior pupils and staff were to move to Troedyrhiw Secondary Modern School on Thursday, December 1st, 1966. Three days were given to move equipment and stock.

The Aberfan Social Club organised a Christmas Party for all children on Thursday, 22nd December, 1966.

Mr. and Mrs. Jones kindly arranged, at the Gordon-Lennox Club, a farewell party for the Seniors on Tuesday, December 6th, 1966. Mr. and Mrs. Jones spared no costs and excelled themselves with the arrangements. To quote:

3 gross each of assorted hats, masks, paper blowers, balloons, streamers and serviettes.

For food: 18 large tins of salmon, 15lbs of boiled ham, 200 trifles.

Minerals: 15 dozen orange, 15 dozen lemon.

Sausage rolls, pastries and fancy cakes.

Mrs. Jones prepared this colossal party with only seven helpers. The Rev. Kenneth Hayes, Baptist Minister at Aberfan, kindly loaned from the Baptist Church 200 knives, 200 spoons, 200 tea-plates and tables to accommodate 80 pupils.

Mrs. M. Hayes kindly arranged a small present for each child, delivered from the Baptist Church.

O. P. Chocolates, Merthyr kindly donated 300 novelties.

The party was a momentous occasion, thoroughly enjoyed by all.

The Juniors and Infants had their party on Thursday, 15th December. Mr. Wilding, Manager of Morlais Bus Services, kindly placed at our disposal a number of coaches to transport the children free of charge to see the pantomime *Mother Goose* at the New Theatre, Cardiff.

To climax all the proceedings and to bring our eventful month at the Gordon-Lennox to a close, the Bath Trades & Labour Institute Social and Democratic Club arranged a memorable day's entertainment.

Saturday, 3rd December, 1966

Two hundred and ten children left Aberfan at 8.30 a.m., accompanied by Mr. H. Watkins, Mrs. T. Watkins, Mr. Cyril Vaughan, Miss G. Evans, Miss M. Morgan and Mrs. N. Morgan, with eight club members to Bath.

At 11 a.m we crossed the Severn Bridge, where we were met by members in a black car bearing a large Union Jack and proceeded to Bristol, where we assembled at OLDLAN COMMON, where tea and biscuits were kindly provided. Each coach was then escorted by two people of the Bath Welsh Speaking Society. The party was honoured in having a police escort into Bath, where we assembled outside the old Police Station. A party of 100 pupils and staff went directly to the Roman Baths for a conducted tour. Fifty went to see the Roman Abbey and 50 to the Pump Rooms.

After a short tour it was back to the coaches for a short ride to the Bath Trades & Labour Institute, Green Park, where we were kindly met by Mr. Felton, President and Chairman and his Committee members. The children were entertained to a hot lunch of fish and chips, a sweet, etc.

At 1.30 p.m. we were given a short tour of the beautiful city of Bath, before arriving at Hillside Hall for a cinema show, entertainment from a comedian and a Beat Group. At 4 p.m. the children were given a delightful tea. After a most delightful day and having thanked Mr. Felton, Mr. A. Downing, Vice-Chairman, and Mr. W. Wedlock, Secretary, for their kind hospitality, we departed for the return journey to Aberfan.

Thursday, December 1st, 1966

The momentous day arrived when we moved as a school to Troedyrhiw Secondary Modern School to be accommodated in nine mobile classrooms. Here we were to remain until our final move to become part of Merthyr's first Comprehensive School.

People all over the world still expressed their kindness in many ways. Invitations for holidays abroad, to Greece, Italy, France, Brittany, Germany and many holidays in many parts of the British Isles.

The boys and girls who went through that dramatic period in their lives are now parents themselves, whose sons and daughters now attend Afon Täf High School.

Over the years the pain has diminished with time but can never wholly be wiped away.

The name "Pantglas" will always be remembered.

A Visit to Llanthony Abbey with the Aberdare Naturalists, 1891, The Brecon and Merthyr Railway explored

The Aberdare Naturalists' Society visited most of the places of interest in the immediate neighbourhood in the summers of 1889 and 1890. They decided to visit Llanthony Abbey in 1891. This trip involved journeys on interesting old railways long since abandoned. An account of the trip appeared in the *Merthyr Express* for 6.6.1891 p.6 col.4.

"Splendid weather was enjoyed. Mr. J. Morris, superintendent of schools, Aberdare, was selected to guide the party, his intimate acquaintance with the science of botany and his keenness in catching sight of rare plants and flowers made the long tramp, which would otherwise at times have become monotonous, thoroughly enjoyable.

"Mr. W. D. Phillips, solicitor, also delighted the company with historical references, coupled with much knowledge of the legislation of the past.

"Mr. W. Notton, Abernant Schools, was always ready to instruct the other members of the Society on geological and other scientific subjects.

"Messrs. J. Griffiths, Park Schools, and I. A. Lloyd (Gwladgarwr) taking occasion at each stopping place to inform the rest of the party on Welsh archaeology, etymology and folk-lore. At 9 a.m. the party, who, in addition to the leaders referred to, included a number of learners, left Abernant by train for Merthyr, by way of the Abernant Tunnel. From Merthyr they proceeded by the Brecon and Merthyr Railway to Talyllyn.

"At Merthyr, the party were exeeedingly fortunate in securing the company of Mr. W. Davies, Maerdy Place, Aberdare, for the first portion of the journey, and his intimate knowledge of the Taff and Usk Valleys made the railway journey most enjoyable. After passing Cyfarthfa Castle, Cefn Coed Viaduct, pretty Pontsarn, Pontsarn Viaduct, we reached Pontsticill Junction, thence to Dolygaer.

Aberdare Junction was at Abercynon, so a journey down the Merthyr Valley and back up the Aberdare Valley to Aberdare, on the Taff Vale Railway system, was involved.

See also *A Pilgrimage to Llanthony Monastery. Father Ignatius Interviewed. South Wales Weekly News*, Saturday 8.5.1880 p.5 col.6+7.

Also, Father Ignatius at Merthyr Tydfil, conducted three mission services at the Drill Hall. *Merthyr Express* 22.9.1894 p.7 col.7.

Foundations, 1893-1902

by T. F. HOLLEY AND V. A. HOLLEY

Introduction

The decade 1893-1902 saw a positive explosion in building activity in South Wales. Many new public buildings were erected or restored.

In 1887 the Bishop of Llandaff responded to a toast at a Dinner in Cardiff, to honour Merthyr Tydfil-born Sir Samuel Griffith, Premier of Queensland, Australia. The Bishop stated that he was opening Churches at the rate of one a month. (*Merthyr Historian*, Volume Five.)

The South Wales Institute of Engineers was founded in 1857 and Incorporated by Royal Charter in 1881. Work on new premises, in the Renaissance style of architecture, designed by architect Edwin Corbett, Bute Estate Offices, was started in Park Place, Cardiff, in July 1891, the imposing landmark was completed in 1894. These premises served as the home, not only of the South Wales Institute of Engineers, but also of the Monmouthshire and South Wales Coalowners Association. (*W.M.* 13.1.1894 p.6.)

At the Opening Service for the rebuilt Llanwynno Parish Church in 1894, it was stated that the cost had been generously defrayed by Miss Olive Talbot, of Margam, who within a few years had financed the restoration of Parish Churches at Llangynwyd, Bettws, Llangeinor, Llandyfodwg, Llanilid and Nicholaston and was at that time erecting at her sole cost a large Church at Abergwynfi. (See *Central Glamorgan Gazette* 29.4.1892 p.6, *Pontypridd Chronicle* 20.7.1894 p.7., *Merthyr Express* 21.7.1894 p.7.)

In an after-lunch speech at Pant, Merthyr, following the dedication of Christ Church, Pant, in June 1896, the Bishop stated that he had attended the Opening Ceremonies for more than one hundred and twenty Churches in the past fourteen years.

At the Offical Opening for Merthyr County School in 1897, Principal Viriamu Jones mentioned that about seventy new Intermediate Schools had been opened in the Principality in the past two years.

This National trend, the building and rebuilding of public buildings, was apparent also in Merthyr Tydfil and surrounding districts. The decade 1893-1902 was a time of FAITH, HOPE and CHARITY. Many notable public buildings, including Chapels, Churches, Inns, Libraries, Schools, Reservoirs, a Town Hall, a Truant School, were built, rebuilt or restored. Many generous benefactions of land and money were made, to assist and promote the building programme.

For example, Peter Williams, in an essay in *Merthyr Historian*, Volume Six, gave an account of the visit of Bishop Hedley to Merthyr Tydfil in 1893, to lay the foundation stone for St. Mary's Catholic Church, Brecon Road. This Church replaced an earlier building, also designated St. Mary's, situated on a busy and noisy tramroad at Georgetown. The site was obtained by a Father Ross, who was succeeded in 1884 by Canon Wade. The Canon and his not-very-rich parishioners amassed £6,000 in ten years, to build the new St. Mary's.

In this essay we have located and summarised accounts of Stone-laying Ceremonies and/or Opening Ceremonies for the following Merthyr and district public buildings:

1.	Hope Chapel, Opening Ceremony	1893
2.	Truant School, Quaker's Yard	1894
3.	Merthyr Town Hall	1896
4.	Dedication of Pant Church	1896
5.	Tabernacle Baptist Church, Brecon Road	1896
6.	Restoration of Parish Church, New Bells	1896
7.	Opening Ceremony, County School	1897
8.	New Library, Cefn Coed	1898
9.	Swan Inn, Old and New	1899
10.	Smyrna Chapel, Aberfan, Stone Laying	1901
11.	Smyrna, Aberfan, Opening	1902
12.	Bethania, Aberfan, Silver Jubilee	1902
13.	English Baptist Chapel, Penydarren	1902
14.	Calfaria, Heolgerrig, Stone Laying	1902
15.	Upper Neuadd Reservoir	1902
16.	Penydarren Reading-Room, Opening	1902.

A Chronological Date Sequence of these and other building events in the area has been compiled and is given at the end of our essay. It is hoped that it will act as a pointer to and encouragement for further research by interested persons.

Sincere thanks are tendered to John D. Holley for voluntary assistance with field work, photography and typing, for this essay.

1. Hope Chapel, Opening Ceremony, 1893

"The spacious and elegant new Chapel erected by the Church and congregation of Hope upon the site of the old edifice in High-street, opposite the Castle Hotel, was inaugurated for public worship on Sunday last, under the happiest auspices. The opening service was conducted by the pastor, the Rev. D. C. Edwards.

"The new building was designed by Mr. Thomas Roderick, architect, Aberdare, and has a Gothic character, though representing no particular style of architecture. Its dimensions are 80ft. long by 45ft. wide, and the height from the basement to the apex of the roof is 54ft., and to the wall plate 32ft. It is constructed throughout of native stone, with coigns of Grinshill stone from the neighbourhood of Shrewsbury. The flanking turrets, the principal Gothic window in the front, the lobby windows beneath, and the two pointed windows at the sides, are built entirely in Grinshill stone, which is also used for the arches of the doorways and the coping of the gables, and harmonises nicely with the native stone. The coigns of the lesser windows are in buff brick, which, we think, was a mistake. It would have been better had all the coigns been in stone alike. The boundary wall in front is coped with a stone somewhat similar in colour to the Grinshill stone, but which comes from Yorkshire. The basement, entered by the central door in front, contains the schoolroom, 50ft. by 40ft., with two classrooms at one end and at the other end a kitchen, fitted with boilers for tea parties, heating apparatus, lavatories and other conveniences, and there are staircases ascending therefrom to the Chapel above. This commodious room will enable the Sunday School to be held without resort to the Chapel, and it will be available for a variety of purposes in connection with Church work and the numerous gatherings, social and otherwise, constantly occurring.

"The old pulpit platform has been utilised as a rostrum here, and the seats are all movable, so that the room can be converted into many uses without difficulty.

"Over the school-room is the Chapel, which has the same dimensions in length and breadth, and contains 62 pews on the floor and 34 in the galleries, giving sitting accommodation for 750 persons. It is approached by two entrances from the front, a flight of steps on each side leading into an outer lobby, which communicates with an interior lobby with doors leading to each aisle of the floor, and others by short flights of steps to the galleries. Behind the pulpit is a room for the minister and deacons, with necessary adjuncts. The gallery is continuous all round, the sides having three rows of seats, and the portion at the front double that number.

"At the other end over the minister's room is the organ loft, with massive pointed arched opening, with three rows of seats for the choir in front, and communicating on both sides with the main galleries. The walls are cemented, small portions here and there being done in ordinary plaster, and coloured white to give relief to the grey granite tone of the rest.

"The roof is of high pitch, and is ceiled in panels on the rafters up to the point at which the proper ceiling commences. This also is divided into panels with pendant mouldings stained and varnished, the panels being in diagonal match boarding varnished upon its own finish. All the interior woodwork is in pitch-pine, varnished upon its own grain, but a tasteful and effective relief to the front panelling of the gallery has been imparted by the introduction of alternate upright small niches in mahogany with oblong panels in the wood principally used. The same alternation of woods has been used in the construction of the pulpit, which has three seats, and is, together with the stairs and balustrades, in pitch-pine, relieved by deep niches in mahogany. The communion seat is enclosed by a railing in pitch-pine, and is covered with Brussels carpet, the furniture including a pair of handsome black oak carved chairs, upholstered in crimson.

"The galleries are borne by cantilevers from the walls, supported at the front by elegant fluted cast-iron columns, with Corinthian capitals. The columns are painted in chocolate colour, the capitals in light blue picked out with gold.

"The lighting is admirable. The side windows are glazed with a rolled glass that excludes the glare of the sunshine, and a similar effect is produced by the beautiful stained glass windows, of which there are three, one of noble proportions at the front and two smaller ones at the sides. The light which streams through these windows is beautifully mellowed, and is reflected from the soft grey cement, with which the walls are chiefly covered, with a pleasurable sensation of comfort to the eye, the general effect being harmonious and agreeable. The artificial illumination of the building is provided for by two massive coronas pendant from the ceiling, and fitted with Cowan's high power burners, with white enamel reflectors. There are twenty-five jets to each corona, and when they are lighted, the interior is flooded with light that reaches effectively all parts of the Chapel, except those beneath the galleries, for which side lights are provided.

"The gas fittings were supplied and fixed by the Merthyr Tydfil Gas Company. Immediately over the coronas are the ventilating arrangements. For admission of fresh air there are sixteen of Boyle's patent inlet valves fixed in the walls; and to carry off the waste products of combustion and human exhalations there are three circular ceiling ventilators, painted in sea green and picked out with gold.

"Above the ceiling these are boxed in and convey the up currents of impurities into a central shaft that communicates with the external ventilator in the apex of the roof. The Chapel will be heated with hot water, the boiler for this purpose being placed in the kitchen in the basement. The ventilating arrangements were put to a good test on Sunday night, when the building was crowded to its utmost capacity, and yet there was no sense of heaviness in the atmosphere or of that condition which produces drowsiness and depression, nor was there any sense of discomfort from an excessive rise of the temperature.

"The acoustic properties of the Chapel are excellent, and from every part of the auditorium the preacher can be heard fully and distinctly and without the slightest confusion of sounds. The general appearance of the interior is exceedingly pleasant and tasteful. There is sufficient embellishment to remove all the dullness of strict simplicity without a particle of excess, and the beautifying of the house of prayer has not been carried to gaudy extremes.

"The organist for the opening service was Mr. Edward Lawrence, formerly organist of St. David's Church. A beautiful solo was sung by Miss Mabel Davies, Courtland-terrace, who surprised her friends by the brilliance of her singing. A collection yielded over £200.

"In the afternoon, a service was conducted by Rev. Ellis Edwards, Bala, who officiated again at night. The Chapel at the evening service was crowded to excess, and many failed to obtain admission. There were large numbers of friends from other denominations present to testify their sympathy with the congregation in their important undertaking, and the day closed under circumstances of genuine satisfaction and rejoicing amongst the members of the Church."

(Condensed from the *Merthyr Express*, 15.7.1893, p.3 col.4+5.)

2. Truant School, Quaker's Yard, 1894

For many years prior to 1894, difficulty was experienced in South Wales and Monmouthshire in dealing with children who, whilst not having been detected in actual crime, could not be induced to attend school.

With the object of providing a suitable place in which the truants could be kept for a period of about three months, and then released on license, Alderman Thomas Williams, J.P., Chairman of the Merthyr School Board, called a Conference of School Boards at Merthyr Workhouse on December 5th, 1889. This led to the purchase of a site at Quaker's Yard from Lord Windsor for £300.

A general Committee was appointed with Alderman Thomas Williams, J.P., as Chairman, Mr. W. W. Wood was Vice-Chairman, Mr. E. Stephens, Clerk to the Merthyr School Board, was Secretary, Mr. C. Dauncey, Clerk to the Bedwellty School Board, was appointed solicitor and Dr. W. W. Jones, Wellington Street, Merthyr, accepted the post of Medical Officer.

The architect was Mr. W. H. Dashwood Caple, Cardiff, the contractors were Messrs. Stephens, Bastow and Company, of Bristol, the Clerk of Works was Mr. C. M. Davies, Merthyr, contractors for the steam fittings were Messrs. Bradford and Perkins, Peterborough.

The cost of the building was £6,600, including boundary walls and roadways.

A detailed description of the School building, which comprised two storeys and a basement, appeared in the *Merthyr Express* for Saturday 13th January, 1894, p.4.

Facilities included a detached Laundry, workshop, large drill shed (60ft. long) and drill yard. A range of steam jacketed cooking pans were fitted in the kitchen, and a six foot roasting range was also provided. The schoolroom, classroom, dining hall, office, waiting room, dormitories (three, housing 33, 31 and 26 boys), sick and infectious diseases rooms , and linen rooms were heated singly and collectively by steam. The rest of the rooms had open fireplaces. The steam required was generated by a four-horse power boiler, fixed in a boiler house between the main building and Laundry.

The whole site was surrounded by a wall or railings nine feet high, to prevent escapes, all windows had locked sashes, and could only be opened six inches at top or bottom for ventilation. Fire extinguishing appliances and hydrants were fixed on each floor.

Mr. W. Davies, North London Truant School, was appointed Superintendent, Mrs. Courtney, late of Cardiff, was Matron.

The beds taken by the various School Boards were as follows:

Merthyr	15
Bedwellty	15
Ystradyfodwg	12
Aberdare	7
Llanwonno	6
Aberystruth	6
Llantrisant	4
Eglwysilan	3
Llantwit Fardre	3
Llanelly (Breconshire)	2

79

Llangynidr	2
TOTAL	75

Originally fifteen additional beds were unallotted, total accommodation, ninety beds.

The Opening Ceremony was performed by Lord Aberdare on Monday 8th January, 1894,, he was presented with a gold key by Alderman Thomas Williams. Lord Aberdare gave a lengthy address on the subject of juvenile offenders and their treatment. In responding to the vote of thanks, Lord Aberdare mentioned that on the following Friday he would have the honour of introducing an influential deputation to the Chancellor of the Exchequer, inviting his assistance in taking the necessary steps for founding a University of Wales, the Charter for which had been issued by Her Majesty Queen Victoria a short time ago.

That Truant School might be called the basement of the great educational building, and with their Intermediate Schools and a University the structure would be complete.

Lunch, provided by Mrs. Howfield and Son, Merthyr, followed the Opening Ceremony. Colonel D. R. Lewis, High Constable of Merthyr, in an after-lunch speech, remarked that School Boards had the power to compel parents to send their children to school, but they did not possess much power over the child. He would like to see a short Act of Parliament passed which would give the police authority to catch children in the streets and take them to school. This system had been adopted in America and worked well.

The proceedings concluded with a vote of thanks to Chairman Alderman Thomas Williams, J.P., proposed by Mr. C. H. James, J.P., and seconded by the Rev. S. R. Jones.

Another account of the Opening Ceremony of the Quakers Yard Joint Truant School appeared in the *Western Mail* for Tuesday, 9.1.1894, p.7 col.4+5.

See also *Cardiff Times and South Wales Weekly News*, Saturday 13.1.1894, p.5 col.6.

3. Merthyr Town Hall, 1896

New municipal buildings were erected in Merthyr Tydfil in 1896. These buildings are today (1994) referred to as the old Town Hall, or Chambers Nightclub.

The laying of the foundation stones for the old Town Hall took place in May 1896. A report appeared in the *Merthyr Express* for 23.5.1896 p.8. The foundation stones were fixed in a prominent position at both ends, and were some distance from the ground, so that they could easily be seen. The stone on the right was laid by Mr. Thomas Jenkins, who was High Constable when the building was actually commenced and was also the oldest member of the local governing bodies.

The stone near the left corner was laid by the Chairman of the Merthyr Urban District Council, Mr. D. W. Jones.

In this latter stone a receptacle was made for the storage of a sealed bottle containing a copy of the *Merthyr Express*, the *1896 Express Almanac*, the *Standard Time-table*, the *Merthyr Times*, and a copy of the day's programme, together with a small parchment on which was detailed the day's proceedings.

The following history of the events which led to the eventual construction of the old Town Hall, appeared in the *Express Almanac* for 1896.

"The agitation was started in the late 1850s, when a committee, which had among its members Mr. Frank James and the late J. D. Thomas, acquired the leasehold property opposite the Castle Hotel and demolished it. This committee handed over its rights and liabilities to the Local Board, which in 1865 obtained an Act authorising the expenditure of £10,000 upon a Town Hall. There the matter rested for years. Public opinion was divided upon the question of sites. Mr. Robert Crawshay offered £1,000 towards the cost if the Market Square was selected. That offer was not accepted.

"Nothing definite was done till 28.12.1870, when a letter was read at the Board from Mr. Linton, Aberdare, on behalf of his wife and Mr. John Russell, former owners of the property occupied by the Board, in which application was made for the payment of the purchase money. The Finance Committee considered the application, and decided to recommend to the Board the advisability of borrowing £6,000 to buy out the reversionary interests of Mr. Richard Thomas, Rev. John Griffith and Mrs. Kirkhouse. The Board borrowed the money on 18.1.1871. Nothing was done to utilise the site till 1886, when a prize was offered for the best design. Mr. E. A. Johnson, Abergavenny, beat fourteen other competitors.

"In February 1887 Mr. Harvey, surveyor, presented an estimate of the cost to the Board for the erection of the buildings, namely £11,239. Nothing much happened till 20.1.1892, when special terms were made with Mr. Johnson, the architect, and on 3.8.1892 protracted negotiations with the Rector, Rev. D. Lewis, for the purchase of some additional glebe land, were concluded. The Board originally offered £500 for the land but was forced to pay £2,500 for it, and pay all legal expenses.

"In 1894 Her Majesty's Office of Works sanctioned an allowance of £200 per annum to be paid, in consideration of the County Court being accommodated in the Town Hall. On July 18th, 1894, Mr. Johnson sent completed plans to the Board. The work was put out to tender and Mr. Gibbon, Cardiff, was suc-

81

cessful at £11,668. By 20th February, 1895, the Board had not sought to borrow money to enable the work to proceed. A District Council had by this time been elected, its members were keen to support the building of a Town Hall.

"Eventually powers were obtained to borrow the money and on Thursday, September 5th, 1895, Messrs. D. W. Jones, David Davies and Dan Thomas met Mr. Gibbon, the contractor, on the ground and the contractor signed the agreement. Not long afterwards building operations commenced."

Amongst others, present at the stone-laying ceremony for the Town Hall were
> Mr. Frank T. James, the High Constable,
> Mr. D. A. Thomas, M.P. (later Viscount Rhondda),
> Colonel David Rees Lewis.

Another account of these events appeared in the *Western Mail* for Friday, 22nd May, 1896 p.6 col.4+5.

4. Dedication of Pant Church, 1896

This event was reported in the *Merthyr Express*, 13.6.1896, p.8. "At Dowlais, where the Rev. Llewelyn M. Williams is rector, the work of Church extension has been swift and certain in its progress and on Thursday, St. Barnabas' Day, the dedication of a new Mission Church at Pantyscallog was performed by the Lord Bishop of Llandaff.

"In April 1893, Dowlais Church grand bazaar took place at the Oddfellows' Hall. The event, which lasted four days, had for its object the furthering of the work of Church extension in the parish. At that time in the three mission centres, congregations of Churchpeople had to worship in buildings quite unsuitable for the purpose. At Pengarnddu and Gellyfaelog divine service was conducted (and is still conducted in the case of Gellyfaelog) in schoolrooms, and at Pantyscallog no better accommodation was provided than the Cemetery Chapel. In all the districts also the buildings were absolutely too small, and the discomfort of the worshippers who attended the services was great. A project for the erection of three new Churches was inaugurated, involving the outlay of £3,000, the bazaar was held, about £1,000 was realised by sales, and £500 by donations.

"The Officers of the bazaar were

President	E. P. Martin
Vice president	Rev. Llewelyn M. Williams
Secretaries	Dr. Pearson R. Cresswell
	A. W. Houlson
Treasurers	J. King Price

Thomas Jones, J.P.

"The foundation stone for Pengarnddu was laid by Mrs. George Martin in August 1894 (Bank Holiday) and in December this Church was opened for public worship. During 1894 the Parish Church of Saint John was rebuilt and extended, the whole cost was borne by Lord Wimborne, proprietor of Dowlais Works. On October the fourth 1894 the Lord Bishop of Llandaff publicly consecrated St. John's, Dowlais, and on the same day laid the corner stone of Pant Church.

"Gellyfaelog Church building will commence in 1897."

Mr. William Jenkins, of Consett, gave £500 towards building the chancel, and his family subsequently gave many valuable items, including the altar and reredos of carved oak, and a stained-glass window in the chancel.

The site on which Pant Church stands was also a most important gift, as the land occupies a valuable situation. The owner, Mr. Edward Davies, Bassaleg, very readily and generously offered the site for the purpose required.

In responding to the toast of "The Bishop and Clergy" at the public luncheon which followed the dedication of Pant Church, the Lord Bishop commented very favourably on the fact that the site and other items had been freely donated. It gives food for thought to reflect that the acquisition of a site for Merthyr Town Hall was long delayed by protracted negotiations with successive Rectors of Merthyr, who drove a very hard bargain.

Landowner, MR. EDWARD DAVIES, J.P., Bassaleg, was a very interesting character. He married Miss Ella Georgina Abdy, daughter of General Abdy, at Bonchurch, Isle of Wight, in 1889. (*Western Mail*, Wednesday 1.5.1889 p.3 col.3.) At that time he was a Captain of the Second Volunteer Battalion, South Wales Borderers, a prominent member of the Newport Board of Guardians, and Chairman of Rhiwderin School Board. Edward Davies was a lifelong friend of Viscount Tredegar.

Captain, later Major, Davies had four children

> Edward Davies, junior,
> Henry Charles Abdy Davies,
> Gwladys Margaret Abdy Davies and
> Margaret Elizabeth Abdy Davies.

An account in 1882 of a "Great land sale at Cardiff" mentioned that Edward Davies, Newport, had purchased Caeracca Farm, Pant, Merthyr, for £2,000. (*Cardiff Times*, 27.5.1882 p.5 col.4.)

Mr. Edward Davies, then of Machen House, Newport, J.P. for Brecknockshire and Monmouthshire, a former High Sheriff of Brecknockshire (1907), died aged sixty-nine on October 19th, 1914. He left estate of the gross value of £114,456, of which the net personalty was sworn at £53,161. In his Will he made provision for his wife and daughters, left £500 to his god-daughter Leila Lang Brown, and £100 each to his god children, Lilian Llewellyn, Wyndham Smith, Basil Knight Stratten and Francis Williams.

He left several properties on trust for his son Edward, namely
> Maes y Faenor (Vaynor), Llwynrodin,
> also his share and interest in properties known as
> Pengelli Fawr, Vaynor,
> Pantyscallog, Merthyr Tydfil,
> Felindre Fields, Llanilid and
> Gwt Llanilid and Coichurch.

Real estate known as
> Ynisygerwn,
> Cair Bach,
> Brynmawr,
> Llyngeron,
> Coed Cae, Vaynor and
> Caeracca, Merthyr Tydfil,

were left on trust for younger son Henry Charles Abdy Davies and his issue. As parts of the farms of Brynmawr, Llyngeron and Coed Cae had been sold to Merthyr Tydfil Corporation for Waterworks, £5,000 was to be substituted in H. C. A. Davies' portion for that land so sold.

(Brecon County Times 31.12.1914, B.R.E. 31.12.1914 p.3 col.2)

See also *B.C.T . 22.10.1914 p.3 col.6.*
> *Brecon and Radnor Express, 22.10.1914 p.2 col.7*
> *B.C.T. 24.1.1908 p.5.*

Major Edward Davies owned a pack of foxhounds, the Maes-y-Faenor Hounds, which were normally kenneled at Vaynor, for an outing with these Hounds see the *Merthyr Express* 16.2.1884 p.5.

Captain, later Lieut. Colonel H. C. A. Davies, became Master of the Talybont Hounds at Christmas, 1918, and had a long association with the Gelligaer and Talybont Hunt. When H. C. A. Davies departed for London to become a barrister, Lord Buckland and his daughter Miss Eileen Berry took over Mastership of the Hounds. (See *Tails of Old Merthyr, A History of the Gelligaer Hunt, 1898-1939*, Holley, 1983.)

Lieut. Colonel H. C. A. Davies died aged ninety-one in 1987, leaving children, grand-children and great-grandchildren.

5. Tabernacle Baptist Church, Brecon Road, 1896

Kelly's Directory for 1891 listed a Tabernacle (English) Baptist Chapel at Ivor Street, Dowlais. Also listed was a Tabernacle (Welsh) Baptist Chapel, location not specified.

A movement was set in motion to provide more central and comfortable accommodation for Tabernacle Church. The idea was first mooted by Mrs. David Davies, wife of Alderman David Davies and when that lady died, Alderman Davies took up the movement with characteristic zeal. A strong Committee, with the pastor, Rev. David Price, as Chairman, and D. L. Jones and Evan Morgan as Secretaries, was formed. The self-sacrificing nature of the congregation, composed mainly of working men, was revealed when £1,000 was quickly raised.

The plans for the new Chapel were entrusted to George Morgan of Carmarthen, who designed a building in the Norman style, containing, in addition to the main body of the structure, a spacious schoolroom. The main building comprised a handsome portico (porch with columns), a Chapel capable of seating nine hundred, with gallery on three sides and an organ chamber and rostrum (pulpit) on the fourth side. There was also a minister's room, vestry and offices. The contract was given to John Jones, Glanynant, the cost when completed was expected to be £5,000.

The foundation stones were laid at a ceremony held in July 1896, the event was reported in the *Merthyr Express* for 11.7.1896 p.8.

A large assembly gathered, composed of members of all Nonconformist denominations. Present were

> Rev. David Price, pastor of Tabernacle,
> Mrs. Gwilym James, Miss Dora James,
> Alderman David Davies and Miss Nellie Davies,
> Alderman Thomas Williams, J.P.,
> Colonel D. R. Lewis,
> Mr. William Harris,
> Rev. T. Salathiel,
> Rev. J. G. James, B.A.,
> Rev. Alfred Hall,
> Rev. John Thomas, Zoar,
> Rev. D. L. Jones,
> Mr. Rees Abraham, precentor,
> Councillors J. Lewis and W. Lewis,
> Rev. Jason James, Penydarren,
> Mr. Gilleland,

Mr. T. J. Rice,
Professor Edwards, Cardiff.

In an address, Rev. David Price detailed the acquisition of the site from Mr. John Vaughan, solicitor. He wanted the new building to compare favourably with others in the district (perhaps St. Mary's?). Rev. Price stated that his congregation comprised four hundred members, plus three or four hundred other adherents, who were regular attendants. On Sunday evenings the congregation averaged seven hundred people.

Six foundation stones were laid in front of the building, and one on the left side; they were laid in the following order:

By the pastor, for Mr. D. A. Thomas, M.P.	(Ten guineas)
Colonel David Rees Lewis	(Fifteen pounds)
Miss Nellie Davies, daughter of Ald. Davies	(One hundred pounds)
Mr. William Harris	(Ten guineas)
Mrs. Gwilym C. James, for her husband	(Twelve guineas)
Mr. Thomas Williams, J.P.	(Twelve guineas)
Mr. David Davies	(Four hundred pounds).

Each "mason" was presented with a handsome silver trowel, suitably inscribed, and a boxwood mallet, and they all declared in the usual formula that "this stone is well and truly laid".

The amounts subscribed by those who laid the stones are shown. Mr. T. H. Thomas, Twynyrodyn, sent two guineas.

Letters of apology for inability to attend were read by Alderman David Davies. Mr. D. A. Thomas, M.P., telephoned that he regretted he could not possibly attend, as he was engaged on the Railway Bills Committee. Mr. Gwilym James wrote to say that he could not attend, as he had to attend with the Urban Council at the Pentwyn and Neuadd Reservoirs. The High Constable, Mr. F. T. James, Mr. William Evans, Cyfarthfa, and Mr. W. L. Daniel also wrote, the latter being in London on behalf of the Chamber of Trade in support of the Bute-Rhymney Bill. Mr. John Vaughan also sent a letter of regret, enclosing a cheque for five pounds for the building fund.

Dr. Edwards, Cardiff, terminated the proceedings by proposing a vote of thanks to those who had assisted in the day's events.

In the evening there was a large congregation at the old Tabernacle Chapel when the Rev. C. Davies (Cardiff) and the Rev. G. Griffiths (Rhymney) preached Welsh sermons.

The collections were for the Building Fund.

Biographical

The Obituary of John Jones, Glanynant, builder of Tabernacle, appeared in the *Merthyr Express* for 15.6.1901 p.5.

That of Alderman David Davies, Merthyr, appeared on 2.9.1899 p.5 and 9.9.1899 p.5.

6. Restoration of Merthyr Parish Church, New Peal of Bells, 1896

Summary of a report which appeared in the *Cardiff Times*.

"A comprehensive scheme of restoration, or rather rebuilding, of the Merthyr Tydfil Parish Church was proceeding in 1896.

"The old tower, built in 1829, had one bell of medium size, which was cast in 1844. This old tower was replaced by the present (1896) stone structure, and the bell was deposited on the floor of the nave.

"The old Church, rebuilt in 1807, has been succeeded in part by the present fine building, the chancel has not yet been rebuilt.

"Thanks to the eight gentlemen who have so frequently been mentioned as 'eight old Merthyr boys', a peal of eight bells has been erected aloft in the new tower, the bell-founders were Messrs. John Taylor and Company, Loughborough. Each bell contains a record of the donor's name and a quotation or verse, Tennysonian couplets occurring in four instances:

> Ring out the thousand wars of old
> Ring in the thousand years of peace.

> Ring out false pride in place and blood
> Ring in the common love of good.

> Ring out the false, ring in the true
> Ring out the feud of rich and poor.

> Ring out the grief that saps the mind
> Ring in redress to all mankind.

"All are excellent sentiments and ought to be found in practice everywhere.

"As a commencement of the dedicatory proceedings on Sunday afternoon, a procession was formed outside St. David's Church, at the conclusion in that place of the children's service. The band of the Merthyr Detachment, the 3rd V.B. Welsh Regiment, Mr. R. Jones, bandmaster, took the lead and among those who followed were

Rev. Daniel Lewis, rector,

Rev. David Jones, curate,

Rev. J. Williams, curate,

Mr. T. L. White, Churchwarden, St. David's,

Mr. T. Flooks, Churchwarden, St. David's,

Sir W. T. Lewis, Baronet,

Colonel D. Rees Lewis,

local detachments of the Church Lads' Brigade, etc.,

The parish wardens,

Mr. David Williams, Henstaff Court, Groesfaen, and

Mr. T. W. Lewis, Sir William's father, were unable to be
present.

"The rector conducted the service, the worshippers included the following donors of bells:

Sir W. T. Lewis, who gave the tenor bell,

Mr. Herbert Kirkhouse,

Mr. W. Thomas, J.P., Brynawel, Aberdare,

Colonel D. Rees Lewis,

Mr. E. P. Martin,

Mr. William Jenkins, Consett.

Mr. Edward Williams and Mr. Tom Morgan, Ohio, were
represented.

Lady Lewis was also present.

"A hymn was sung commencing with the verse

'Treat them fairly in the steeple

Let our bells ring out on high;

There fulfil their daily mission

Midway 'twixt the earth and sky.

"The rector gave an address, in which he cursorily commented upon the more
silent and miscellaneous methods which had preceded the use of bells, for some
of the purposes to which bells were now put.

"Bells were first used in the eighth century, and since that time they had been
in use in the Eastern and Western and Anglican Churches. Up to the time of the
Reformation there was scarcely a place in this country without a peal of bells,
but then the Commissioners of the King turned many of the bells and the vessels
of the Churches to monetary account, and this was repeated in the time of
Cromwell, when it was recorded that the bells of Merthyr Parish Church were

sold for sixpence a pound, the Rev. Nathaniel Jones adding quaintly to his record that they were worth at least fourteen or sixteen pence a pound. It was probable, the rector suggested, that the present was the third peal of bells erected in their parish Church. The rector expressed deep gratitude to the donors whose hearts had been moved to make so generous a gift.

"An offertory was taken in aid of a fund for a new pulpit, the band playing a march meanwhile. After the Benediction had been pronounced, Mr. Silver, the St. David's organist, played the concluding voluntary on the harmonium, and the new bells rang out right merrily."

(Condensed from the *Cardiff Times*, 7.11.1896 p.3 col.8.)

7. Formal Opening Ceremony, Merthyr County School, 1897

The new Intermediate or County School started work in October 1896 and was formally opened in January 1897 by Principal Viriamu Jones, of Cardiff University College. A report of these proceedings appeared in the *Merthyr Express* for January the 16th, 1897, page 8, columns 1 and 2.

Mr. D. A. Thomas, M.P., (later Viscount Rhondda) acted as Chairman.
Amongst those present were

> Miss E. P. Hughes, Cambridge Training College,
> Mr. W. M. North, Stipendiary Magistrate,
> Alderman Aaron Davies, Chairman of the County Governing Body,
> Alderman D. P. Davies, J.P., Chairman, Board of Guardians,
> Mr. G. C. James, J.P.,
> Mr. H. W. Southey, J.P.,
> Mr. W. Harris, F.R.G.S.,
> Mr. W. Edwards, H.M.I.S.,
> Rev. J. Thomas, Zoar,
> Rev. D. Lewis, Rector of Merthyr,
> Mr. Frank T. James, High Constable,
> Rev. J. Hathren Davies,
> Mr. D. W. Jones, Chairman of the District Council,
> Dr. Biddle, Dr. Cresswell, Dr. Hughes and many others.

Mr. Charles Owen, M.A., the Principal of the School, said that they began work with fifty-five pupils in October 1896, and ended with one hundred at the close of the term. They hoped to open with one hundred and thirty pupils during the ensuing week.

Mr. Owen appealed to benefactors to provide a school library, a playfield for boys, a tennis court for girls, on the ground at the back of the School, and works of Art to adorn the School interior.

Mr. Owen pointed out that it was a low and sordid view of education, which regarded it merely as a means to material success and quoted Mr. Goschen's saying "Education is needed not only for livelihood but for life". He said the aim of the School should be to give the boys and girls not only useful knowledge and practical habits, but also to cultivate high tastes and interests which alone imparted elevation and refinement, breadth and depth to life, which might irradiate obscurity and dignify and ennoble poverty.

Principal Viriamu Jones, of Cardiff University College, gave the inaugural address and mentioned that about seventy new Intermediate Schools had been opened in the Principality in the past two years. He mentioned the benefits to be obtained from physical education and gymnastics, and advocated the study of Natural History and the Welsh Language.

Miss E. P. Hughes (Cambridge) then gave an address on "The higher education of girls". She defined education as "Preparation for life by a cultivation of the whole mind". She gave four "warnings" to the assembly:

1. Do take care in Wales of your higher education.
2. Do not forget that secondary education must of necessity be more expensive than elementary education.
3. Take care of the teaching of literature in your schools.
4. Do not forget the girls!!

In conclusion Miss Hughes hoped the School would be a grand fortress for all things good and wise and great.

Professor J. M. Davies, M.A., said it was always a pleasure for him to hear of any improvement in his native district. The nineteenth century, he said, had been the most important in the history of the Principality. Firstly, they had the great religious awakening, and they saw chapels and churches in every nook and corner. Then they had the great industrial revolution, in which the Merthyr district had shared so largely, springing from a petty village to become the great Iron Metropolis. Then they had the political enfranchisement movement. And lastly, this great educational movement.

Wales had had to wait a long time for its University, and they knew what a curse mental poverty had been to the land. Was it then to be wondered at that the national genius should have slumbered and slept so long, only to break out here and there in exceptional instances?

But the "winter of their discontent" was past and the higher education question was going to exercise a beautifying and refining influence on their education.

90

Alderman Thomas Williams, Chairman of the Governors, moved a vote of thanks to the speakers. He stated that fifty-five years ago (ca. 1842) there was only one elementary school in the parish, with accommodation for only 300 children. Merthyr now (1897) had on the register in the elementary schools, 12,506 children, the average attendance being 9,860. Alderman Williams stated that there was no debt on the building. The vote of thanks was seconded by Mr. Edwards, H.M.I.S., supported by Mr. W. M. North, and was carried with acclamation.

The Rev. Aaron Davies proposed a vote of thanks to the subscribers and the Building Committee. He thought that the fact of their having to pay £1,200 for the site of the School WAS A BLOT ON THE HISTORY OF LANDOWNERS. The landowner should have given the ground free.

Alderman D. P. Davies seconded this vote of thanks. Mr. Gwilym C. James acknowledged the compliment on behalf of the subscribers and Colonel David Rees Lewis on behalf of the Building Committee.

A vote of thanks to the Chairman, Mr. D. A. Thomas, M.P., was moved by Mr. W. L. Daniel, and seconded by Mr. F. T. James, High Constable, supported by Mr. D. W. Jones, and carried with applause.

Mr. D. A. Thomas, M.P., replied, then terminated the proceedings. Those present adjourned for tea, provided by the Governors.

See also "County School Opened at Merthyr", *Western Mail*, Thursday, 14.1.1897 p.7 col.1.

8. New Library at Cefn Coed, Stone-laying Ceremony, 1898

In May 1897 the Rev. Hathren Davies convened a meeting of leading inhabitants of Cefn Coed to consider the best means of celebrating the Queen's Jubilee there. A Committee was formed and it was decided to build a Reading Room and Library. Those involved included:

Major J. J. Jones, Chairman, Jubilee Celebration Committee,
Rev. J. E. Jenkins, rector of Vaynor,
Mr. J. Rogers, Glanyrafon,
Mr. J. Harpur,
Captain H. V. Jones,
Mr. Matthew Owen, Secretary,
Mr. Watkin Williams, Treasurer,
Rev. T. Salathiel,
Mr. D. E. Jones, and Mr. J. C. Lee.

A sub-committee entered into negotiations with Mrs. Pearce to purchase a plot of land held by her under a lease of nearly sixty years and situated opposite the existing Reading Room and Library. The plot was bought for £605, free of every ground rent, for the unexpired term of the lease.

Mr. R. C. Jenkins, the surveyor to the Vaynor and Penderyn District Council, was instructed to prepare plans, and these were adopted by the Committee. A Subscription List was opened, great impetus was given to the movement by the gift of £100 from Messrs. Crawshay Bros. At the time of the stone laying, half the required sum was in the hands of the Treasurer.

The following were appointed trustees of the new building: Major J. J. Jones, Mr. John Rogers, Capt. H. V. Jones, Mr. Watkin Williams, Maesyrhaf, and the Rev. J. Hathren Davies.

Members of the Committee and interested persons met at Fron Heulog, the beautiful home of Major J. J. Jones, who was to lay the stone. They then marched to the new building, escorted by the Band of the 1st Batt. South Wales Borders. Amongst those present:

> Mr. and Mrs. T. Morris,
> Mr. and Mrs. Rogers,
> Misses A. Jones, Olive Jones, Norah Jones,
> Misses Rogers (3),
> Misses Mann (2),

Messrs. Watkin Williams, C. W. Pearce, T. L. Pearce, W. Hughes, B. R. S. Frost, J. Llewelyn, Lewis Jones, Fred James, R. C. Jenkins, M. Owen, Isaac Powell, W. P. Benson (*Merthyr Times*), J. G. E. Astel (*South Wales Daily News*).

Mrs. Morris, Taff Brae, presented Major Jones with a beautiful silver trowel, and the gallant Major, in performing the interesting function of laying the stone, delivered an admirable address, brimful of most apposite quotations, on the advantages of reading good books and the value of Libraries.

Sweet music was played by the Band and also by the Cefn Male Voice Party, conducted by Mr. Tom Jones, which sang well *The Soldiers' Chorus* by Gounod and *Come, bounteous May*.

Over £6 was laid on the stone by ladies and gentlemen present.

(Condensed from *Merthyr Express*, 30.4.1898 p.6 col.8.)

The following publications by the Rev. J. Hathren Davies, mentioned above, were listed in *Guide To The Local History Collection, 1982*, published by Merthyr Tydfil Public Libraries.

69.   Hanes Dowlais, *Welsh Language*, Handwritten, Dowlais, 1891. 129pp.

70.   *History of Dowlais*, Translated by Tom Lewis from original 1891 manuscript.

71.   *The Tramways of Merthyr Tydfil*, 15 pages, no date.

9. The Swan Inn, Old and New, and Tidings of Old Friendly Societies, 1899

"The Swan Inn at Merthyr, now in process of reconstruction, is probably amongst the oldest houses in the town. During the work of demolition recently, evidence was found that the house existed as a hostelry over one hundred years ago, in the time, too, when the inhabitants even acknowledged Merthyr to be a village.

"Some men at work on the building found lodged in the roof, just above the rafters, a bundle of paper and a little earthenware jar. As the papers dealt almost solely with friendly society work in byegone days, it may be safely judged that the little jar was the cash box of some whilom secretary, who, according to the custom of his times, utilised the hole in the roof as a 'safe deposit' for his petty cash and papers.

"Mrs. Owen, the present landlady, allowed us to examine three of the papers. One is a balance sheet of an organisation named 'The Young Bucks Society' and the others are both copies of rules of two other Societies held at the Inn.

"The earliest bears the date of 1786, when we are told 'A Society of Tradesmen and others, called the Faithful Friends, met at the dwellinghouse of John Davies, in the said village, known by the Sign of the Swan.' There are forty-nine rules, signed by Thomas Price, clerk, and beginning with an 'Imprimis', which states the hours of meeting to be later in summer than in winter, and the subscriptions are '1s. a month for the good of the fraternity, and 2d. to be spent', the latter sum, presumably, being for the good of the house. The second rule says 'Every member shall pay down every club night 1s. to the box and 2d. for ale.' Any person suspected of being over forty-five years of age was ineligible, and emigration abroad meant a forfeiture of all claims. We have here also an old age pension scheme, for 'when any member of the Society is grown old and infirm and unable to procure his livelihood by his daily toil, there shall be paid to him out of the box 3s.6d. per week, so long as he lives.' The public peace is considered, too, for 'if any member be disabled by fighting, and it appears to be his beginning, and he demands relief, he shall be excluded,' and any member in liquor placed himself in similar danger, because the Society sought 'the preservation of good manners and the suppression of vice. The uncertainty of individual liberty is brought to mind by reading a reference to 'any member impressed into the King's service, or balloted in the militia', which shews that the operations of the press gang had been heard of in the village, and was regarded as a fearsome thing.

"The old feast was observed on the first Monday in August when members had to attend and answer the roll call, and proceed in decent form to Church.

The landlord, finally, is admonished to keep a good fire in the room from Michaelmas to May Day.

"The second document is entitled 'Rules and orders to be observed by the Dowlais Female Society meeting at the dwelling house of John Davies, known by the Sign of the Swan, commenced on April 15th, 1806. This Society allowed 3s. a week to aged members. It is not surprising to find a special rule in a women's Society against 'back biting', as a fine of 2s.6d. was mentioned for 'reflections on a member'.

"Both of these documents were set off with a kind of preamble or preface, which, being worded exactly alike, was possibly inserted in all such club rules: Whereas it has been an ancient and laudable custom in this kingdom of Great Britain for divers persons to meet together and form Societies, to promote friendship and true Christian love, and upon all just occasions to assist and support each other. It is therefore agreed by us, who have entered our names in a book, to be kept in the care of a clerk of the said Society as follow.

"The third paper was the printed balance sheet for 1827 of another club held at the Swan, called 'The Young Bucks Society'. This little Society had a turnover of £700 and £400 in hand.

"These three documents have the names of three different Merthyr printers, all of them long ago passed out of memory. One dated 1825 gives the name of 'J. James, printer, Merthyr'. Another paper is printed by J. Jenkins, who occupied a house in Bridge-street, where he issued several well-known books. The third name was T. Price, printer, High-street, his shop was where the old *Merthyr Telegraph* was printed later on, and several printers known to the present (1899) generation were apprenticed there. From Mr. J. P. Lewis we gather that his father was one of Mr. Price's apprentices, and the venerable Mr. Thos. Thomas, who worked in Mr. Lewis's office for so many years, was an old employee of the Price establishment."

(Condensed from the *Merthyr Express* 10.6.1899 p.3 col.6.)

10. Memorial Stone Laying, Smyrna Chapel, Aberfan, 1901

The memorial stone laying service at Smyrna new Chapel, Aberfan, took place on 23.5.1901.

Stones were laid by

Mrs. R. T. Griffiths, Aberfan House	£21
Mr. Charles Price, grocer, Troedyrhiw	£5.5s.

Miss Griffiths, Aberfan, and Master M. D. Evans, Windsor-place, and subscriptions were given as follows:

Miss Griffiths (Navigation), Aberfan	£10.10s.
Mrs. Griffiths, Navigation	£2.2s.
Mrs. Davies, Sunnybank	10s.
Mr. Rowley Davies,	10s.
and as shown.	

Collections were made at each meeting, with very good results. Each person who laid a stone was presented by the Smyrna Church with a silver trowel with ivory handle, suitably inscribed, and ebony mallet, all in case.

Speeches were given by the Rev. Wm. Lewis, pastor, Rev. D. W. Jones, Dinas, Rev. Hughes, Moriah, Dowlais and Mr. Charles Price, Troedyrhiw. In the evening a preaching service was held at Aberfan Chapel, kindly lent, when eloquent sermons were delivered by Revs. D. W. Jones and Hughes.

(*Merthyr Express* 1.6.1901 p.3 col.4.)

When examined in 1994, only two of the four memorial stones, laid in 1901, have withstood the ravages of time and weather, one to Master M. D. Evans and one to Mrs. R. T. Griffiths, Aberfan House, Aberfan.

Mr. Rowland T. Griffiths, Aberfan House, Master of the Aberfan Hounds, a small pack, was a landed proprietor and coalowner, with land at Merthyr Vale adjoining the pit (worked by Messrs. Nixon, Taylor and Cory).

Griffiths was a member of the Local Board of Health and the Merthyr Board of Guardians, and was an Overseer of the Parish of Merthyr Tydfil for many years. He died in 1887 and was buried at Llanfabon, where his mother's family originated.

See *Western Mail* 5.7.1887 p.3 col.8.

Merthyr Express 9.7.1887 p.5 col.4.

11. A New Chapel at Aberfan, 1902

February 1902 saw the opening of the new Welsh Baptist Chapel, Smyrna, at Aberfan. Spratt Brothers were the builders, the cost about £1,800. The pastor was Rev. W. Lewis

On opening Sunday the Rev. T. Hughes, Mountain Ash
Rev. Phillips, Cilfynydd, and
Rev. T. Davies, Aberaman,
preached to crowded congregations. In the morning sixteen persons were baptised by immersion, by the Rev. Mr. Lewis.

Preachers for the following Sunday and Monday were
Rev. William Thomas, Dowlais,

Rev. J. T. Hughes, Dowlais,

Rev. H. E. Jones, Penygraig.

A short report appeared in the *Merthyr Express* for 22.2.1902 p.5 col.6. In 1910 and 1920 services were held at Smyrna on Sundays, Mondays and Thursdays.

12. Bethania Chapel, Aberfan, 1902

Members of Smyrna Chapel, Aberfan, held an Opening Ceremony in February, 1902. At this time members of nearby Bethania Chapel were celebrating the Silver Jubilee of the Chapel, which opened in 1876.

Three former pastors attended,

the Rev. B. D. Davies, Gwaencaegurwen,

the Rev. G. Griffiths, "Penar", Pentre Estyll, and

the Rev. Robert Evans, Penmaen, near Blackwood.

The services were conducted throughout by the Rev. D. Johns.

Mr. B. M. Thomas, Secretary of the Church for the past fourteen years, gave financial statements and progress of the Church from the commencement, of which the following figures are of interest.

Total collections 1876-1902	£4,199.3s.6d.
Total expenditure 1876-1902	£4,172.1s.8d.
BALANCE	£27.1s.10d.

Cost of erection of Chapel and Vestry £1,724.12s.0d.

The cause was commenced in 1876 with four members, and at the time of Jubilee there were 243 members.

Bethania Chapel was used as a temporary mortuary for the Aberfan Disaster. The old Chapel has now been replaced by a new building.

(See *Merthyr Express* 22.2.1902 p.5 col.6.)

13. Foundation Stone Laid, English Baptist Chapel, Penydarren, 1902

In 1901 the congregation at Beulah English Baptist Chapel, Dowlais, decided to establish a branch at Penydarren. A successful start was made in the Penydarren Board Schools, the pastor was Rev. James Williams, a congregation of fifty members and one hundred Sunday School members soon built up.

A site for a new Chapel was given by Mr. Thomas Williams, J.P., Gwaelodygarth, on ground adjoining the new Free Library, and immediately fronting the Penydarren Board Schools.

The foundation stone was gracefully laid by Miss Nellie Davies, Merthyr, daughter of the late Alderman David Davies. Handed a handsome silver trowel, suitably inscribed, by Miss L. J. Harris, Graig-terrace, Dowlais, Miss N. Davies declared the foundation stone to be "well and truly laid".

Addresses were delivered by

    Revs. James Williams, T. W. Chance, High Street, Merthyr,

    H. Jenkins, Ainon, Georgetown, Merthyr,

    Edwin Aubrey, Morlais Chapel, Glebeland St., Merthyr,

    D. Price, Tabernacle, Brecon Road, Merthyr,

    Owen Owen, Elim Welsh Baptist Chapel, Penydarren,

    J. D. Hughes, Moriah, Mount Pleasant, Dowlais and

    J. H. Williams, Brynfarrd.

A letter of apology was received from Mr. Thomas Williams, J.P., Gwaelodygarth, who was unable to attend due to illness.

A report appeared in the *Merthyr Express* for 10.5.1902 p.3 col.3.

14. Stone Laying at Heolgerrig, 1902

The ceremony of laying the memorial stones in connection with the new Baptist Chapel, Calfaria, Heolgerrig, was performed in the presence of large numbers of the residents and others on Monday afternoon.

The structure is a substantial building, to accommodate 450 persons, and is fast approaching completion. The interesting proceedings commenced at 2.30 p.m., and were presided over by Mr. Richard G. Price, schoolmaster. The Rev. David Price, Tabernacle, first read a portion of Scripture, and offered a prayer. The following ladies and gentlemen then placed a stone in position, and declared it "to be well and truly laid":

    Mrs. D. A. Thomas, Llanwern,

    Miss Cissie Harris,

    Miss R. M. Evans (Tarian), Aberdare,

    David Hughes, C.C., Aberdare,

    John Morgan, C.C., Merthyr,

    Griffith Hall, Thomas Williams, Henry Harris, Thomas

        Richards, Rees Harris and Rev. T. Davies, Treforest.

Appropriate addresses were then delivered by the Chairman, Mrs. D. A. Thomas, the Revs. Stephen Williams, T. Chance, E. Aubrey and H. Jenkins, Messrs. D. Hughes, John Morgan and D. Cope Harris.

Each of those who took part in the stone laying was presented with a beautifully bound Bible by Mr. Spratt, the contractor. After the ceremony tea was provided in the Heolgerrig Schools, etc.

(Condensed from *Merthyr Express* 28.6.1902 p.4 col.6. See also *Merthyr*

Express 18.10.1902 p.4 col.6.)

15. *Merthyr Waterworks, Opening of the Upper Neuadd Reservoir*

A Thursday in July 1902 witnessed the formal completion and opening of one of the most important undertakings ever carried out by the Sanitary Authority of Merthyr Tydfil - the Upper Neuadd reservoir. This reservoir is the third constructed by the Merthyr Tydfil Local Board of Health and its successor, the Merthyr Urban District Council.

In the year 1875 a provisional order was obtained to construct a reservoir to contain eighty million gallons at Lower Neuadd, about four miles above Pentwyn, from which Dowlais and the Treharris district could be supplied by gravitation. The late Mr Samuel Harpur, surveyor to the Board, was the engineer. The order was obtained and the reservoir made, Messrs J. Pickthall and Sons being the contractors. The embankment was of the usual character earth with a central puddled clay trench. Shortly after its completion, after Mr Harpur had retired from the office of surveyor, and when Mr Harvey had succeeded him, some grave defects were discovered. It was found that storm waters accumulated with such extraordinary rapidity that the bye-wash was much too small to discharge them, but more serious than that was a leakage in the embankment on the west side of the tunnel. These defects necessitated the lowering of the level of the water to about one fourth the capacity of the reservoir, and there would never be any possibility of utilising it to the full until those defects were effectually remedied. Then came another disagreeable surprise. The mill owners wanted to know by what authority the council impounded water in the new reservoir and then it was discovered that the provisional order which conferred the authority to make the reservoir, gave no authority to impound water. For several years this grave error of omission was the subject of correspondence between the Council and the millowners and finally led to the latter initiating litigation to assert their own rights. The action did not come to trial but the outcome was an agreement to apply to Parliament for powers to construct a new reservoir at Upper Neuadd on a site which had been indicated as most favourable by Mr Thomas F. Harvey the surveyor, out of which the millowners were to receive as compensation a daily discharge increasing in proportion to the body of water impounded. Plans were prepared by Mr Harvey which were submitted to Mr G. F. Deacon C.E., for his approbation and ultimately Mr Deacon was appointed as engineer of the scheme, Mr Harvey being the resident engineer in charge. The dam designed was not the old fashioned bank of earth, with a clay trench in the centre, but a solid wall of well-built stone masonry of the same character as the dam at Vrynwy,

98

but differing in certain important details of construction. The Act of Parliament was obtained in 1895, and the contract for the work was let to Messrs Holme and King, Limited, in November of the following year. The contract was peculiar in nature, the Council taking exceptional precautions to ensure the quality of the work being sound throughout. The contractors supplied all materials, and performed most of the work except the actual building of the dam, that is to say the laying of the stones in their places. That was done by workmen employed by the Council by the day so that there was no inducement to hurry anything, and every layer had its proper time for setting before the next was put on. The result has been eminently satisfactory, since, although the period of construction exceeded the time limit named in the contract, the work has been thorough from beginning to end, and the dam holds back a vast body of water behind it without the slightest trace of a flaw. The overflow is in the centre of the dam. It is a magnificent example of engineering, both in design and in execution, and reflects the greatest credit upon the engineers and constructors. The height from the bed of the river at the vertical face of the dam to top water is 67 ft. 3 in. - the overflow level being 1,506.5 ft. above ordnance datum. The total length is 1622 ft of which 232 ft are in the breasts of the mountains out of sight. The reservoir, when full, has a surface area of 59 acres, containing 350 million gallons, and the drainage area is 2,018 acres. The total cost of the reservoir has been £138,000, which is about £18,000 above the original estimate. The Council decided while the contractors have their plant on the ground, to have the Lower Neuadd Reservoir made watertight and secure by a larger bye-wash and that work has been carried out at an expense of nearly £20,000. Altogether the Council and its predecessors have spent upon waterworks for the parish upon the original scheme £82,000; upon Lower Neuadd £80,000; upon Upper Neuadd £138,000; total, £300,000; for which it now has a storage capacity representing 770 million gallons. The compensation flow for the ironmasters today is practically represented by what is discharged from Pentwyn in as much as the discharge from Upper Neuadd mainly serves to prolong the supply from Pentwyn, and it is not an addition thereto. The sale of the plant used in the construction took place a few weeks ago, and before the branch line to Torpantau is removed, Mr Gwilym C. James, Chairman of the Council, very properly considered that the satisfactory completion of a great and important undertaking was worthy of a formal opening ceremonial, and to that end he issued invitations for the event on Thursday.

The guests invited were

        Mr G. F. Deacon, C.E. the engineer-in-chief of the works;

        Mrs Deacon and Miss Deacon;

        Sir Alex. Binnie;

        Sir W. T. Lewis;

        Sir B. Baker;

        Mr E. P. Martin and Mrs Martin;

        Prof. Boyd Dawkins;

        Colonel Gwynne, Chief Constable of Breconshire;

        Mr H. W. Martin;

        Mr J. P. Gwynne Holford;

        Mr J Plews;

        Mr W Griffiths, Messrs Holme and King;

        Mr E. Jones, L and P Bank;

        Dr Biddle, High Constable;

        Mr Christmas Evans;

        Mr T. Marchant Williams;

        Mr W. L. Daniel;

        Mr E. A. Johnson;

        Dr Webster;

        Mr R. Owen traffic manager B. & M. R.;

        Mr R. J. Rhys, coroner;

        Dr Ward;

        Mr C. Wilkins;

        Dr W. W. Jones;

        Mr A. W. Houlson;

        Mr Jno Rogers, Cyfarthfa;

        Mr C. Russell James;

        Col. Cresswell;

        Dr Williams Cardiff;

        Dr Savage Cardiff;

        Mr Baker;

        Mr T. Aneuryn Rees and Mrs Rees;

        Mr and Mrs Evan Evans;

        Mr and Mrs T. F. Harvey;

        Dr Thomas M.O.H.;

        Mr H. M. Richards Abercriban;

        Mr John Williams Blaentaf.

The whole of the members of the council were invited but only the following were able to be present;

Messrs:

T. E. Morgan

D. Evans

N. Hankey

J.M. Berry

J. Roberts

V. A. Wills

Dan Thomas

D. John

Mrs G. C. James and Miss James were also present.

The guests proceeded by the 12.10 p.m. train, a saloon being provided for them. Though the weather was threatening it held up fine until Torpantau was reached. Then, while the party were waiting for the "Neuadd special" to back into the station it began to drop and Jupiter Pluvius, thinking nothing could be more appropriate than for him to participate in the function of opening a reservoir, raised the sluices of his own waterworks to some purpose as soon as the train began its journey on the contractor's line. Most of the passengers were in a covered carriage, which had the lamp holes on the roof open, and the hail and the rain came down with such force that umbrellas were opened for protection. But a number of gentlemen were seated in open trucks, and they had the full benefit of the storm, which lasted until the reservoir was reached. Then it fortunately ceased, and continued fine with one short interval during the remainder of the day. The wind blew with tremendous force across the water and on the embankment, everybody found it no light matter to keep a good footing. The water, which was within six feet of the overflow, was very choppy. Arrived at the valve tower, through which the wind whistled like a tempest.

Mr G. F. Deacon, the engineer-in-chief of the works, said the Merthyr District Council had many reasons to be proud of that reservoir. They would be able to carry by aqueducts along the valleys a water supply to mining populations twenty miles away, the works being at an altitude at which no supply had ever been provided before. Then the water was pure - and it was not likely to be contaminated in the future for no one would think of making his home above the reservoir. With the exception of those of Vyrnwy and Thirlmere it was placed at the highest altitude of any reservoir in this country. Then it was a masonry dam, which was more lasting than one of earth would be. Not that a masonry dam was the right thing anywhere and everywhere, but it was the right kind of dam for that place. Further, it had been built mainly of Welsh materials - very little indeed that went into its construction having been brought from England or abroad. Welsh stone and Welsh hydraulic lime had proved the equals of Portland cement. Then it had two sets of valves, one for the regulation of the compensation flow, and the other for the town's supply. They could not turn off the town supply but the compensation water had been stopped for half-an-hour, and now he invited the Chairman to turn on a double dose.

Mr Gwilym C. James then turned the valve, and others followed him, until a copius discharge was observed flowing from the conduit into the bed of the river below. He then said he had much pleasure in declaring those waterworks open for the requirements of the inhabitants of the Merthyr Tydfil Urban District, and he desired to congratulate them upon the completion of the work. He then invited them all to lunch with him at the Mission House.

The guests completed the perambulation of the dam, and went down to the overflow and the chamber where huge pipes for the discharge of the water are contained. Outside a photograph was taken of the party. Arrived at the Mission House we found it prettily decorated, and the tables beautifully and elegantly laid for luncheon. Mr Gwilym C. James presided, having on his right Mr Deacon, Dr Cresswell, and Mrs James, and on his left Mrs Deacon and E. P. Martin. Grace having been said by the Chairman, ample justice was done to the good things placed before the guests. The post prandial proceeding commenced by

The CHAIRMAN giving the health of "The King."

The toast was heartily drank, and the CHAIRMAN then gave the health of the Queen, the Prince and Princess of Wales, and the rest of the members of the royal family.

The CHAIRMAN then said that life like the weather was full of sunshine and storms. They had had it exemplified that day in the atmospheric conditions around them, and it held good too in the history of the Merthyr Water Works, whose prospects had been sometimes rosy and at others dark. It was ten years come December next since he first interviewed Mr Deacon at Liverpool with respect to the action of Messrs. Crawshay Brothers to restrain the District Council of Merthyr from the use of water gathered in the Lower Neuadd reservoir, but he would not inflict upon them a history of that. It was fifty years ago that a body of gentlemen first moved together with a view of securing an efficient supply of pure water for the district. At that time it contained about 42,000 inhabitants who had to go long distances for water from impure sources and carry it home in tin jacks. Amongst the gentlemen who banded themselves together to get the necessary powers for obtaining a water supply were some gentlemen whose sons were with them today. There was:-

Sir John Guest, a name always honoured in the district;
Mr William Crawshay, father of Mr Robert Crawshay;
Mr Robert Crawshay himself;
Mr W. Meyrick, a solicitor of long standing;
Mr John Evans, whose son was still with us;
Mr Benjamin Martin, an uncle of Mr E P. Martin;
Mr Edward Purchase, with whose family Dr Cresswell is
connected by marriage;
Mr William Norton, a brewer;
Mr Sam Thomas, father of Mr D. A. Thomas;
Mr Charles Herbert James, his own father;
Mr Geo. Martin, father of Mr E. P. Martin and
Mr H. W. Martin;

and dear old Captain Russell. These gentlemen obtained an Act to enable them to supply the town with water, though he did not remember where the reservoir was to have been; but they did not carry that scheme out, and in 1858 the Local Board obtained an Act under which they constructed Pentwyn Reservoir. In 1876 Neuadd Reservoir was authorised and made, but after impounding water it was found that though a provisional order could authorise the acquisition of land, it could not empower the taking of water. Then Messrs. Crawshay Bros. intervened, and it was at that juncture that he became the clerk to the Local Board. He felt it to be his duty to resist Messrs. Crawshay's claims strenuously, and he did so. In the result after long litigation, they came to an agreement with the millowners, under which they were able to acquire the whole of the water above Neuadd for the uses of the inhabitants and for other purposes, subject to the provision of compensation. The quantity claimed was at first very large, but ultimately it was fixed to one million gallons per diem, to be discharged into the bed of the river below the Lower Neuadd.

Merthyr Express 12 July 1902
Page 5 columns 6,7,8
Waterworks

For further biographical information on George Martin and his sons Edward Pritchard Martin and Henry William Martin, mentioned above, see "The Martin Family of Dowlais", *Merthyr Historian, Volume Six* pp. 109-134.

16. Merthyr Free Libraries, Opening of Penydarren Reading-Room by Mr. D. A. Thomas, M.P., 1902

On a Monday afternoon in September, 1902, Mr. David Alfred Thomas (Gladstonian Liberal, elected Member of Parliament for Merthyr Tydfil in 1892, 1895, 1900 and 1906), accompanied by his wife and Alderman Thomas Williams, J.P., Gwaelodygarth, formally opened the Penydarren Reading-room, one of six to be built and maintained by the Merthyr District Council under the provisions of the Free Libraries Acts. The building was situated just above the Penydarren Schools, and contained a commodious reading-room, a game room and necessary outhouses. The cost was £600. There was some additional land beside the Library, for future use. The land was donated by Alderman Thomas Williams, J.P., Gwaelodygarth.

Councillor F. S. Simons, Chairman, Free Libraries Committee, referred to the struggles the Council had met with, since the adoption of the Free Libraries Acts, first of all in obtaining sites and then in getting the necessary money to build Free Libraries. Alderman Thomas Williams had generously given land for the Penydarren Free Library, that example had been followed by Lord Windsor, who had given a site for a Troedyrhiw Free Libarary. Councillor Simons said that he lived in hopes that the large firm of Iron Masters, Messrs. Guest, Keen and Nettlefolds, would give a site in Dowlais at no distant date. So far that was all they had been able to do.

Councillor Simons also thanked Mr. D. A. Thomas (who later became Lord Rhondda) for influencing Mr. Andrew Carnegie to donate £6,000 to Merthyr for Libraries.

Mr. Simons stated that it was not at that time the intention to make each Reading-room a circulating library, anyone wanting a book could apply and the book would be obtained from the Central Library.

Mr. D. A. Thomas hoped the example of Mr. T. Williams and Lord Windsor would be followed by other landlords in the parish. The condition laid down by Mr. Carnegie was that THE SITES FOR THE READING-ROOMS MUST BE FREE. It would be a scandalous thing if they could not avail themselves in Merthyr of Mr. Carnegie's generosity, by landowners not complying with this condition. D. A. Thomas regarded Andrew Carnegie as one of the greatest of living men of his day. Carnegie's ambition was to do good whilst he was living. He had said that TO DIE RICH WAS TO DIE DISGRACED, and he intended dividing his wealth among good philanthropic objects, so that he might see them flourishing. Carnegie's sympathies were international and the immense good he had done would live after him.

Alderman Williams referred to the need to supply counter attractions, to encourage temperance and provide alternatives to dependence on public houses and alcohol for sociability and entertainment.

Mr. W. Edwards, His Majesty's Inspector of Schools, said that the Free Libraries Act had been in force for a long time, but this was the first concrete exemplification of it in the shape of bricks and mortar.

Mr. Edwards commented adversely on the fact that the Merthyr Central Library was to be left till the last. He jocularly suggested Mr. Carnegie be approached for a further £2,000. Due to problems in acquiring a site, the Merthyr Central Library was not opened until 1935.

(Condensed from the *Merthyr Express* 20.9.1902 p.3 col.3.)

A biography of D. A. Thomas, Viscount Rhondda, was written by his daughter, Rhondda, and others, and published by Longmans, Green and Co., 1921.

Alderman Thomas Williams, J.P. (1823-1903), Gwaelod-y-Garth House, Merthyr Tydfil, present at Stone Laying or Opening Ceremonies for

> The Truant School, Quaker's Yard, 1894
>
> Tabernacle Baptist Church, Brecon Road, 1896,
>
> Merthyr County School, 1897,
>
> English Baptist Chapel, Penydarren, 1902, and
>
> Penydarren Reading-room, 1902,

was the subject of a comprehensive biographical essay, by W. R. Lambert, in Stewart Williams' *Glamorgan Historian, Volume Eleven.* Thomas Williams's memory was honoured by the erection of the Williams Memorial English Congregational Chapel at Penydarren, officially opened in October, 1906.

Discussion

The erection of public buildings was often a protracted affair, but was occasionally accomplished with ease and speed.

The following processes have been briefly examined for the buildings studied:

1. Decision to build.
2. Acquisition of sites.
3. Finance.
4. Architects.
5. Builders.
6. Foundation Stone/Memorial Stone Ceremonies.
7. Opening Ceremonies.
8. Maintenance.

Buildings still standing include

Hope Chapel, Truant School, Merthyr Town Hall, Pant Church, Tabernacle (Brecon Road), Parish Church (Merthyr), Swan Inn, Smyrna, Bethania (Aberfan, New Building), Calfaria (Heolgerrig), Upper Neuadd Reservoir.

Demolished buildings include

County School, Bethania Aberfan (Old Chapel), Penydarren Reading-room and adjoining English Baptist Chapel.

We conclude our account with one last Stone Laying Ceremony, which has fascinating historical overtones.

A new Tabernacle Congregational Chapel at Treharris was in course of erection in 1893, on the site of the old Tabernacle Chapel. The congregation gathered at the site and headed by a magnificent banner, marched to the Great Western Station to meet Alderman Thomas Williams, J.P., Gwaelodygarth, Merthyr. The marchers then paraded the streets, singing stirring hymns. A service was held and stone laying proceeded.

The first two stones were laid by

Mrs. W. T. Jones, chemist, and

Mrs. B. P. Evans, The Schools.

They were presented with beautiful electro-plated trowels and polished rosewood mallets. Each lady placed a twenty-pound donation on her stone.

Mr. J. T. Morgan, Rhigos House, Treharris,

Councillor D. Prosser and

Mr. Edward Edwards, J.P., Penlan House,

also laid stones and made donations.

Alderman Thomas Williams, J.P., then placed in position a fine mural marble tablet commemorating the tercentenary (1893) of the martyrdom of the Welsh Nonconformist, John Penry, and after completing his work Mr. Williams delivered an impassioned address, giving a summary of Penry's life and death.

Born in Breconshire, John Penry was a Roman Catholic who attended Peterhouse College, Cambridge, for four years, then went to Oxford. There he was drawn into a circle of Puritans.

On 21st of May, 1593, John Penry was arraigned before the judges in London, charged with being "a seditious heretic". On May 25th, 1593, sentence of death was formally passed and four days later the Archbishop and three others signed the death warrant. He was hanged at Southwark on May 29th, 1593, aged thirty-four years. Penry left behind a widow and four small children, the eldest five years of age. The only legacy Penry had to leave his children was a Bible each.

KEY TO PEN Y DARREN MAP

1. Reading Room.
2. English Baptist.
3. Williams Memorial.
4. Horeb.
5. Mission Hall.
6. St. Johns.

PEN Y DARREN

1910.

See "Foundations".

Chronological Date Sequence of Events, Merthyr Tydfil Public Buildings, 1893-1902

Events	References
Special Services at Bethesda to Celebrate Clearance of Debt.	M.E. 25.2.1893 p.3 col.4.
Dowlais Parish Church Bazaar for Rebuilding Fund.	M.E. 22.4.1893 p.8 col.5.
Lord and Lady Windsor Opened Dowlais Bazaar. Huge Success.	M.E. 29.4.1893 p.8 col.3-6.
Extension of St. Illtyd's Catholic Church, Dowlais, who was St. Illtyd??	M.E. 3.6.1893 p.8 col.4.
Hope Chapel Opened.	M.E. 15.7.1893 p.3 col.4+5.
Water Litigation at Merthyr, Crawshay and others versus The Merthyr Local Board. Terms Agreed.	M.E. 15.7.1893 p.8 col.1-3.
Sale of Work, New Mission Hall, Penydarren, to cost £1,200.	M.E. 22.7.1893 p.4 col.8.
Bishop Hedley Laid Stone for St. Mary's Church.	M.E. 5.8.1893 p.5 col.7 and p.8 col.4.

See also, Peter Williams, *Merthyr Historian, Volume Six*, 1992.

Truant School, Opening Ceremony.	M.E. 13.1.1894 p.4. W.M. 9.1.1894 p.7 col.4+5. C.T.. 13.1.1894 p.5 col.6.
St. Mary's, Brecon Road, Opening.	M.E. 29.9.1894, p.8.

Tabernacle Chapel, Troedyrhiw, Opening. M.E. 2.11.1895 p.8 col.2.
Penywern Chapel Reopened after Renovation.   M.E. 9.11.1895 p.8 col.3.

Ivor Chapel, Dowlais, New Organ.   M.E. 28.12.1895 p.8 col.2.

Merthyr Town Hall.   M.E. 23.5.1896 p.8.
                                              W.M. 22.5.1896
                                              p.6 col.4+5.

Christ Church, Pant. dedication.   M.E. 13.6.1896 p.8.
                                              *A History of the Church in
                                              the Parish of Dowlais,
                                              Christ Church, Pant,
                                              1896-1986,*
                                              Huw Williams, 1977.
                                              W.M. 13.6.1896 p.7 col.1.

Tabernacle, Brecon Road, Stones Laid.   M.E. 11.7.1896 p.8.
                                              W.M. 10.7.1896 p.6 col.8.

Deml Baptist Chapel Abercanaid.
Replaced Shiloh. Stones Laid.   M.E. 12.9.1896 p.3 col.7.

Restoration, Parish Church, New Peal.   C.T. 7.11.1896 p.3 col.8.
                                              W.M. 2.11.1896 p.3 col.3.

Reopening, Bethania Chapel, Dowlais.   M.E. 21.11.1896 p.8 col.2.

Merthyr County School, Formal Opening.   M.E. 16.1.1897
                                              p.8 col.1+2.
                                              W.M. 14.1.1897 p.7 col.1.

Diamond Jubilee Ward, MGH, Sir W. T. Lewis. M.E. 27.2.1897 p.8 col.1-3.
                                            C.T. 22.2.1897 p.7 col.3+4.

Memorial Window to Martin Family,
St. John's, Dowlais.   M.E. 5.6.1897 p.8 col.3.

Christ Church, Pant, Window to Mr.
and Mrs. W. Jenkins, Consett Hall.　　M.E. 20.11.1897. p.8 col.5.

Monument at Pant Cemetery to
Rev. John Jones,, "Matthetes".　　M.E. 20.11.1897 p.8 col.5.

Stone Laid, New Library, Cefn Coed.　　M.E. 30.4.1898 p.6 col.8.

New Jewish Mortuary at Jewish
Cemetery, Cefn Coed.　　M.E. 8.4.1899 p.8 col.4.

Restoration, Old Parish Church,
Grand Bazaar at Drill Hall, Opened
by Sir W. T. Lewis.　　M.E. 29.4.1899 p.8 col.3.

"Captains of Industry" Window Dedicated,
Parish Church.　　M.E. 13.5.1889.p7.col.4

Swan Inn, Old and New.　　M.E. 10.6.1899 p.3 col.6.

Tender for Taking Down and Rebuilding
The Parrot Inn, Ynysgau.　　M.E. 10.6.1899 p.5 col.8.

Thomastown Tips to Become
Recreation Ground.　　M.E. 24.6.1899 p.8 col.2.

Amateur Dramatics, Temperance Hall,
for Parish Church Funds.　　M.E. 24.6.1899 p.8 col.3.

Alderman David Davies. Obituary.　　M.E. 2.9.1899 p.5 col.7+8.

Grand Bazaar for Christ Church, Pant.　　M.E. 11.11.1899 p.5 col.8.

Street Improvements, Owners'
Appeal to the Magistrates.　　M.E.. 25.11.1899 p.7 col.6.

One Hundred and Fifty Years,
Ynysgau Chapel Anniversary.　　M.E. 2.12.1899 p.7 col.6.

High Street Baptist Chapel Rebuilt.	M.E. 23.6.1900 p.5 col.7+8.
New Union Infirmary, a Palace for the Sick and Infirm.	M.E. 7.7.1900 p.2 col.7.

See also
The Story of St. Tydfils Hospital, *Merthyr Historian, Volume Six.*

Consecration of Taff Fechan Church by the Bishop of St. David's.	M.E. 4.8.1900 p.3 col.3.
Dedication of St. Luke's Church, Gellifaelog, Dowlais.	M.E. 6.10.1900 p.8 col.3+4.
St. James's Church, Pentrebach.	M.E. 23.3.1901 p.7 col.3.
Morlais C.M. Chapel, Reopening.	M.E. 20.4.1901 p.8 col.3.
Smyrna Chapel, Aberfan, Stones Laid.	M.E. 1.6.1901 p.3 col.4.
Reopening, Merthyr Parish Church.	M.E. 15.6.1901 p.5 col.7+8.
Reopening, St. Peter's, Abercanaid.	M.E. 22.6.1901 p.7 col.6.
Parish Bell Ringers on Strike.	M.E. 6.7.1901 p.4 col.8.
New Organ, Christ Church, Pant.	M.E. 21.9.1901 p.3 col.7.
Jerusalem Baptist Chapel, Pentrebach, Stones Laid.	M.E. 12.10.1901 p.8 col.5.
New Unitarian Chapel.	M.E. 7.12.1901 p.7 col.5+6.
Smyrna, Aberfan, Opening.	M.E. 22.2.1902 p.5 col.6.
Bethania, Aberfan, Silver Jubilee.	M.E. 22.2.1902 p.5 col.6.

Penydarren, English Baptist Chapel,

Stone Laid.	M.E. 10.5.1902 p.3 col.3.
Calfaria, Heolgerrig, Stones Laid.	M.E. 28.6.1902 p.5 col.7+8.
Free Libraries, Andrew Carnegie's Gift.	M.E. 28.6.1902 p.5 col.7+8.
Upper Neuadd Reservoir, Opening.	M.E. 12.7.1902 p.5. W.M. 10.7.1902 p.7. S.W.D.N. 11.7.1902 p.6.
St. Mary's New Mission Church, Penydarren.	M/E. 19.7.1902 p.5 col.6. See also *Merthyr Historian, Volume Three*, p.23.
Site for Free Library at Aberfan not available as a Gift.	W.M. 21.7.1902 p.6 col.3.
Petition for Removal of Pant Fever Hospital.	M.E. 6.9.1902 p.8 col.2. W.M. 4.9.1902 p.3 col.5.
Opening Ceremony, Penydarren Reading Room.	M.E. 20.9.1902 p.3 col.3. W.M. 16.9.1902 p.6 col.7. S.W.D.N. 16.9.1902 p.6 col.2.
Calfaria, Heolgerrig, More Stones Laid.	M.E. 18.10.1902 p.4 col.6.

The Standing Conference of the
History of the South Wales Valleys
by JOSEPH GROSS

The Standing Conference was started to promote research and create interest in the history of the Valleys of South Wales. For this purpose an annual one-day Conference is held which features lectures about various facets of Valleys' history. There is no formal membership. An Executive Committee is elected annually and meets a few times during the year to arrange a programme for the next Conference. Admission fees charged for each Conference are designed to cover cost and are kept to a minimum.

The Standing Conference has its origin in the Aberfan Disaster of 1966. Aberfan is a small village some 4 miles south of Merthyr Tydfil. For more than a hundred years coal mining was carried out in the area, centred on the colliery at nearby Merthyr Vale. The spoil from mining operations was deposited in large, cone-shaped tips on slopes above the valley floor. On 21st October, 1966, one of the tips collapsed and water and slurry rushed down the mountain side with enormous force and speed. Farm cottages in its path were destroyed and Pantglas Junior School engulfed, Pantglas Senior School was severely damaged and a number of houses in the village were destroyed. In Pantglas Junior School alone 5 teachers and 100 children died. In all 144 persons perished, among them 116 children. It was said that a whole generation was wiped out on that day in the village.

The disaster stirred the compassion of the world. Large sums of money were raised to aid the victims. However there was also a great need to provide spiritual and counselling assistance to the stricken community as a whole. The General Secretary of the Church of Christ, Walter Hendey, recognized the need and asked the Rev. Erastus Jones, who at that time served on the Ecumenical Council in Blaendulais, to visit Aberfan. Among the funds received in Aberfan were contributions from the Welsh Church in Toronto sent to the Welsh Council for Churches. They invited Mr. Jones and his wife to work in Aberfan as Community workers. A caravan named Ty Toronto was provided as an office. Later a house was provided. Mr. Jones had no church nor congregation, his brief was simply to do what the situation required. When the money from Toronto ran out, funds were given from the Disaster Fund until 1972.

Rev. Jones not only dealt successfully with the problems of groups and individuals, he also set up an organization to deal with problems of social and economic aspects in the South Wales communities. He assembled a small group of researchers who operated from Ty Toronto. During the next few years they enquired into many aspects of Valley life, arranged Conferences and published several valuable reports. In March, 1973, they arranged a Conference "Call to the Valleys". It was followed in 1974 by "The Year of the Valleys". A socio-economic strategy for the Valleys of South Wales was published under the title: "Choosing our future". In 1974 a Conference for Valleys' Historians was organized. It was held at the Glamorgan Polytechnic on 30.3.1974. Another publication followed in 1975: "The Valleys' Call". On 23.9.1976 the *Western Mail* called Ty Toronto "the centre for South Wales Valleys' Studies" and reported that the centre was sponsoring a meeting of Valley Historians with the aim of setting up a Standing Conference for historical studies. The article continued: "Eventually Ty Toronto plan to produce a comprehensive history of the Valleys as a whole." A consultation took place at the Aberfan Community Centre on 23.10.1976 which inaugurated the Standing Conference for Valleys' Historical Societies. Those attending decided to form a Steering Committee for the purpose of getting the movement off the ground. Some twenty persons attended, representing various Historical Societies and Institutions from all parts of South Wales. A further meeting was held on 20.11.1976 to clarify the aims of the Standing Conference. This led to a temporary Committee Meeting on 29.1.1977 attended by Dr. Raymond Grant, Dr. Joseph Gross, Mrs. Etta Lewis, Miss Kate Olwen Pritchard, Mr. Delwyn Tibbott, Mr. Douglas William and from Ty Toronto Rev. Erastus Jones, Mrs. Eiluned Jones, Miss Elaine Mahoney and Mr. Len Roberts.

It was agreed to draft a Constitution to be placed before the Inaugural Conference on 26.2.1977. The main provisions of the Constitution were as follows:

Name: Cynhadledd Sefydlog Ar Hanes Cymoedd De Cymru. Standing Conference of the History of the South Wales Valleys.

Aims: To provide a focus of concern for the history of the Valleys and their future.

Membership: Membership will be open to individuals and groups who accept the aims of the Conference.

Conference: An open Conference will be arranged as frequently as the Executive Committee deem necessary.

Annual General Meeting: An Annual General Meeting shall be held in May. Other General Meetings may be held as the Executive Committee may deem necessary.

Officers: President, elected at an Annual General Meeting for five years, who would normally chair the open Conference.

Chairman, Vice Chairman, Secretary, Treasurer elected annually at the A.G.M.

Executive Committee to consist of the Officers and six other members elected at the A.G.M. for three years.

Finance: Money shall be raised by membership subscription, donations and special activities.

Changing the Constitution: Rules are laid down for changing the Constitution, briefly as follows: A motion must be sent to all members prior to the next A.G.M. and be voted on by members at the A.G.M.

The Inaugural Conference was held on 26th February, 1977, at the Aberfan and Merthyr Vale Community Centre. The draft Constitution was adopted. The following Officers and members of the Executive Committee were elected:

President:	Professor Glanmor Williams
Chairman:	Rev. Erastus Jones
Vice-Chairman:	Dr. Raymond Grant
Secretary:	Mr. John Mear
Treasurer:	Dr. Joseph Gross.

Six Committee Members:

Mr. Howard Jones

Dr. Tony Jukes

Mr. D. Tibbott

Mrs. Etta Lewis

Mr. Adrian Babbidge

Mr. Hywel Francis.

Papers on the following topics were presented to the Conference:

Historical Societies: Mr. John Mear, Cynon Valley Historical Society.

Record Offices: Mrs. Patricia Moore, Glamorgan Record Office.

Schools: Dr. Raymond Grant, Mid. Glamorgan Education Department.

Museums: Mr. Dafydd Gwylon, National Museum of Wales, Schools' Service.

Academic Departments: Mr. E. D. Evans, South Glamorgan Institute of Higher Education.

The Committee met for the first time on 21st March, 1977 at Ty Toronto. Ty Toronto was to remain the venue for Committee Meetings until the retirement of the Rev. Erastus Jones in 1986. It was decided to issue a leaflet explaining the aims of the Conference. It was also decided to publish a newsletter from time to time, giving details of what was going on in local history, as well as records of publications, projects and acquisitions for the Gwent and Glamorgan Record Offices. Dr. Jukes undertook the editorship of the Newsletter and subsequently six Newsletters were published. The Minutes Book was kept by Rev. Erastus Jones till May, 1978, when Dr. Joseph Gross took over.

At the Committee Meeting of 16.5.1977 it was decided to hold the first Annual General Meeting and Conference on 13th May, 1978. At the next Committee Meeting on 26.9.1977 the A.G.M. and Conference were further discussed. Professor Glanmor Williams was to be asked to give an address in the morning, and four talks were to be given in the afternoon. The first Newsletter was issued on 21.11.1977. The venue for the Conference was to be Aberdare Swimming Pool. The matter of registration with the Charities Commission was discussed, but it was decided to leave the matter in abeyance.

The first Annual General Meeting and Conference was held on 13th May, 1978 at the Assembly Rooms of the Aberdare Swimming Pool. The fee for admission, coffee and luncheon was £2.50. Forty-nine persons attended. At the election of Officers, the Rev. Erastus Jones indicated that he did not seek re-election. Dr. Raymond Grant was elected Chairman, Dr. A. Jukes Vice-Chairman, Dr. J. Gross Secretary and Treasurer, Mr. Egan was co-opted to the Committee. Mr. Howard Jones resigned.

At the following Conference Professor Glanmor Williams gave the Presidential address. He dealt with the respective roles of professional and amateur historians. After luncheon, four papers were given:

Mr. Adrian Babbidge, Director of the Torfaen Museum Service, introduced a plan of action for the Standing Conference, stating that one of its objectives was to work towards a History of the Valleys.

Dr. Anthony Jukes of Oxford House Industrial Archaeological Society described the restoration of the Melingriffith Water Pump.

Mr. John Mear, assisted by Mr. Geoffrey Evans and Mr. Lyndon Harries, gave a semi-dramatised presentation of the dispute between Dr. Price and Vicar Griffiths - the Treachery of the Blue Books.

Messrs. David Maddox and Gwyn Evans gave a talk describing their methodology in mounting an exhibition on part of Tonypandy's history.

At the Committee Meeting of 4.10.1978 it was decided to circulate a letter, in accordance with the plan outlined by Mr. Adrian Babbidge at the Standing Conference in May, inviting various Societies and individuals to contribute to the history of the Valleys. The letter was duly sent out but produced very little response and the plan was not further pursued by the Committee.

Newsletter Number Two appeared, Newsletter Number Three was issued on 20.11.1978 and Number Four on 19.3.1979. It was decided that the theme for the 1979 Conference, to be held on 12.5.1979, should be "Transport in the Valleys".

The Second Annual General Meeting and Conference was held on 12th May, 1979, at the Assembly Rooms of the Aberdare Swimming Pool. The fee for the Conference, including admission, coffee and luncheon, was £3. Thirty-five members attended. At the A.G.M. it was decided to leave the annual subscription at £2. At the election of Officers and Committee Members, Mr. Tom Evans and Mr. Huw Williams, Research Assistant at the Merthyr Tydfil Heritage Trust, were co-opted to the Committee.

The Presidential Address at the Conference was given by Professor Glanmor Williams, who eloquently contrasted the character of the people of the Vale of Glamorgan with the sturdy, more self-reliant inhabitants of the Uplands of Glamorgan in the seventeenth and eighteenth centuries. Talks given in the afternoon were as follows:

Mr. Ian Milne, Secretary of the Neath and Tennant Canals' Preservation Society spoke on the work of the Society.

Mr. Terry McCarthy gave a talk on "Railway History in the Rhymney Valley".

Mr. Chris Taylor spoke on "Road Transport in the South Wales Valleys".

Newsletter Number Five was issued in November, 1979, and Number Six in April, 1980.

The Third Annual General Meeting and Conference was held on 17th May, 1980, at the Blaenavon Recreation Centre, Blaenavon, Gwent. The fee of £1 included admission and Morning Coffee. Twenty-seven persons attended. At the

The Thomas Williams's Memorial Chapel, Penydarren, Merthyr. Opened in October 1906. 1994. See "Foundations".

The Mission Hall, Penydarren, Merthyr, 1994.

Merthyr Old Town Hall, nowadays used as a Nightclub, 1904. The foundation stone laid by Thomas Jenkins, Pant, can be clearly seen, under the bay window.

Merthyr Tydfil New Town Hall, 1994.

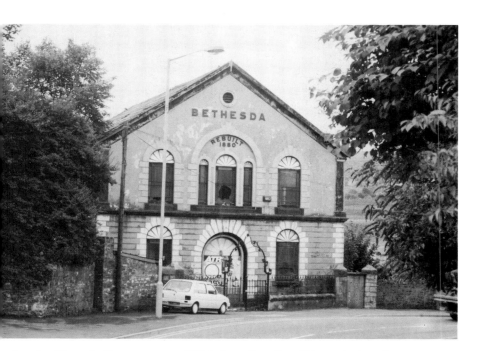

ethesda Chapel, Georgetown, 1994. Derelict. See "Foundations".

*ethesda Chapel, Georgetown, 1994. A sad sight, served as a community cen-
e in recent years.*

The Priory, Brecon Road, priests' house, regarded by architects as a model of architectural correctness.

Gwaelod-y-Garth House, Merthyr Tydfil. This was once the home of Alderman Thomas Williams, J.P. Now used for Therapy.

. *Mary's Church, Brecon Road.*

John's Parish Church, Dowlais. The large plaque commemorates Sir John
iest.

Parish Church Exterior, Merthyr Tydfil.

Parish Church Interior, Merthyr Tydfil.

Graig Chapel, Abercanaid, 1994.

Sion Chapel, Abercanaid, 1994.

St. Peter's Church, Abercanaid, 1994.

St. Paul's Church, Abercanaid, 1994.

Carnegie Reading Room, Alexandra Place, Abercanaid, 1912.

Disused Free Library, Alexandra Place, Abercanaid, 1994.

Free Library, Treharris, 1994.

Carnegie Free Library, Treharris, 1913.

Plaque commemorating Alderman Andrew Wilson, J.P., Mayor of Merthyr, at Treharris Free Library, 1909.

Stone commemorating John Penry, Martyr. Tabernacle Chapel, Treharris.

Brynhyfryd Chapel, Treharris, Mid-Glam, a Memorial Stone laid by C. H. James, M.P., can be clearly seen to left of door. 1994.

Close-up of Memorial Stone, Brynhyfryd Chapel, laid by Charles Herbert James, M.P. for Merthyr Tydfil. 1994.

Pant Fever Hospital, drawn from an old photograph, by Merthyr artist David Lewis Jones.

William Menelaus.   *Photo courtesy of Merthyr Central Library.*

Cattle in Landscape. A. F. Bonheur. NMW 21. Menelaus Collection. National Museum of Wales.

The Challenge Refused. J. E. Hodgson. NMW 35. Menelaus Collection. National Museum of Wales.

Cardiff Free Library, 1904. First home of the Menelaus Collection. See "William Menelaus of Dowlais".

The National Museum of Wales, Cardiff, present day (1994), home of the Menelaus Collection.

A.G.M. Dr. Jukes stated that he did not wish to serve as Vice-Chairman. It was decided to leave the Office of Vice-Chairman in abeyance for the time being. Mr. Bob Gulliford was elected a member of the Executive Committee.

The theme of the Conference which followed was "Social and Cultural Conditions in the South Wales' Valleys in the Mid-Nineteenth Century". Professor Glanmor Williams, the President, took the Chair.

The lectures given were as follows:

Professor Ieuan Gwynnedd Jones, University College, Aberystwyth: "Social Conditions in the Valleys in the Nineteenth Century". (*Note:* This lecture was later published as a Monograph in 1981.)

Mr. John E. Hilling, Dip.Arch., R.I.B.A.: "Architecture in the Valleys".

Mr. Adrian Babbidge, Director, Torfaen Museum Trust: "The History of Blaenavon".

Note: The Annual accounts for the year ending 30.4.1980 showed a surplus of £35.02p. The Conference funds stood at £87.94p.

At a Committee Meeting held on 20.10.1980, Dr. Grant resigned as Chairman and Mr. Douglas Williams was elected Chairman. It was agreed to print the lecture of Prof. I. G. Jones given at the previous Conference as a Monograph. Mr. Babbidge agreed to finance it through the Torfaen Museum Trust. The Monograph was printed by the Gomer Press in Llandysul in 1981.

At a Committee Meeting held on 19.1.1981, members were informed that the President, Professor Glanmor Williams, had been awarded the C.B.E. in the New Year's Honours List. It was decided to send Professor Williams a telegram of congratulations. After a Committee Meeting held on 4.6.1981, members visited the Coke Ovens at Cefn Glas Pit, near Quakers Yard.

The Fourth Annual General Meeting and Conference was held on 13.6.1981 at the Assembly Room of the Aberdare Swimming Pool. The fee charged was £4.50 for admission, coffee and luncheon. Twenty-seven persons attended. Professor Glanmor Williams took the Chair. At the A.G.M. the Secretary reported that the Committee had decided to discontinue the publication of the Newsletter and would instead publish Monographs concerning comparative studies of given aspects of the history of the Valleys. The first such publication was Professor Ieuan Jones's lecture given at the last Conference, "Social Conditions in the Valleys". This was in print now and would be sent to all members of the Conference free of charge. The publication was financed by the Torfaen Museum Trust, to whom the Conference expressed their thanks. The Treasurer reported that the accounts for the year showed a surplus of £19.28p. Our funds stood at

£107.22p. The Conference decided to keep the annual subscription at £2 per person.

In the following elections, Mr. Douglas Williams was elected Chairman, Mr. Adrian Babbidge Vice-Chairman, Mr. Tom Evans and Mr. Bob Gulliford had been previously elected till 1983, Mrs. Etta Lewis, Mr. Leo Davies and Mr. Mor O'Brien till 1984. Mr. C. J. Drew was appointed auditor.

The theme of the Conference was "Economic Aspects of the South Wales' Valleys". The following lectures were given:

Mr. Philip Riden, Lecturer in History, Department of Extra Mural Studies, University College, Cardiff: "The South Wales Iron Industry 1750-1850. Tasks for the Local Historian".

Dr. Barry Brunt, Lecturer, Department of Geography, University of Cork: "Merthyr Tydfil and the Rhymney Valley. A comparison of economic development". (This lecture was published in the *Merthyr Historian, Volume IV*, 1989. Editor Dr. J. Gross.)

Mr. John Williams, Lecturer, University College, Aberystwyth: "The Coal Industry in the South Wales Valleys".

The Fifth Annual General meeting and Conference was held on 15th May, 1982, at the Torfaen Museum Trust, Pontypool. The fee was £4, which included admission, coffee and luncheon. Twenty-six persons attended. The Chair was taken by Mr. Douglas Williams, in the absence of the President, Professor Glanmor Williams. The Accounts for the year showed a deficiency of £11.06p. Our funds were £96.16p. In the elections which followed, Professor Glanmor Williams was re-elected President for another 5 years till 1987, Mr. Douglas Williams was re-elected Chairman, Mr. Adrian Babbidge resigned as Vice-Chairman and Mr. Tom Evans was elected Vice-Chairman, Dr. Joseph Gross, Secretary/Treasurer. Mrs. Etta Lewis resigned from the Committee. The Executive Committee Members elected were as follows: Mr. R. D. Gulliford (till 1983), Mr. Leo Davies and Mr. Mor O'Brien till 1984. The following were elected till 1985: Mr. B. Hillman, Mr. David Sutton, Mr. Geoffrey Hill. Mr. C. J. Drew was re-appointed auditor.

The theme of the Conference was "Aspects of Administration in the South Wales Valleys". The following lectures were given:

Dr. Anita Jordan: "Children of the Workhouse".

Mr. A. Mor O'Brien: "C. B. Stanton, Member of Parliament for Merthyr Tydfil and Aberdare".

Mr. Adrian Babbidge, Curator of the Torfaen Museum Trust: "Law and Order in the Eastern Valleys".

At the Executive Meeting of 15.11.1982, Mr. Davies resigned from the Committee.

The Sixth Annual General Meeting and Conference was held on 14th May, 1983, at the Guest Memorial Hall, Dowlais, Merthyr Tydfil. The fee was £5.00 per head and covered admission, coffee and luncheon. Twenty-seven persons attended.

The Chair was taken by the President, Professor Glanmor Williams.

At the A.G.M. the Treasurer presented his report. There was a surplus in the Accounts of £14.55p and the Funds stood at £110.71p. At the following elections, the Officers and retiring members of the Committee were re-elected without change.

The theme of the Conference was "The History of the Lordship of Senghennydd in the Middle Ages".

The lectures given were as follows:

The Very Rev. Canon T. J. Pritchard, Rector of Neath: "The Church in Mediaeval Senghennydd".

Dr. J. Beverley-Smith, Reader in History, University College, Aberystwyth: "Political and Economic Aspects of Mediaeval Senghennydd".

Professor T. V. Davies, Professor of Mathematics, Leicester University: "Farms and Farmers of the Merthyr Parish in the late Middle Ages".

The Seventh Annual General Meeting and Conference was held at the Guest Memorial Hall, Dowlais, Merthyr Tydfil on 5th May, 1984. The fee was £5 for admission, coffee and luncheon; thirty-eight persons attended. The President, Professor Glanmor Williams, took the Chair.

At the A.G.M. the Treasurer presented his report. The accounts showed a surplus of £15 for the year. The funds stood at £125.71p. Mr. Geoffrey Hill tendered his resignation from the Committee. At the election the retiring Officers and members of the Executive Committee were re-elected, except for Mr. Hill who, as stated, resigned.

The lectures given at the Conference were as follows:

Mr. H. N. Savory, formerly Keeper of Archaeology at the National Museum of Wales: "Prehistory in the Valleys".

Dr. Prys Morgan, Lecturer in History, University College Swansea: "Iolo Morgannwg; The Vale and the Valleys".

Dr. David Smith, Senior Lecturer, Department of History of Wales, University College, Cardiff: "Ups and Downs, Sport, the People and the Nation".

The Eighth Annual General Meeting and Conference was held on 25th May, 1985 at the RAFA Club, Georgetown, Merthyr Tydfil. The fee was £5 for admission, coffee and luncheon. Thirty-three persons attended. Professor Glanmor Williams, the President, took the Chair.

At the A.G.M. the Treasurer presented his report. The accounts showed a surplus of £26.29p. The funds stood at £152. The annual subscription was then discussed. The number of subscribers was declining, yet attendance at the Conference remained satisfactory. The Committee therefore proposed to discontinue the annual subscription which last year was £2, and instead charge an additional £1 for the Annual Conference. This was agreed. At the elections, the Officers and retiring members of the Committee were re-elected. Dr. F. Holley was co-opted to the Committee.

At the subsequent Conference, lectures given were as follows:

Dr. David Zienkiewicz, Research Assistant of the Department of Archaeology, National Museum of Wales, in charge of the Legionary Museum in Carleon: "Aspects of the Roman Occupation of South Wales".

Professor Harold Carter, Professor of Physical Geography, University College, Aberystwyth: "Merthyr Tydfil in 1851: The structure of an industrial town in the Mid-Century".

Mr. John Edwards: "In a Manner of Speaking".

The Rev. Erastus Jones announced in October, 1985, that he intended to retire at Christmas and to leave the area. Committee Meetings could therefore no longer be held at Ty Toronto and it was decided to meet in future at Yr Hafod, Heol Y Mynydd, Cefn Coed, near Merthyr Tydfil, the home of the Secretary/Treasurer, Dr. Joseph Gross. The first meeting to be held there was on 28th October, 1985. It was decided that the Chairman and Secretary visit Mr. and Mrs. Jones, to thank them for the work they had done for the Standing Conference and to present them with a cheque for £25.

The Ninth Annual General Meeting and Conference was held on 3rd May, 1986, at the AUEW Building, Swan Street, Merthyr Tydfil. The fee was £6 per head for admission, coffee, luncheon and tea. Thirty persons attended. Professor Glanmor Williams, the President, took the Chair.

At the A.G.M. the Treasurer presented his report. There was a deficiency of £21.87p. Conference funds were £130.13p. At the following elections, the Chairman, Mr. Douglas Williams, the Vice-Chairman, Mr. Tom Evans, and the

Secretary/Treasurer, Dr. J. Gross, were re-elected for one year. Mr. R. D. Gulliford and Mr. L. D. Davies were re-elected till 1989.

At Conference, the following lectures were given:

Dr. T. Boyns, Lecturer in Economics, University College, Cardiff: "Raw Materials and the growth of iron production in South Wales to c.1870".

Mr. W. B. Jones, Department of Industry, Maritime and Industrial Museum, Cardiff: "Industrial Emigration from South Wales to the U.S.A., in the late nineteenth century".

Mr. Hywel T. Edwards, Lecturer, Department of Extra Mural Studies, University College, Swansea: "History of the Choirs in the South Wales Valleys".

The Buffet Luncheon at the Conference was provided by Mrs. Barbara Richards. It was of a high standard and Mrs. Richards has continued to provide luncheons for the Conference ever since. The tea and coffee were provided by Mrs. R. L. Gross and Mrs. Carol Gross.

The Tenth Annual General Meeting and Conference was held at the AEU Building, Swan Street, Merthyr Tydfil on 25th April, 1987. The fee for admission, coffee, luncheon and tea was £6 per head. Twenty-four persons attended. Professor Glanmor Williams, the President, took the Chair.

At the A.G.M. the Treasurer submitted his report. The accounts showed a surplus of £36.55p, increasing the funds to £166.68p. At the subsequent elections, the Conference expressed their thanks to Professor Glanmor Williams on completing his tenth year as President and for his continuing support and excellent, courteous and efficient Chairmanship of each succeeding Conference. It was proposed and unanimously agreed that Professor Williams be asked to continue as President for the next ten years till 1997 and he agreed.

The following Officers were elected for a further year:

The Chairman,	Mr. Douglas Williams
Vice-Chairman,	Mr. Tom Evans
Secretary/Treasurer,	Dr. Joseph Gross.

The following were re-elected until 1990:

Mr. Mor O'Brien

Mr. Colin Griffiths.

The following were re-elected till 1988:

Mr. B. Hillman, Mr. D. Sutton, Dr. T. F. Holley.

Elected until 1989:

Mr. R. D. Gulliford, Mr. L. D. Davies.

The following lectures were given at the Conference:

Mr. Richard Hayman, Research Assistant, Merthyr Tydfil Heritage Trust: "The Iron Industry in Merthyr Tydfil in the 18th and 19th centuries".

Mr. John Davies, Senior Lecturer, University College, Aberystwyth: "The Marquess of Bute and the Coalfield of Glamorgan".

Mr. Chris Barber: "Cordell Country".

The Eleventh Annual General Meeting and Conference was held at the AEU Building, Swan Street, Merthyr Tydfil, on 23rd April, 1988. The fee of £6.50 included admission, coffee, luncheon and tea. Thirty-four persons attended. The Chair was taken by Professor Glanmor Williams, the President. An exhibition on Chartism was arranged in the Conference Room. It had been prepared by Mr. Kevin Littlewood, Senior Supervisor of the Heritage Team of the Manpower Services Commission, sponsored by the Heritage Trust of Merthyr Tydfil. The Conference expressed their thanks to Mr. Littlewood and his team.

At the A.G.M. the Treasurer presented his report. The Conference accounts showed a deficiency of £18.80p due to the small attendance. The funds stood at £147.88p. At the elections that followed, the Officers and members due for re-election were re-elected. Mrs. Eira Smith was co-opted to the Committee.

At the Conference, the following lectures were given:

Mr. John van Laun: "Industrial Archaeology: Antiquarian Indulgence or Academic Discipline?".

Mr. J. Barrie Davies: "Llantrisant. A borough for the Blaenau".

Professor T. V. Davies: "Farms and Farming in the Merthyr Parish in the Sixteenth Century".

The Twelfth Annual General Meeting and Conference was held on 22nd April, 1989, at the AEU Building, Swan Street, Merthyr Tydfil. The fee was £6.50 for admission, coffee, luncheon and tea. Thirty-eight persons attended. The Chair was taken by Professor Glanmor Williams, the President.

At the A.G.M. the Treasurer presented his report. The accounts showed a surplus of £54.69p, increasing the funds to £202.57p.

At the elections, the Officers and retiring members of Committee were re-elected. The Secretary expressed the Conference's thanks to Professor Glanmor Williams for his continuing support. Mr. Douglas Williams, the Chairman, proposed a vote of thanks to Mrs. R. L. Gross and Mrs. Carol Gross for their contributions to the refreshments.

At the Conference, the following lectures were given:

The Very Revd. Canon Roger L. Brown, M.A., Rector of Tongwynlais: "Like a Pelican in the Wilderness. The established Church in the Valleys c.1830-1900".

Mr. Keith Thomas, Local Historian and Publisher, Blaenau, Gwent: "English Iron Masters in Blaenau, Gwent".

Professor T. V. Davies, Professor Emeritus, Leicester University: "Quakers in the Valleys".

The Thirteenth Annual General Meeting and Conference was held on 21st April, 1990 at the AEU Building, Swan Street, Merthyr Tydfil. The fee of £6.50 included admission, coffee, luncheon and tea. Thirty-two persons attended. The Chair was taken by Professor Glanmor Williams, the President.

At the A.G.M. the Treasurer reported that the Conference Accounts showed a surplus of £52.65p. The funds stood at £255.22p. At the elections, the Officers and Members due to retire were re-elected. There were no changes in the Committee.

At the subsequent Conference, the following lectures were given:

Mr. D. L. Davies, Teacher in History, Afon Taf High School, Troedyrhiw, Merthyr Tydfil: "Vision or Mirage. The story of the first Glamorgan settlers in Patagonia 1865-1875".

Professor David Smith, Department of History of Wales, University College, Cardiff: "The Writers of the South Wales Valleys".

Professor T. V. Davies: "The History of Cwm y Glo".

The Fourteenth Annual General Meeting and Conference was held on 20th April, 1991 at the AEU Building, Swan Street, Merthyr Tydfil. The fee of £7 per head included admission, coffee, luncheon and tea. Thirty-eight persons attended. The Chair was taken by Professor Glanmor Williams, the President.

The President paid tribute to Professor T. V. Davies, who died on 7.1.1991. The President asked all present to stand in tribute to Professor Davies. Professor Davies had given lectures to the Conference in 1983, 1989 and 1990. His exhaustive and scholarly researches into the farms in our area were published in two volumes after his death. Their title is: *The Farms and Farmers of Senghenydd Lordship, prior to the Industrial Revolution.*

At the A.G.M.. the Treasurer reported that the annual accounts showed a surplus of £35.40p and the funds stood at £290.62p.

The Secretary announced with regret the resignation of Professor Glanmor Williams as President, after this year's Conference. Professor Williams had been President for 14 years.

At the following elections, the Officers and retiring members were re-elected.

Mr. Douglas Williams, the Chairman, then presented Professor Williams with an inscribed silver salver to express the gratitude of the Conference to Professor Williams for his services as President.

At the Conference, the following lectures were given:

Mr. R. E. Bowen: "The Railways of South Wales".

Miss Joanna Brown, Curator, Torfaen Museum Trust: "Pontypool Japanned Ware".

Professor Glanmor Williams: "My boyhood recollections of Merthyr and Dowlais". This lecture was published in *Merthyr Historian, Volume Six*, with the title "Bachgen Bach O Ddowlais".

The Fifteenth Annual General Meeting and Conference was held on 25.4.1992 at the AEU Building, Swan Street, Merthyr Tydfil. Twenty-five persons attended. The fee of £7 per head included admission, coffee, luncheon and tea. Mr. Tom Evans, Vice-Chairman, took the Chair in the absence of the Chairman, Mr. Douglas Williams.

At the A.G.M. the Treasurer presented his report. The accounts for the 1991 Conference showed a deficiency of £42.23p. The Balance at the Bank was £248.39p. At the subsequent elections, Mr. Colin Griffiths tendered his resignation.

The Officers and retiring members were duly re-elected. The composition of the Committee was as follows:

Chairman:	Mr. Douglas Williams
Vice-Chairman:	Mr. Tom Evans
Secretary/Treasurer:	Dr. Joseph Gross.

Committee Members elected until 1993 were

Mr. R. D. Gulliford and

Mr. D. L. Davies.

Committee Members elected until 1994: Mr. D. Hillman, Mr. D. Sutton, Dr. F. Holley, Mrs. Eira Smith. It was proposed to co-opt Mrs. Judith Jones to the Committee.

At the Conference, the following three lectures were given:

Dr. Peter Stead, Lecturer, Department of History, University College, Swansea: "Wales and Films".

Dr. Derek Webley: "The Life and Work of Penry Williams".

Dr. Glynne Jones: "Caradoc and his Choir".

The Sixteenth Annual General Meeting and Conference was held on 24.4.1993 at Canolfan Cymraeg Merthyr Tydfil at Zoar Chapel Hall, Pontmorlais, Merthyr Tydfil. The fee was £7 per head to cover admission, coffee, luncheon and tea. Forty-five persons attended. The Chair was taken by Mr. Douglas Williams, the Chairman.

At the A.G.M., the Treasurer reported that the accounts showed a deficiency of £17.88p and that funds stood at £231.31p. At the elections, the Officers and retiring members were re-elected.

The following lectures were given at the Conference:

Mr. Charles Hill, Principal Archaeological Officer (Curatorial), Glamorgan and Gwent Archaeological Trust: "The Nantgarw Pottery Site".

Mrs. Tibbott, Assistant Curator, Welsh Folk Museum, St. Fagan's: "The Rhydycar Cottages, Merthyr Tydfil".

Mr. A. J. Moreton: "The History of the Pandy Farm, Merthyr Tydfil".

The Seventeenth Annual General Meeting and Conference was held on 23.4.1994 at Canolfan Cymraeg Merthyr Tydfil at Zoar Chapel Hall, Pontmorlais, Merthyr Tydfil. The fee for the Conference was £9.50 and included admission, coffee, luncheon and tea. Thirty-three persons attended. The Chair was taken by Mr. Tom Evans, Vice-Chairman, in the absence of the Chairman, Mr. Douglas Williams.

At the A.G.M. the Treasurer presented his report. The accounts for the 1993 Conference showed a surplus of £31.49p. The funds stood at £262.80p.

At the following elections, the Officers and members due to retire were re-elected.

At the Conference, the following lectures were given:

Mr. Tony Moreton: "The Newspaper Industry in Merthyr Tydfil".

Mr. Brian Davies, Curator, Historical and Cultural Centre, Pontypridd: "Dr. William Price".

Ms. Sue Price, Director, Merthyr and Cynon Ground Work Trust: "The Taff Trail".

At the close of the meeting, the Chairman proposed a vote of thanks to Mrs. Rhoda L. Gross and Mrs. Carol Gross for their help with the catering.

Members then visited Zoar Chapel.

Yr Hafod, Cefn Coed
Merthyr Tydfil
July, 1994

Recollections of three Merthyr Artists

by CHARLES WILKINS

Introduction

From 1846 to 1866 Charles Wilkins (1831-1913) was the librarian of the Merthyr local subscription library of which Thomas Stephens was Secretary. Wilkins succeeded his father as postmaster of Merthyr and served from 1871 till retirement in 1898.

Charles Wilkins wrote various books and newspaper articles on the local history of Merthyr Tydfil and we owe our knowledge of many of the old Merthyr characters and stalwarts to the writings of Wilkins.

Three newspaper biographical sketches, by Charles Wilkins, of the Merthyr artists Joseph Edwards, Penry Williams and William Jones, were located. These anecdotal accounts make very interesting reading and are reproduced in full.

An essay appeared in *Merthyr Historian, Volume Six* (1992), on the life and work of Merthyr Tydfil-based Painter of Portraits, William Edward Jones, who should not be confused with William Jones, the sculptor, subject of Charles Wilkins's third sketch. William Jones had a brother, Watkin, also a sculptor, and another brother John Emrys, a professional photographer. John Emrys was a personal friend of Charles Wilkins.

The lives and works of the three talented Jones brothers are the subject of ongoing protracted research by Merthyr genealogist and television personality, Mrs. Eira Smith. The Historical Society hope to be accorded the opportunity to publish this work at a later date.

1. Joseph Edwards, The Sculptor

There are few moments in life of more profound interest than to stand by the side of a bubbling spring, amidst the magnificent, yet lonely mountains of Wales,

126

and there listen to the tale that this is the source of a great river. Here, a child could divert its wanderings, but winding on, and increasing in volume and in beauty, laving (washing) the skirts of hamlet, town and city, it is whelmed at length - bearer of yacht and brig, of steamer and warship - into the mightier sea.

Weighty the reflections opened out to the mind, yet still, how puny compared to those presented to one by the dawn of a human life, its early aspirations, its meridian of action, and of usefulness, and then the decline of years when the poetry of the world has faded, and all silently, the object of affection and reverence passes away and becomes simply a memory.

The life of Joseph Edwards is one that might be written, so far as his ancestry is concerned, by the novelist, but with reference to himself, to the building up of his own character, to the formation of his mind, to the number and importance of his achievements, he would more fully and more as he would have wished, figure in the list of self-made men and earnest workers.

Let me just glance at the romantic side. Speaking to him one day in his own London studio, he said, and it was tacitly understood that no direct reference should be made to it in his own lifetime, that there was an incident in his family history not unworthy of the old three-volume productions.

"Here are the materials," he said: "A cosy, old-fashioned country inn amongst the hills of Glamorgan; the landlord dead; the place kept by his widow, and several daughters. The family an old and respected one; the inn a resort for the sportsman and angler. To the inn came one autumnal day a stranger, a gentleman, young, fond of sport. He liked the inn, and lived there, and soon became one of the family. The daughters were pretty - one in particular struck his fancy - and when he left there was a parting, emotional and fervent on both sides, for the love was mutual. He came again. There was a clandestine marriage, and then a little after a complete disappearance. In time a daughter was born, and great was the effort to find the father, but he was never seen at the country inn again, and though there was more than a suspicion that he was the scapegrace son of a noble Welsh family, he never claimed his wife and child. The daughter grew up to womanhood, and alas! in obscurity, and in due time linked her fortune to a poor stonecutter."

This was the parentage of Joseph Edwards. He told me this not without feeling, as he spoke of the wronged mother, but with a smile in referring to noble ancestry, for to him pure thought and virtuous act were higher than lineage, and it was "only noble to be good".

127

Shon o Penlan, the father, was an insignificant man. The mother, on the contrary, had not only a devotional mind, but was also artistically inclined, and could paint flowers with considerable skill. She was, in addition, an amiable woman, and to her Joseph Edwards was indebted for that gentle manner and almost winning refinement which characterised him to the last.

Joseph Edwards's early life was one of patient endurance: in poverty at first, culminating in earnest and determined effort. Drudging in towns, musing in mountain churchyards, such as Vaynor, he finally made a bold effort to be free, and failing to win success at Swansea after trudging thirty weary miles to that place from Merthyr, he made his way to London.

Here the retiring boy, for he was only seventeen at this time, almost realised the fate of Chatterton. He was reduced to his last shilling, when a model of his in clay caught the eye of a sculptor and, thenceforth, though he had to labour and to wait, yet he was placed above positive want.

The roamer amongst the Welsh mountains, who had poetised on clouds and drunk in deeply of the beauty of nature, now entered into another school of the mind, and all accessible literature was devoured. This was systematically done; whenever a book took his fancy he made copious notes. Here are a few extracts from the earliest which he took as texts for his guidance:

> O spirit that dost prefer
> Before all temples the upright heart and pure,
> Instruct me! What in me is dark
> Illumine; what is low raise and support. (*Paradise Lost.*)

Here is another:

> If I am right Thy grace impart,
> Still in the right to stay;
> If I am wrong, oh! teach my heart
> To know a better way.

The life of the student of classic days was athletic contest and philosophic discourse. That of Edwards was an arduous day labour at his profession, and an exhaustive night study, which he modestly considered as repairing the defects of early education, or lack of it. It was marvellous to note how much he accomplished. It would have been a difficult task to meet a man better read in English literature, and with a few grammars and dictionaries he won a fair knowledge of

Latin, Greek and Hebrew, as well as French and German. He wished to meet the mind of a thinker "face to face", be his own interpreter and, as an example, few more fully comprehended the German School of abstract thought than he did. Few studied more keenly the communist and revolutionary efforts of France, which at one time, aided by Paine's theories, threatened to disturb the peace of Wales.

Few entered more minutely into the lore of the Hindoo, or revelled more keenly amongst the subtle problems that perplex the Christian and the philosopher; but from this lone wrestle with doubt he came forth to hope that the paternal idea of God, the belief in God's providence was right, and would shame after all the learning and scepticism of the schools.

Like as in the illustration given of our great astronomer, the enquirer roamed through the great ocean of investigation, and came back in childlike faith to the early teachings at his mother's knee.

This his extracts show:

The day is Thine, the night also is Thine. (Psalms)

Look up on high and thank Thee, God for all. (Chaucer)

To love and praise be thou alike impelled,
Whatever boon is granted or withheld. (Wordsworth)

Joseph Edwards won distinction in the Royal Academy, carrying off the first prizes year after year, and from the fount of pure thought and graceful fancy, work after work was given to the world, but so humbly that the world knew it not. Only a few kindred minds saw, wondered and eulogised, and in the great stream of kindred efforts, where Dives rules over genius, and the poet and philosopher, the painter and the sculptor, meekly do his behest, Edwards pursued his unambitious, his studious, but his happy way. His greatest wants and luxuries cost little. They were his books. With his cultured mind and wonderful grace of manipulation he would have attained eminence if there had been a leaven (admixture) of the practical in his nature.

But his meridian was a recast of his youth. In early London days he stood at dinner time by a bookstall, one shilling only in his pocket, and an old Homer, valued a shilling, before him. It was a question of dinner or Homer, and Homer won it. So in later years it became the question of making his genius profitable, and, from the abstract philosopher, becoming a man of the world. His life showed the character of his decision, the innocency of youth blended with the love of all lands, highest speculations, and a love for all that was beautiful in the world, remained with him until the "silver cord was loosed, and the golden bowl was broken". "and is this all?" exclaims the practically minded of this prosaic and money-loving age. "The Welsh lad from the mountains became no Michael Angelo, figured simply as the producer of some beautiful conceptions, and died poor." True, O practical mind. "Then, what of all that arduous effort, that mighty struggle for bread, that self devotion for half a century to learning, that greed for knowledge, that constant self denial, waving off even the innocent enjoyments of life, and *cui bono*, for what?"

Let us go back to the illustration with which this biography was begun, the fount that broadened into the health-bestowing and mankind-aiding river, the life that from simplest beginning was matured and dignified. Wales never had a truer or a more gifted son. Edwards built up a pure life, perfected and enriched a grand mind, and his monument is not alone the many creations of his poetic, philosophic or devotional mind, but himself, stainless as the marble from Carrara ere it left his studio.

One of his finest conceptions, that of "Religion", can be seen on the Harris's family vault at Cefn Coed. This is so purely white and beautiful that it is locally known as "The White Lady". Another fine work of his can be admired at Abercanaid Chapel, and one is placed in Vaynor Church, which is deservedly praised. This was a commission for the Penyrhadwy family, and commemorates a daughter whom the sculptor justly thought one of the most amiable and lovely. You may trace Edwards's handiwork in many a historic pile, one or more in St. Paul's Cathedral, and here is just a line touching upon one of the causes which has denied him national honour, upon work which was unquestionably his you will fail to see the true sculptor's name.

Joseph Edwards lacked, unfortunately for himself, the power of self-assertion, of standing up before the world and defending his own fair fame. He had the power of genius and, the gentle, feminine quality, extreme delicacy, preferring to be unknown than to be thought wishful for publicity. As a result, others benefited by his labours and, open-handed as he was, he died poor.

On January ninth, 1882, in his London house, he breathed his last. He was in his 67th year.

1899.

2. Penry Willians, The Painter

The Iron Kings were not so engrossed with their Works as to be unmindful of social duties, and the annals of the town include notice of several kindly actions on the part of the Crawshays, Guests and Hills, which compare favourably with the occasional openhandedness by large employers of labour elsewhere.

This was shown in the case of Penry Williams. He was the son of William Williams, a house painter, who lived in a cottage now (1899) swept away with its garden between the old Iron Bridge and the over-flow. The father was a good tradesman, and had most of the better class of work of house painting in the district, going to Cyfarthfa Castle for example, and to the Williamses of Aberpergwm, and Penry was in the habit of going with him. From anecdotes current years ago, it would seem that the companionship of the boy with the father was more for the youth's pleasure than the father's help. While Williams senior was busy painting windows and doors, the lad would be occupied in using some of the materials for boyish amusement, sometimes to the annoyance of the father. One day it is said that the young fellow was amusing himself at the Castle in drawing figures on one of the windows, and to his alarm William Crawshay, the Iron King, came on the scene, and was so struck by the skill displayed by one so young, that instead of lecturing him he praised the boy and spoke to the father upon the necessity that the talent of the lad should be fostered. This was hopeful.

Young Penry was told to bring up to the Castle the sketches he had done, and a view of these confirmed the ironmaster that Penry was no ordinary boy. The next step was to get him proper instruction. William Crawshay must himself have had artistic inclinations and associations, for he appears to have been one of an art circle, of which Fuseli was a member. Fuseli was an official of the Royal Academy, and to him, and several others, Crawshay sent Penry with letters of introduction, and the day was arranged when the village boy should present them. What a day this was in the hopes and anticipations of the Williams family. The journey was long. There was no railway, none of the many conveniences for travel that we have (1899). The boy's route was to Caerphilly, and by the "Old Passage" to Bristol and then coach to London - a journey, in its danger and inconvenience, greater than now to any town on the Continent. Penry reached London safely, and his first course was to go to the Royal Academy, where the eccentric, clever, but good-hearted Fuseli met him.

There is only a hint in local history concerning the moment of meeting. Fuseli does not appear to have been sanguine. The young Welshman, judging from his appearance, was rough and somewhat stolid, but when Fuseli opened the book of sketches he was astounded. His delight was so great, it is said, that he there and then wanted to buy the lot. The scenes were of various kinds, principally of the Welsh mountains. Here the gray old hill, scarred by storms, and arousing thoughts of vastness and loneliness; there a typical mountain stream, fretting and churning amongst the rocks; and, again, the peasant girls in the fanciful attire of the Neath fisherwomen, the "Merchad y Mera". "You did these, boy?" we can imagine the keeper (Fuseli) shouting and, when assured, both by ingenuous face and words, that it was so, Penry's introduction to the great school was certain. He was required, of course, to give proofs of his ability, which were soon forthcoming, and then the course was open for winning the laurel and the bay.

Before being classed amongst the students he had the entry to the Academy, and in a short time was able to write home and tell his parents of his success. It was a proud day for him when he was able, after a time, to take a little leisure and go home just for a brief holiday, and give them fuller details of his progress than he could do by letter. Then he returned to the city and plunged into work. The novelist generally runs over the time necessary to win fame by a line, but in art, in music, in song and in literature, no one knows who has not been in the mill, of the weary unlit years through which one must toil to gain success. Paderewiski, we are told, often, even now, exercises for sixteen hours at a stretch. One of our own gifted artistes, all too suddenly lost to us, Miss Scott, would frequently practise for twelve hours. And so with the brush; and when the painter can mirror nature so truthfully that the effect is like a stolen bit of sky, or slice of cornfield, or breadth of woodland, then comes the reward, often only when it is too late to be of use.

Penry was fortunate in having a wealthy patron, and not one, but several. The very works which secured him notice in the Academy were bought directly William Crawshay and Sir John Guest saw them. And then, with sufficient finances, he was enabled to struggle on again and produce more and better. He felt it his duty to bring his performances before the patrons at home, and they were only too pleased, and Sir John gave him commissions in particular, which lead to the production of some very fine works, which first graced the Institution in Pall Mall, and afterwards adorned the walls of Dowlais House or Cyfarthfa Castle.

It must often have puzzled William Crawshay, the bluff ironmaster, to account for the gems of art which Penry brought to him. He could account for a Georgetown boy attaining proficiency as a fitter, a puddler, a railman, brought up from youth first to observe the method of work when he took the father's dinner to the mill, the forge or the rolls, then to begin his prentice hand and work a turn himself. That he could understand: but how a lad, untrained, should acquire that witchery of portrayal by which the glittering pool amongst the mountains gleamed before one, and the restful silence of the woods was imagined; how that was done was only to be accounted for by inborn gift, and then endless practice.

However done, done it was, and very hearty and encouraging was the welcome given to the artist whenever he came down. Many years passed in the upward climb. He had to suffer, often to labour, and to wait. He had to see his young manhood pass and middle age come on in the struggle, made easier as it was by William Crawshay and Sir John Guest. Penry had to visit continental cities and study art in many a foreign scene before he could be said to have graduated through his school.

When he had done this it must have recompensed much for all his labour to find himself recognised at last as a worthy brother in art by such men as Sir Thomas Lawrence, Sir Charles Eastlake, and by Gibson, who was his lifelong friend.

As the Iron Kings grew old, so did the painter, and the visits to Merthyr grew few and far apart. Eventually Penry lived nearly always in Rome. London saw him at rare intervals, Wales scarcely ever. His father died, and was buried at Cefn, his mother, several of the family, amongst them his brother, the deaf and dumb artist, said in his brief life to have been even more clever than Penry. Nearly all were gone but a sister Sophie, who had a dancing academy, and who herself was in the decline of life, and then, all unexpected, Penry appeared.

I always recall the visit with pleasure, for we had corresponded frequently, and were in letters the best of friends. It was a summer day, and I was sent off from a neighbour's hayfield, and was told that a stranger wished to see me. Entering I noticed an old gentleman with a nimbus of white hair, a grave kindly face, and the bearing of one at home in any surroundings. He stepped quickly towards me with an open hand and a smile, exclaiming, "You are —— and I am Penry Williams!" We had a delightful hour and then the parting, and we never met again. One of his last letters gave me details of an attempt to assassinate him in Rome. He was mistaken for a nobleman who lived in an adjoining villa.

The ruffian, muffled up in a cloak, stole quickly after Penry one dusky night, mounted the steps, and struck him with a stiletto, which grazed his arm. Penry turned in alarm, shewing his face, and the villain, finding his mistake, flew.

For years Penry remained in Rome, the doyen of an English community. Whenever the Prince of Wales visited the eternal city, he always went to Penry's Studio, the place for a brilliant throng.

Now and then one of the peculiar blue-tinted paintings of Penry would find its way to the Academy, and be welcomed, and honourably noted. Then, as time went on, little was heard, only that he was living, until, one day, came intelligence of the death of Gibson the sculptor and the notice that at the grave, as one of the chief mourners, was his lifelong friend, Penry. He himself died at an advanced age, having survived, to the best of my recollection, all of his household, and the last letter he ever wrote expressed a wish, some day, I hope, to be granted, that a humble memorial of his father and mother and of the family should be placed in the Old Church of Merthyr Tydfil.

1899.

3. William Jones, The Sculptor

Merthyr boys have taken a high place as sculptors. First and foremost, Joseph Edwards, whose graceful works in many parts of the country, in addition to Vaynor, Cefn Cemetery, Abercanaid Chapel, Ynysgau, are his memorials; and second to him William Jones, and the brothers William (Mynorydd) and David Davies, London.

William Jones was brother to John Emrys Jones, so well known to old inhabitants. He was the son of humble parents, the mother being associated as caretaker with St. Tydfil Church. Early in life William exhibited considerable ability, and London being then the great Mecca of all aspiring men, thither he went in the year 1836. I have many atime heard from the lips of his brother, John Emrys, an old friend of mine, of his varied abilities. William was not only a good sculptor, but a good artist as well, and of a very inventive turn of mind. He had the misfortune, like many men in his day, and afterwards, to devote a great deal of thought to the invention of weapons of warfare, and to dream dreams that some day a generous Government would reward him with a fortune for so doing.

But Governments, Liberal or Conservative, are never generous. One of his ideas was to bring in magnetism as a motive power, not only with his weapons, but with printing blocks.

Fortunately for him, instead of growing grey, and haunting the government offices until poverty and death claimed him, the fate of so many a child of genius, he appears to have discarded inventions for his first love, and to have exhibited with success at the Royal Academy. In 1840, filled with a great desire to try his fortune in a new world, he left London for Australia. William Jones bore excellent testimonials, in addition to the specimens of his own work which he was able to demonstrate were truly his own.

There was a long silence after his departure. The mother mourned her promising son, and dreamed that in time to come he would return with substantial evidence of his success, but time passed, and only very tardily came the news at

134

length that his abilities had been recognised. His studio in Melbourne became one of the principal, and a fashionable resort of the city, where clever men and women went to note and criticise his efforts, and to gossip of art and of society's doings.

In the course of William Jones's Melbourne career he was presented with a gold medal in token of the admiration which his artistic labours elicited.

And so the years passed in honourable effort, and Jones achieved distinction. Then came the unrest of genius. Men of the "two and two are four" description, who patiently build up fortune, and quietly retire to enjoy it, have none of that so-called flighty disposition which affects the child of genius, be it in poetry, in song, or in art; too often leading as surely to destruction as the bright light which lures the heedless gnat.

Not satisfied with the success which he had won in Melbourne, William Jones's attention was directed towards Sydney, as likely to offer still greater honour, and so, to the sorrow of many, he broke up his home, bade adieu to his friends, and started one day along the coast like an adventurer. That he had prospered was shown by driving his own carriage, and thus, laden probably with necessaries required on a long and lonely journey, he disappeared from the sight of Melbourne.

At that time lawlessness was rife, and his fate is only open to conjecture. No tidings ever came to Wales of that fate. The years went by; the mother, hoping, longing, died in her old age. Another son, Watkin, also a promising sculptor, left too for London, and made strenuous efforts to glean news of his brother, but also without success, and so the veil remains drawn.

The last surviving brother, John Emrys, a man of considerable intelligence, with a strong philosophic bent, came to an untimely end, the result of a railway accident, and lies with a brief record in Cefn Cemetery.

One fact of the family history is of interest. They claimed, and it was asserted by John Emrys Jones to be no baseless claim, to be descendants, humble and distant was not denied to have been, of the line of the doughty Rhys ab Thomas, so conspicuous in Welsh history and the Wars of the Roses.

After the death of John Emrys, the family left for the North of England, and with their departure the link between them and Merthyr appears to have been indissolubly broken.

1900.

The Merthyr Tydfil Naturalists' Society, One Hundred Years Ago

by T. F. HOLLEY

The Cardiff Naturalists' Society was formed in 1867. The Aberdare Naturalists' Society was formed in 1888. In September, 1889, a letter appeared in the *Merthyr Express* proposing the formation of a Naturalists' Society in Merthyr Tydfil and a meeting was convened at the Victoria Street Coffee Tavern to discuss this proposal (Ref.1). Mr. C. Henry James, High Constable, presided and among those present were Mr. B. R. S. Frost, Mr. H. W. Southey, Mr. Fleming (headmaster of Dowlais Advanced School) and Mr. Ernest Daniel. A committee was formed and it was agreed to prepare a circular, setting forth the objects of the Society and to approach people to join the proposed Society.

A further meeting was convened in October 1889 at the Morlais Hall (Ref.2). There was an encouraging attendance and a large proportion of those present were ladies. Mr. C. Russell James proposed Mr. J. C. Williams as Honorary Secretary, the proposal was seconded by Mr. J. L. Cocker and Mr. Williams eventually accepted and was elected. The following were elected to a committee in order to draft Rules: Mr. C. Henry James, Dr. Creswell, Mr. C. Russell James, Mr. H. Dewdney, Mr. Fleming (Dowlais) and Mr. T. F. Harvey.

A further meeting was held in November 1889 (Ref.3). About eighty ladies and gentlemen expressed a wish to join the Society. Mr. C. Henry James was elected President of the Society, and Vice-Presidents appointed were Colonel Cresswell, Mr. W. Edwards, H.M.I.S. and Mr. C. Herbert James. Mr. B. R. S. Frost was appointed honorary curator; Mr. Gilbert Davies, National Bank of Wales, hon. treasurer; and Mr. J. C. Williams, hon. secretary. The following gentlemen were appointed a committee: Rev. J. G. James, Messrs. C. Russell James, H. Dewdney, W. Lintern (Dowlais), T. F. Harvey, C. Biddle, J. C. Fleming, H. D. Pearce, D. Abraham, B. Michael, J. Rees and Ernest Daniel.

136

Mr. C. Henry James agreed to deliver a lecture to the Society on November 15th, 1889, entitled "Welsh Maps and Old Writers on Wales".

The 1890 Annual General Meeting of the Society was reported in the *Merthyr Express* (Ref.4). The report of the secretary is given here in some detail as it defines the scope of the Society's indoor and outdoor activities.

"The committee have pleasure in submitting to the members a report of the past season just concluded. It will be remembered that the Society was established in November, 1889, after several preliminary meetings had been called by the then High Constable, Mr. Charles Henry James, to ascertain the amount of support likely to be forthcoming. The attendance and enthusiasm shown was not promising, yet in the face of gloomy misgivings another frail bark (boat) was launched amongst the billows that roll and sport over the wrecks of so many fair literary and social ventures with 'Merthyr' on their bows (laughter). So far, however, the Society has had a fair measure of success. We had several very interesting lectures during last winter, and it may recall pleasant recollections to briefly enumerate them.

"First of all we had an inaugural address by the President, Mr. Chas. Henry James on 'Welsh Maps and Old Writers of Wales', illustrated by a series of early maps and ancient works on the subject. This was followed shortly afterwards by an admirably appropriate and thoughtful paper by Mr. Charles Russell James on 'Shakespeare as a Naturalist'. Then came a lecture of a scientific order, but in a popular style, on 'The Physiology of Food' by Mr. F. Millett, B.Sc., of the Gelligaer Grammar School.

"Later on came another literary treat by Mr. T. H. Thomas, R.C.A.., of Cardiff, on the 'Wonders of the Yellow Stone National Park', illustrated by perhaps the finest sketches and mammoth photographs ever exhibited to a Merthyr audience. A few weeks later on Mr. Acomb, of Aberdare, assisted by Dr. Morris with magnificent limelight apparatus, favoured the Society at short notice with a lecture on 'Coins'. At all the lectures, the attendance, both of members and visitors, was most encouraging, a noteworthy feature being the number of ladies who graced the proceedings by their presence. In this latter respect the 'outings' of the Society were still more successful. Several excursions to neighbouring points of interest were made, during the summer. The time-honoured ruins of Morlais Castle were visited by a large party, and the vaulted roof of its ancient crypt echoed with an interesting address by the President, on its history and association.

"On another occasion the members, again under the leadership of the President, enjoyed a personally conducted trip to the Beacons and to Brecon, characterised by several amusing incidents graphically chronicled in the following week's *Express*. An excursion to the Ystradfellte Caves and Waterfalls was not also without its memorable features 'of moving accidents by flood and field' (laughter). *A propos* thereof, your secretary's modest estimate of the distance from the station proved considerably at fault, the 'pleasant walk of three miles from Hirwaun' turning out to be rather more than the 'bona-fide traveller' usually understands by the phrase (laughter). On another date the heights of Cilsanws Mountain were triumphantly scaled and a careful note taken of the signs of glacial action there to be seen. A Roman road and the site of a Roman camp at Dolygaer were the objective points of another excursion, and in spite that day of more than 'gentle dew from heaven' several enthusiastic naturalists betook themselves to Pentwyn to investigate these little-known remains of the Roman occupation. Additional outings were in contemplation but fell through owing to a short summer and bad weather. It is manifest that in the past summer we have not exhausted all the spots even around Merthyr which may profitably be visited, and we therefore hope that next summer we may find besides 'fields and pastures new'.

"The committee are pleased to announce that the usual winter series of lectures (postponed until the close of the valued Gilchrist course) will be resumed before Christmas, the Society having already secured gratifying promises of lectures on interesting and appropriate subjects." (Ref.4.)

An account of the Society's Annual General Meeting for 1891 was not located. A report of the A.G.M. for 1892 was, however, located (Ref.5). This revealed that the Society was very well established and had organised an overseas excursion. The following is an extract from the *Merthyr Express report*:

"The Committee have pleasure in submitting to the members of the Merthyr Naturalists' Society their THIRD annual report. The season now ending began as usual with a course of lectures delivered during the winter. Of these, the first was on the 15th December last by Dr. C. E. G. Simons on 'Our Unseen Foes'. Under this title were introduced, on the lantern screen to his audience, magnified photographs of different deadly germs of disease invisible to the naked eye, but appearing under the microscope as berry shaped, rod shaped and comma shaped bacilli. Specimens of the apparatus used for their cultivation, under laboratory conditions, were arranged on the platform, and enabled his hearers to follow with interest his description of the processes. Recent advances of science in the direction of preventative medicine were dwelt upon with satisfaction, and hopes held out that ultimately other diseases besides anthrax, small pox, etc., might, by their gradual extinction, shew the sanitarian victorious in his struggle for supremacy over 'Our Unseen Foes'.

"On the 26th January, Mr. Abraham Houlson of Dowlais, gave the Society a lantern lecture entitled 'Wanderings in Wales and the Border Counties'. This consisted of a chatty description of various places of interest and beauty in and about the Principality, and the views exhibited were greatly admired.

"On the 12th February, Mr. Thomas Evens, M.E., of Cardiff and the Werfa Colliery, Aberdare, favoured the members with a lecture on 'Coal and Collieries', which, for an audience belonging to a mining district, he invested with an unusual degree of interest. His description of the mode of coal getting was greatly enhanced by an admirable series of photographs, taken by himself with the aid of artificial illuminants, of scenes in coalpits with men, trams, etc. in situ. These pictures, and Mr. Evens' account of the difficulties he experienced in taking them, were much appreciated.

"On the 2nd March, the Rev. William Seward, of Cardiff, delivered an able lecture on 'Atoms and Natural Forces, or the soul that works in all things', illustrated by chemical and philosophical experiments and astronomical slides.

"On the 24th March, the Society became indebted to the Rev. J. G. James, B.A., for an eloquent and instructive lecture entitled 'Before the Dawn, or the Story of Prehistoric Man'. This was a valuable review of the evidence from race, language and remains, of the antiquity of man and the innumerable ages before history. The stone, bronze and iron ages were effectively illustrated by sketches, drawn by the lecturer, of implements discovered. The Rev. Mr. James concluded with references to the mental and moral characteristics, politics and religion of these early progenitors of the human race.

"With summer came the 'outings'. These were this year to no distant places, but afforded those who desired it opportunities for culling wild flowers and searching for antiquarian relics amidst such roads and lanes as might be traversed in the compass of a summer's afternoon.

"The first Thursday and third Saturday in the months of May, June and July were devoted to these excursions, which included Ystradfellte Falls and Caves, Hirwaun and Dolygaer, with its Roman camp and road. It is to be regretted that the attendance at some of these meetings was very limited. Perhaps the spots visited were too close at hand, and that it may be advisable next year to arrange for more distant excursions, say to such historical ruins as Caerphilly, Raglan or Tintern. That greater success may possibly attend greater aims is evidenced by the fact that more members of the Society joined the Society's trip to Brittany than mustered at the station for an outing to Ystradfellte.

"The Brittany trip, a unique excursion for a provincial Society, came off in

August, and its salient features have already been brought under the notice of the members in the attractive little brochure which Miss Francis Evans has kindly presented for circulation amongst them. With a graceful and facile pen this young lady has so ably delineated the varied adventure of the party that an 'official' version of a most delightful holiday tour can well be dispensed with. It should, however, be mentioned that another gifted lady of the party, Mrs. Rogers, also wrote a narrative of the trip, which the readers of the *Merthyr Express* greatly enjoyed. As her account contained interesting and valuable notes on the botany of the places visited, she, like Miss Evans, was asked to favour the Society with reprints, and kindly consented to do so but, unfortunately, it was found that the type in which the articles had been set had been 'distributed'. Recognising the services these ladies had rendered the Society by their contribution, the Committee had much pleasure in passing a very hearty vote of thanks to them for their kindness." (Ref.5.)

Merthyr Express References

1.   M.E. 28 September 1889, p.6 col.4
2.   M.E. 26 October 1889, p.5 col.4.
3.   M.E. 9 November 1889 p.5 col.3+4.
4.   M.E. 13 December 1890 p.8 col.1
5.   M.E. 5 November 1892 p.7 col.8.

Thanks are due to the Committee of the present-day (1994) Merthyr Tydfil and District Naturalists' Society for permission to publish this essay, which previously appeared in Newsletter Number Thirteen of that Society.

Charles Henry James, J.P. (1838-1914), mining engineer, was a son of Job James, Ironmonger, Merthyr.
Charles Russell James, solicitor, was a son of Charles Herbert James (1817-1890), Liberal Member of Parliament for Merthyr Tydfil from 1880 to 1888.
Job James and Charles Herbert James, M.P., were brothers, sons of William James, maltster, Merthyr Tydfil.

The Rector of Merthyr and the Channel Tunnel, 1882

TRANSCRIBED

"The annual church parade of the Merthyr detachment rifle Volunteers took place on Sunday morning, the men falling in at the drill-hall, and headed by the band, marching to St. David's church. The muster consisted of about two hundred, the officers present being Captain and Commandant D. R. Lewis, Dr. Ward, Captains White and Davies, Lieutenants T. Evans, J. O. White, A. P. James, and L. P. Jones. There was a large congregation in addition to the Volunteers. A number of suitable hymns were sung, which were printed in leaflet form for the convenience of Volunteers.

"As customary, the sermon was preached by the Rev. J. Griffith, rector of Merthyr, who, without giving out any text, delivered one of his characteristic addresses.

"Having combated the objections which some persons took to the Volunteer movement, the rector proceeded to say that he was ashamed of those who looked upon the completion of the CHANNEL TUNNEL as the greatest blessing that could be bestowed upon them by Providence. It seemed to him blasphemous to bring in the name of Providence at all.

"He looked upon it in a totally different way. He looked upon it as tempting Divine Providence to bring about our own destruction. Let them just see what it was. The arm of the sea was supposed to divide them from their neighbours across the Channel, and was their natural defence in time of war. Should they tempt Divine Providence by breaking off this arm, in fact, bridging over the passage in order that the enemy might come here? Having referred to the fact that the gathering of the English fleet in the Channel prevented Napoleon invading this country, he remarked that, knowing the blue jackets (sailors) were doing all the work, the people of this country slept safe as long as Nelson was alive and the sea did not run dry.

"With this great fact before them, could they not see the danger of tunnelling a way under the Channel for France to come over? What was the question at issue? Nothing else but to satisfy the cupidity and avarice of men who would drive a tunnel through their grandmothers' graves if they could sell their bones for phosphate at a profit. It was not for the benefit or the interest of the English people.

"And the worst of it was there were so many dupes of these people, and he was afraid that Parliament, seeing that the country was so indifferent upon the subject, would allow the tunnel to be made. If the tunnel were made tomorrow, only thirty-five minutes in transit would be saved, and the reverend gentleman proceeded to urge that the making of the tunnel would be of no benefit to this country, all the exports of which were taxed by France.

"After a few words of advice to the Volunteers, the reverend gentleman brought his discourse to an end.

"The detachment was subsequently dismissed at the armoury."

Cardiff Times, Saturday 22.4.1882 p.3 col.9.

Pant Fever Hospital

by ANN LEWIS

The Pant Fever Hospital was built in 1869, due to an epidemic of typhoid and typhus fever, that started in Dowlais in October, 1868. It gradually spread until, by April 1869, it had reached Merthyr town centre.

The Local Board of Health under Section 37 of the Sanitary Act, 1866, had the power to provide hospitals, or temporary places for the reception of the sick, but not places for the admittance of persons not affected with the disease. It was hoped that once they had provided a place for the sick to be nursed, the people that had been in contact with them could remain in their homes, if a policy was adopted of cleaning, whitewashing, and of disinfecting the houses from which the sick were removed.

The living conditions were poor, many houses were small and overcrowded with no proper ventilation, having windows that could not be opened. Many were also without proper toilet facilities, some having to share with three or four other families. The practice of throwing waste matter onto the road was still undertaken, so polluting the vicinity. Many were fined for continuing to do so.

One Dowlais family in which the mother and four of her children were suffering from typhus fever were being nursed in a bedroom which measured eleven by seven foot. During this epidemic three of the four nurses employed and a doctor died after contracting one of the diseases.

By the end of March the deaths numbered fifty-three, and the reported cases of the disease, three hundred and sixty. The Board of Health decided they had to open a hospital to stem the spread of the disease and try and relieve the appalling suffering of the local people.

At first it was suggested that a large tent would be ideal for the purpose of a hospital, after all, stated one member of the Committee, tents had been well used by the troops for years, but another member of the Committee added that he knew where they could obtain a building or part of a building for the sum of £1,000. It was decided to go ahead with the purchase. It was arranged with Messrs. Eassis of Gloucester for the delivery to take place in four days' time, and to appoint a Mr. John Williams of Morgan Town to find carpenters for the erection of the buildings on the chosen site at CAERACCA, Pant, the ground being readily granted on sufferance from the Dowlais Company. Today the site is occupied by the Queen Street houses.

It was clear that the cases of typhus and typhoid should not be mixed, so it would be necessary to have a separate hospital for the typhus and typhoid patients, and these again must be sub-divided into male and female wards, so as to keep the sexes separate. Besides that, they would have to erect suitable out-of-fices, such as a kitchen, wash-house, etc., but if these were placed between the two hospitals they could be used by both. It was also decided that the site should be fenced in by post and rail fencing for the purpose of preventing trespassing on the adjoining grass land. After the foundation was completed, the building itself took just four weeks to complete, being a wooden structure with a felt roof. By late July the furnishing of the hospital was also completed and ready for use, at this time the epidemic had subsided so the building remained unused until the next epidemic occurred.

During the time the building was being erected and furnished, the death toll had risen to seventy-seven deaths, with the number of cases reaching four hundred and twenty-six. The hospital was large enough to nurse 32 patients in total.

Mrs. Clark of Dowlais House obtained permission from the local Board of Health, for the private use of part of the hospital for 8 male and female patients. It was decided that there would be no compulsory admissions, that patients would only be admitted with their permission. This was thought to be a wise decision, as the chances of recovery would be very poor in patients who were terrified of being admitted, believing they were being taken there to die instead of to recover their health and strength. This fear was somehow connected with Mrs. Clark's Hospital at Dowlais and was largely due to the ignorance of the people, as to the type of nursing required.

There was great concern among the Committee as to whose responsibility it was to pay for the patients' food while at the hospital. They wrote several times to the Home Office, the Chairman of the Committee also wrote privately to the Home Secretary dealing solely with the question of feeding. No satisfactory answer was obtained, so the Board of Health decided that they would have to bear the expense themselves. When the question was asked, who would pay for the

144

beef tea? the Clerk replied: "Can't you make the beef tea medicine?" "We must," came the reply, "and take the consequences."

In 1903 Matron Davies earned thirty pounds per annum, while a Nurse Stephen five pounds more, so a request for Matron's salary to be increased to forty pounds was accepted. At this time only a Matron and a probation nurse were employed by the Council, other nurses required when the epidemics occurred were from the Institute in Cardiff, which meant extra pay for travelling expenses and quarantine fees.

I lost a photograph during developing that I took of the grave stone at Pant cemetery, one of the Matrons that had worked at the hospital; when I returned to take another, the grave stone had been removed.

In 1902 one patient suffering from smallpox escaped from the hospital and was found talking to several small children; the parents were most upset and sent a letter of complaint to the Committee. Another time, two other smallpox sufferers during their convalescence, escaped and visited the local public house and on returning to the hospital broke several windows and some furniture. In due course they were fined for the damage caused and for exposing themselves whilst suffering from an infectious disease. In 1906 my grandmother was fined five shillings (twenty-five pence) for allowing my father, Joseph Williams Thomas, aged three years old at the time, to sit on the front door step of their home while suffering from scarlet fever.

One poor man who died from typhus fever at the hospital had tramped all the way from Glasgow looking for work, only to arrive in Merthyr destitute, to survive for twenty days after contracting the disease on the walk.

The residents of Pant and Dowlais were greatly concerned that the patients were able to receive parcels, and converse with outsiders over the wall of the hospital, and also with the question of the precautions taken by the nurses and others for disinfecting themselves before leaving the hospital. A petition signed by six hundred and forty-four persons, was presented to the Council asking that a temporary hospital be erected away from the vicinity of Pant and that the present structure be removed.

So fearful were some people, like the late Mrs. Margery Jones, that they carried Canfa tablets in a little bag tied around their neck to keep the infection away while passing the hospital.

My uncle, Mr. Morgan Lewis, ninety-four years old and today living in Brecon, has vivid memories of his stay at the hospital as a small child.

When the new Mardy Central Fever Hospital was officially opened in 1907, the old Pant Fever Hospital was no longer required, much to the relief of the

145

people of Pant and Dowlais. The hospital was destroyed by fire on the 24th of August, 1907, as planned by the Committee.

A well-known local man, the late Mr. Dick Llewellyn, father to Malcolm and Pauline Phillips (née Llewellyn), stated that while on his way to school as a young lad, he saw the fire and was requested by the police sergeant to run to the Bush fire station at Dowlais for the horse-drawn fire engine; he was given three old pence for his trouble.

The patients that were in the hospital at the time of closure were transferred to the Mardy Hospital, but that Hospital has a story of its own. A temporary iron structure was sited on the Mardy Estate for nursing smallpox patients just a few years earlier.

An Account of the Merthyr-born Artist, Penry Williams

by Thomas Henry Thomas

This account appeared in the *Western Mail* for 26.3.1904, page seven, and is given verbatim.

"The Editor having kindly afforded the writer all that is truly difficult, namely the dates of the events in the life of this well-known Glamorgan artist, it is easy to write an appreciation of his work and the position he attained in the world of Art.

"Penry Williams was one of a group of intellectual men produced by Merthyr Tydfil during the first half of the nineteenth century, men who have made their mark in industry, literature, music, law, the arts, and in other directions, and among them Penry Williams took a high position. The artist lived a long life. Born, it is thought, in 1800, he survived till 1885, when he died in the place of his long residence, Rome, where he, like his greater compatriot John Gibson, the sculptor, lived a long, laborious, quietly distinguished life.

"Penry Williams early showed liking for and some skill in Art, and early efforts are still prized by some remaining personal friends and patrons of his youth, or their families. More of these might remain but that later in life Penry exchanged a good many for works of his prime, destroying the youthful efforts as not representing his talent. Such works were, however, the tests by which friends judged of his promise. Among these friends were the late Lord Aberdare, Sir John Guest, and members of the Crawshay family, and through their appreciation Penry was sent to London, where he obtained entry to the schools of the Royal Academy of Arts, then under the keepership of the vivid eccentric genius, FUSELI. We find Penry Williams in 1821 obtaining the silver medal of the Society of Arts for a drawing from the antique. The training of this period gave him a certain ease

147

and distinction of figure-drawing, which added greatly to the merit of his later works. In 1822 he began to exhibit portraits and landscapes at the Royal Academy, British Institution, and Society of British Artists.

"For a few years he worked considerably in water-colour, producing small pictures of landscape and peasant figures of very high finish in the soft stippled manner then in vogue. An example of these may be seen in the gallery of the Welsh Museum among the Pyke Thompson water-colours. It has to some extent lost colour (1904), but otherwise represents him. Others are in the possession of Mr. Marchant Williams.

"In 1828 Penry Williams was elected Associate of the Society of Painters in Watercolours, now the Royal Society of Painters in Watercolours, and exhibited annually until 1833, when he resigned, and devoted himself almost entirely to his oil-paintings, which had become highly esteemed during the earlier years of his residence in Rome, whither he went in 1827.

"The same quality shows itself in his painting. Although it was then the fashion to give to paintings of genre a certain air of laborious finish, which marred some of his work, there yet remained a pleasant atmosphere, sunny, yet not arid, a dexterity of composition and an aptness of character, which made all his works highly pleasing at first sight and pleasant to live with when acquired.

"Rome was at that time the Mecca of all artists. It was, indeed, a kind of artistic sanctuary. Artists from all parts of the world flocked to it. A great colony of artistic *forestieri*, foreigners, existed, which each winter was enlarged by others of the same aims who were passing guests, yet stayed long enough to make a part of the hard-working, yet jovial and easy, life of the place, not a few of those without ties each year becoming entranced with the city and people and remaining there. Of these Penry Williams was one. To a man wholly devoted to Art the Holy City was a paradise. In the winter, work not too exhausting, being broken into by travellers, most of them of gentle class, who visited the open studios, frequently with open purses, and who carried away memorials of their visit in sculpture and painting to the ends of the earth, whither they had come.

"In the summer, there were sojourns in the hill country, where beautiful and characteristic scenes were thrust upon the painters. Add to this all convenience and material for the artist, and a personal respect to the poorest artist only second to that paid to the ecclesiastic, and the practical Italianisation of many artists is not surprising. To a Welshman it would be specially fascinating. The very simple life, with its sense of equality among all, had much in common with that lately characteristic of our own country (Wales).

"To Penry Williams, with his taste for painting pictures of incident, it was an admirable position. He brought to it a very facile pencil, capable of quick rendering of landscapes, animals, and of the human figure. He could draw anything with ease and with very bright characterisation. His studies of peasant life in England and Wales had prepared him to appreciate fully the life surrounding him in Rome; he was in sympathy with the movement and grace of Italian life as it showed itself in and about Rome, a city which, to compare small things with great, was like an idealised British country town, with costume and colour added.

"Once away from the main streets, picturesque costumes abounded; markets full of country people were held in the great piazzi: great country carts, drawn by wide-horned, soft-eyed oxen, rolled slowly in at early morning, the farmers and peasants in heavy cloaks and satyr-like, goat-skin leggings. There were brightly-harnessed horses and mules; children played everywhere; the women dressed their stalls, and when ready for the customers, whiled away the time by sitting in rows dressing each other's long, black tresses. There was practically no street regulation; the people just roughly regulated themselves. As a background to this half-vehement, half-indolent life, mediaeval palaces, quaint dwelling-houses, and the crumbling ruins of ancient Rome stood up in dim tones of brown and grey, touched into gold and azure by the light and shadow thrown by the Southern sun.

"This may stand as a description of Penry Williams's paintings, for this life was ever his theme. The artist's industry was habitual: unremitting he went on painting 'without haste, without rest'. The pictures were never of very large size; a canvas the size of a page of the *Western Mail* would give space enough for an ambitious effort and, in fact, some of Penry Williams's finest things are on canvasses and panels of one-quarter of that size. The great ease with which he composed, drew and painted, together with his industry, allowed him to produce a really vast number of works, and their elegance and beauty made them popular and so saleable that his commissions exceeded his production.

"It was the good fortune of the writer (Thomas Henry Thomas) to spend a winter in Rome during the time of Penry Williams's greatest popularity, and to carry with him an introduction from one of the painter's oldest Merthyr friends, the late Charles Herbert James, afterwards M.P. for that town.

"The artist then had a fine studio in the Piazza Mignanelli, and many visits there gave great opportunity of judging of the man and his work. Of the artist himself, kindness and quiet geniality are the qualities that stand conspicuous. Nothing that would aid a student seemed to him a trouble to do, and there was withal a mode of personal companionship which was most attractive. He would explain everything in his methods of work without the smallest reticence, and would allow himself to be watched while painting. These methods were simple and direct. Having the subject clearly in his mind, he would lay his sketch-book before him and draw the composition upon the canvas or panel in pencil almost without an error, and this he would slightly modify from the model, but these modifications were rarely great.

"Then in the same simple, definite way, he would put in a first painting in a bright, fresh series of tints, upon which he could work until it attained its final tone, which was golden in the lights, and bronze in the darker portions.

"It would be interesting to know where Penry Williams's sketch-books now exist, for they contained a wealth of slight, elegantly-drawn studies, chiefly of moving figures, jotted down from the ever-changing panorama of Roman life as it then was. One of the favourite sketching grounds was the Piazza Navona, and we have a delightful remembrance of a morning spent there among the street merchants and *contadine*, when the sketch-book was in constant use and the incidents of life were sketched with unfailing facility.

"The studio in the Piazza Mignanelli had two large rooms, the walls of one of which were hung with a great number of sketches and studies in oil, many of the latter very highly completed. These formed the artist's type collection, and were in continual requisition for his compositions. It may be said that among them was much of the painter's most artistic work. Untied by conventions more or less necessary in works for sale or required by the exigencies of composition, these studies had a brilliance and freshness of most attractive character. Many of them passed into the collection of Miss Yates at the sale of his works at Christie's in 1886, and were exhibited in that year at the Bethnal Green Museum.

"Besides the charming characteristics of Roman life above described, there was another of a less pleasant kind. The great places of artistic resort were certain restaurants, and specially the *Caffe Greco*, where in the evenings all artists called. It was the habit of all who might be out at all late to go homewards accompanied, as a good deal of ruffianism was endemic. Nearly all houses were arranged in flats, to which there was a common stair. Occupants used to provide themselves with *cerina*, a knot of wax taper, which they lit to ascend the stair.

"One night a sad adventure befell our artist upon his stair. From a corner a robber suddenly flung himself upon him, extinguished the light, struck him down by a violent blow in the face, and rifled his pockets.

"This severe shock incapacitated the victim for several days, but he fully recovered, fortunately, without any scar remaining of the wound he sustained, probably from a ring upon the hand of the criminal.

"Penry Williams lived on his industrious life in the city of his adoption until 1885, when he died on July 24th, aged 85. He had become a well-known figure in that city, and was highly esteemed by all, both as an artist and a man.

"Beside the paintings of peasant life, upon which his reputation chiefly rests, the artist's hand had not lost its cunning in portraiture, and many persons of note were painted by him. One of the best of these works is in the collection of portraits in the Accademia di San Luca, Rome, and a replica in the Academy of Urbino. It is a half-length portrait of his countryman and close friend John Gibson, R.A., who then held the position of one of the foremost sculptors of Europe. The work is an admirable likeness, and has been well engraved by Wagstaffe.

"It is not claimed for Penry Williams that he attained first-class rank in art, but that he was an artist of eminence no one can dispute. In placing artists it is necessary to consider the style of the times in which they lived, and the conventions of the period. Of these Penry Williams fully partook, and they are not now admired, so that his works are at the moment (1904) under-estimated; but time, in this respect, brings justice in the end.

"One great quality his works possess is their perfect ease of conception, composition, and execution; they are natural and quite unlaboured, though wrought to a high surface finish. What he attempted he could do perfectly. Above all, there is no affectation of technique. Works of this simplicity always live, in spite of the fluctuation of artistic fashion. This quality carries with it another, durability. Most of Penry Williams's works are still as perfect as on the day they left his easel, and have but improved by time.

"Few artists' works were more widely known in his time. His position in the then centre of the art world, and the current of travellers setting through it year by year, brought him patrons from every country; the brightness and suavity of his compositions did the rest. He has been heard to say that his pictures found a home in every European country; many were in America, and some in Australia; and it is interesting to think of the boy working in the simple cottage at Merthyr Tydfil, destined to carry a refined pleasure into the most cultured circles of the whole world.

"It is, on the other hand, sad to think that hardly any of his work is accessible to his own countrymen. With the exception of his tiny water-colour at the Welsh Museum, nothing of his colour work is to be seen, and in the Deffett-Francis collection of engravings only five examples exist, as few of his works were engraved.

"But a good many of his paintings are in private hands in Wales. Of early sketches, a book is in the possession of the family of the late Mr. Charles Herbert James, M.P.; others of the neighbourhood of Pont-Neath-Vaughan, and one of the cottage of the artist's father at Merthyr, are in the hands of Sir William Thomas Lewis. Others, with finished works, are understood to belong to Lord Aberdare. A picture of Lancaster hangs at Penllergaer, and was kindly lent for exhibition in Cardiff by Sir J. T. D. Llewelyn. Many others are in private collections, and it would be interesting to know them. As has been said, but few have been engraved.

"Two small engravings are in the *Amulet*, 1829-30, and the *Literary Souvenir*, 1836.

" 'Italian Girls Preparing for a Festa' was engraved in 1830 by D. Lucas.

" 'Procession to the Christening' was engraved by Lumb Stocks.

"Of the three pictures in the National Gallery, two from the Vernon Collection, 'Wayside in Italy' and the 'Tambourine' were engraved for the *Art Journal* by C. Rolls. The only portrait we know to have been engraved is that of John Gibson, in mezzotint, by Wagstaffe.

"Would that this slight notice of a man whose memory Wales should not let die might induce owners of works by this artist, so admirable within the limits of his pleasing style, to present an example to our gallery which should fittingly exhibit his taste and skill.

Western Mail 26.3.1904 p.7.

152

William Menelaus of Dowlais

by T. F. HOLLEY AND J. BRYNMOR JONES

William Menelaus was born in East Lothian, Scotland, on the tenth of March, 1818. Educated at a local school, he was then apprenticed to a firm of engineers at Haddington, near Edinburgh. After serving his time, he went to London, where he did not remain long.

In 1839 he was at Middlesborough, erecting, and keeping at work after erection, brickmaking machinery for the Messrs. Pease, who at the time were engaged upon the Middlesborough Dock. Menelaus was afterwards in the service of a Company established for the introduction of improved agricultural machinery, and in 1843 was sent by that Company to superintend some work at Hensol Castle, Glamorganshire, the seat of Mr. Rowland Fothergill, Ironmaster, who governed the Abernant Ironworks, Aberdare, in the days of their prosperity. Fothergill offered Menelaus the post of assistant engineer at the Ironworks, which he accepted.

In 1851, Mr. Rowland Fothergill having retired, Menelaus left Aberdare and entered the service of the Dowlais Iron Company as engineer, becoming shortly afterwards chief manager of their extensive forges and mills. When John Evans, the general manager of Dowlais, retired, Menelaus took his place, and continued to act as general manager of Dowlais until he died.

Menelaus was also a large proprietor in the Tredegar and Treforest Ironworks, as well as in several large collieries, to each of which a share of his attention had to be given.

Under the guidance of Menelaus, Dowlais grew very much both in size and standing. When Mr. Bessemer, at the British Association meeting at Cheltenham in 1856, announced his great discovery, Dowlais was prompt to take it up, and made a series of experiments, over several months, to test its value, but without practical success. Later on, after Mushet had shown how, by the addition of spiegeleisen, the main difficulty in the way of the Bessemer process had been removed, steel-making was resumed at Dowlais, and grew to an extent equal to, if not greater than, that at any other existing works.

Menelaus also established at Dowlais the manufacture of steel by the Siemens process, the plant which he erected being amongst the first designed to carry on the open-hearth process on a large scale in this country.

Menelaus is numbered among the all-time GREATS of the iron and steel industries. His greatest contribution was undoubtedly in commissioning the Bessemer steel making process at Dowlais, for which he was awarded the Bessemer Gold Medal. He also made very significant contributions to puddling by mechanical processes, and as we mentioned in our account of "The Martin Family of Dowlais" in *Merthyr Historian, Volume Six* (1992), the vast deposits of iron ore in South Wales, in Northamptonshire, in Cleveland and in Scotland were unsuitable for Bessemer's process, being phosphoric ores.

Menelaus's former pupil, Edward Pritchard Martin, then manager at the Blaenavon Iron Company, co-operated with Sydney Gilchrist Thomas and his cousin Percy Gilchrist to develop a process to use phosphorus-containing ores to manufacture steel by the Bessemer Process. Menelaus himself got heavily involved in this work, doing large-scale trials at Dowlais. Another former pupil of Menelaus and friend of E. P. Martin, E. Windsor Richards, was in charge of Ironworks in the North of England. E. P. Martin aroused Richards's interest in the Bessemer Process. Richards validated the process and became one of its most active promoters.

A presentation to a Mr. Josiah Richards, Dowlais Manager, took place and was reported in the *Western Mail*, 17.4.1871 p.3. Josiah Richards was appointed manager of the newly-commissioned steel works at Dowlais about 1863, and in 1871 moved to a similar position at Ebbw Vale. Mr. T. Phillips presented the testimonial, a handsome silver tea and coffee service, from the shop of J. D. Williams, jeweller, Merthyr. Mr. T. Phillips described himself as "one of the oldest of the Bessemer workmen".

In accepting the gift Josiah Richards mentioned the coincidence that his father, exactly thirty-five years ago, in that same Dowlais Inn, had been presented by the working men of Dowlais with the handsome gold watch and chain that he (Josiah Richards) now wore.

Menelaus was always on the look-out for talented young men, working at Dowlais, those with the necessary gifts were exposed to all available experience at the giant Works and many in due course made their mark at home and abroad.

E. P. Martin, E. Windsor Richards, William Jenkins, Consett, Edward

Williams, Middlesborough (grandson of Iolo) and William Evans, Bryncae, Pant, mechanical engineer of Dowlais Works (died 11.1.1912), were all Dowlais "boys", tutored by Menelaus and destined to enjoy great professional success.

In 1873 Sir William Thomas Lewis of Aberdare (later Lord Merthyr) acquired the Forest Blast Furnaces from Mr. Francis Crawshay, Treforest; and with Mr. Edward Williams (of Bolckow, Vaughan and Co.), Sir Isaac Lowthian Bell, Mr. Menelaus (General Manager, Dowlais Works), Mr. G. T. Clark (Trustee of the Dowlais Iron Works), and some London bankers, formed the Forest Iron and Steel Company, Ltd., which worked up to 1900, when the Works were dismantled. Mr. Tolfree, the manager, died in 1901. It is stated in *Old South Wales Ironworks* by John Lloyd (1906) that Francis Crawshay erected three blast furnaces at Treforest; but owing to some dispute with his father, William Crawshay, of Cyfarthfa, the blast furnaces were never put into blast until 1873 when, after being modernised, Bessemer pig iron was successfully manufactured up to the year nineteen hundred. A short biographical account of Francis Crawshay appeared in *Merthyr Historian, Volume Four*, 1989.

Those who encountered Menelaus in his chatty moments spoke of his companionship as both entertaining, instructive and totally destitute of egotism. He once alluded to the secret of his success. In his early years he had shown exceptional expertise in cutting cogs. One day his foreman instructed him to cut no more than a fixed daily quota of cogs. Menelaus protested, but that foreman was impervious to argument.

Menelaus then resolved never to be limited as to the quantity of work he could do, but to do as much as ever he could, whatever work he might be engaged in. Menelaus attributed much of his success to this attitude of mind.

Another account attributed Menelaus's great success in managing the Dowlais Works to his GOLDEN RULE which he laid down, and by which he invariably worked. He insisted on having DAILY REPORTS from all the Works Departments under his care, each report was very minutely scrutinised, so that, every twenty-four hours, Menelaus had a full knowledge of all portions of the Works.

Menelaus also brought indomitable perseverance, untiring regularity and exceedingly close application to bear on his work, he was noted for his foresight and grappled at once with improvements likely to be of benefit to the Works.

In twentieth century language, Menelaus was an out-an-out COMPANY MAN, work took precedence over all else.

Menelaus was extremely strict, almost severely so, with those under him; he was also short, blunt and decisive in manner, and no one dared to disobey or question his orders.

Quickness of temper was also one of his most striking characteristics. An unadmitted offence or any endeavour to conceal a fault from his keen eyes, met with his severest displeasure, if not instant dismissal, but a fault readily admitted or acknowledged was passed over, and not noticed again.

If there was one offence more unpardonable than another in the eyes of Menelaus, it was for anyone employed in the Works to give information outside, of what was going on within. This meant instant dismissal for ever, he would trust that person no more. To ask him for information was almost as great a crime.

Menelaus and Learned Societies

When the Iron and Steel Institute was formally constituted in 1869, William Menelaus was elected a Vice-president. He continued in this capacity until 1875, when he was elected President. His distinguished predecessors as President were the Duke of Devonshire, Sir Henry Bessemer and Mr. I. L. Bell.

Menelaus's Presidential Address was devoted to a retrospect and consideration of the position of mechanical puddling, and of the applications and prospects of steel.

Menelaus also contributed a paper to the Proceedings of the Institute on "Improved Machinery for Rolling Rails" (*Transactions for 1869* p.187). This paper described some improvements which Menelaus introduced into the big mill at Dowlais, during the depression of 1867-68, for the purpose of saving labour.

Menelaus was a frequent speaker at the meetings of the Iron and Steel Institute, and the high practical value of his criticisms is amply attested by the Journal in which they are recorded. Menelaus often spoke on the subject of mechanical puddling at these meetings and acted as chairman of the Committee established by the Institute to investigate and report upon the merits of the various systems of mechanical puddling. In May 1881, less than a year before his death, Menelaus was presented with the Bessemer gold medal, in recognition of his services to the manufacture of iron.

Menelaus was a member of the Institution of Civil engineers.

He was also a member, and a Vice-President from 1870-73, of the Institution of Mechanical Engineers. Menelaus contributed papers "On the large Blowing Engine and new Rolling Mill at Dowlais Ironworks" (*Proceedings, 1857* p.112) and "On Mechanical Puddling" (*Proceedings, 1867* p.151), to the Institution of Mechanical Engineers.

William Menelaus was a founder of the South Wales Institute of Engineers. On 29th October, 1857, he was elected first President and was re-elected to the

Presidency in 1864. He contributed, besides his inaugural Address as President in 1857, a paper "On Rolling Heavy Iron", which was read at Newport in 1860.

A Profile of and Interview with William Menelaus of Dowlais

"There is a man now entering through the big doors of the Dowlais Works whom you, a stranger, intuitively know is SOMEBODY.

"The Irish labourer shambles out of his way; old Welsh workers touch their hats, and bow their heads at the same time. He is the Master, evidently. Tall, with strongly marked features, his hair long and black, a huge scarf around his neck, but with nothing in cut or character of dress to indicate consideration for the fashions and usages of society; still there is something about him which constrains attention, commands respect, deference. Who is he? What is he? The answer is soon given, WILLIAM MENELAUS, manager of the Dowlais Ironworks, and its dependent collieries and industries, employer of ten thousand people, who has grasped the details even of one of the largest Works in the world, and holds them like multitudinous reins in his hand as the huge industry rolls around; and who, whether it be the steel made close at hand or the Spanish ore branch at Bilbao, the working profit and loss of the deepest collieries, or the specifications of rails, the texture of steel - has got all, so to state, at his fingers' ends.

"Follow him through the Works. Every man, boy and girl are on their best behaviour as he nears them; hands ply vigorously; even the horses and locomotives seem to catch the contagion, AND THERE IS NO LOITERING HAND OR FOOT OR WHEEL TO BE SEEN.

"They all know that he is no superficial looker on, that he knows how to do it all and which is the best way, and that he has an eye which can seize in a moment the weak point of men or manufacture. Follow him to his home. You are told that he is of the people, and that in early life he laboured with hand as well as with brain. You are surprised, for he is surrounded by the indications of intellectual refinement. His pictures, his books indicate the art critic as well as the thinker. Costly treasures from gifted easels cover the walls, and your host, unlike the wealthy parvenu, who is a collector for the love of collecting or possessing, can discourse (talk) with ability of the special points hidden from all but a few. In the Works you will get from him a thorough practical insight into iron and steel making. You feel that he could take you into the laboratory and explain minutely chemical properties, and the processes by which phosphor, the arch-enemy, is fought, and how good 'make' is ensured at the lowest possible minimum of cost; and take up the role of any of his men, and teach them practically in every branch, as if he had delved or puddled or rolled. But at home this is forgotten, and you are in conversation with a philosophic mind, who takes broad views of God's providence, of nature's laws and human aims and efforts.

Q "Let me limn (paint) a few of Mr. Menelaus's opinions. I hazard the remark that it is a pity our best coal is being given away; that there is a limit to our coal wealth; that a time will come when our great mineral fields will be exhausted; and, then, what then?

A. 'First,' said he, 'if such coals as No.3 Rhondda should run out in a comparatively short period, others as useful will remain, and even at the lowest estimate our stores will last for a couple of thousand years. Quite long enough for us. Nations have a life, the same as individuals, and, judging from the past, and the past is always a guide for the future, for no nation has ever retained its greatness for two thousand years, the duration of our coal will be ample for that of our needs.'

Q. 'Would it not, however,' I suggest, 'be a politic course to improve prices for coal-owners to band in unison?'

A. 'I do not want to use harsh expressions, but it would be simply damnable by any artificial course you name to force prices beyond that rate which is brought about by the law of supply and demand. It is a law of God's providence, as shown by wiser men than you or I, that the price of coal should be dependent upon that of demand, just as that of any other commodity or produce.'

Q. 'But should not coal be exceptionable to that of corn?' I rejoin. 'The field manured and treated with alternate crops, dowered by the rain, the snow and the sunshine, is literally inexhaustible - the gardens of Jerusalem, prolific in the days of Christ, are prolific now, but our coal is not renewed.'

A. 'We have enough and to spare,' he repeated, 'the world is wide, and the mineral extent scarcely guessed at; besides, science advances yearly, and in my time I have seen a wonderful limitation in the use of coal in iron manufacture.'

"I drift away from coal and iron and get into politics.

158

Q. 'Have you seen Gladstone's last speech?'

A. 'No. I take little interest in politics; but your question reminds me of Roebuck's reply to the same query, "I wish to God I had!" I have no faith in the man,' he continued, 'or his class. It is *preposterous* to think that, from beginning to end, the Conservatives have been always wrong. Their opponents do not deny them the possession of great mental power; and to think that such mental power is always systematically used, not only foolishly, but against the best interests of our land, of England, is what no impartial reasoning mind will admit for a moment. The Liberals, in their every-day social and commercial life, do not think so; but touch upon politics, and the men who, as friends, dealers or manufacturers, are trustworthy, become other beings. Do not believe in it. Care little about politics, since the stream becomes so muddied and defiled.'

"I agree with him and lament that the Liberals should decry their countrymen as inhuman in their action against the Zulus.

A. 'Exactly,' said Mr. Menelaus, 'it is the mission of the white man to spread over the earth, just as it is for the weak to give way to the strong. Read by the light of the past it is God's providence, and yet the preacher denounces it as sinful. What would America be if it had been left to the black man and the North American Indian, or New Zealand and Australia to the Aborigines? The black man and the red man must give way to the white. Certainly, individual cases of cruelty exist; you need not go further than Merthyr to find individual cases also; but, generally speaking, they are exceptional, and are lost in the great survey of things.'

Q. 'I refer to the short-sighted notions of preachers of the Gospel, who support the ultra-Liberal and believe, or say they do, that the Conservatives have hounded-on English soldiers to every species of imaginable wrong.'

A. 'Have no faith in them,' said Mr. Menelaus, 'Ministers as a rule are narrow men, and preachers more so. They look at the world as confined to a little circle bounded by the horizon. 'And their God,' I add, 'just such another Jupiter in the clouds immediately over them, listening to the singing and pleased with the harps.' He laughed and the theme was changed.

"At another time the conversation ran into another grove, and English literature became the subject. Mr. Menelaus admitted a hearty belief in Carlyle, 'one of the few great men of the world'. I submitted that he was over-estimated, that his ruggedness was an assumption in great part, as it was seen clearly in *Sartor Resartus* that he could write pure and euphonious English if he liked.

" 'Yes, by way of diversion,' said Mr. Menelaus; 'but the rugged was his native speech. His words are concentrations of wisdom. The flowing language of some writers pass before the eye, but leave nothing to think about. It is not solid enough. Carlyle's, on the contrary, makes you think. You cannot grapple it at first, but when you do, you have something worth holding.'

"No one had read Carlyle more carefully than W. Menelaus, and yet the works of Carlyle, like those of Adam Smith, and of many a sober thinker, constitute only the amusements of those few hours of relaxation which the great duties of Dowlais Works entailed.

"Wonderful is the alteration wrought in the world over which William Menelaus ruled since the days of the early ironmaster and the small furnace. At that time there was more iron left in the waste than was shown in the bar. Ironmaking was only a little advance upon the smithy; but now it is a scientific process, and an ironworks without a good analytical chemist is lop-eared and one-sided. Once ironmaking, like coal working, was easy; the iron ore was to be found in the river bed, and to be had for the getting, and the coal cropped out at your back door.

"Now iron making involves brain work, as well as muscle, and for coal you go down half a mile into the deep. Still, over all operations, as over the ten thousand labourers in a vast field of action, requiring constant attention, keenest knowledge and profoundest thought, laboured William Menelaus, iron in will, as if his nature had become oxidised by the material amongst which he moved; and so regulating the great field of industry that it seemed to move like a vast machine. Thus it continued on and on, through good and bad times, evil report and good report; and even as it continued it expanded, until the question was to what height would not Dowlais attain.

"One may be thankful for all this: *that during a long, terrible stagnation of five years, the Works were retained in operation*; and no measure of praise is too high for the man whose wonderful prescience and skill enabled this to be done until the dark night came to an end. This is the greatest of reputations. *Mr. Menelaus never acted as Justice of the Peace, Chairman of the Board of Guardians, Chairman of Local or School Boards. He kept aloof* from the social arrangements; and while other men made local laws, or aided in carrying them out, he was content to keep the wheels going, and twenty thousand men, women and children were thereby saved from the semi-starvation which has befallen many industrial centres.

"This is high meed, honourable repute, lasting reputation, and, as such, will be associated unquestionably with his name. It is true, in his bluff way, *he would unhesitatingly deny any claim to the distinction of a philantropist*, or question heartily whether he would make a ton of iron in order that the profits went simply to the ironworker, but he has done so notwithstanding, and thus, as a practical philantropist, he has excelled immeasurably the good old spectacled men who pry about in prisons or in quiet lanes, just as they would for butterflies or beetles, and feel their delightful old hearts rejoice in the giving away of a blanket or a Bible.

(This profile appeared in the *Western Mail* on 31.3.1882.)

Menelaus and the Merthyr Art Exhibition, 1880

A major Art Exhibition was organised in Merthyr Tydfil in 1880, to raise funds to establish a local Art School. From far and wide, including South Kensington Museum, items were offered for display in the Exhibition at Merthyr Drill Hall. A "hanging committee" selected items from the huge amount of quality material offered.

The following account was culled from the *South Wales Weekly News* (22.5.1880).

"Foremost among the contributions of the Science and Art Department, South Kensington, are a series of handsome designs of mediaeval figures for execution in Mosaic work, which occupy a conspicuous position at the extreme end of the Drill-hall, facing the gallery at the outer extremity, where are displayed a collection of splendid photographs, the handiwork of some of the first photographers of the day, among them the late Mr. Robert Crawshay, evidence of whose skill in that branch of Art are found in several lovely bits of scenery taken from the neighbourhood of Merthyr.

"The centre piece of the collection is however a remarkable 'composition photograph' by H. P. Robinson of a picture by Hans Makart, which proved one of the greatest attractions of the Paris Exhibition. The subject is 'The Entry of Charles V into Antwerp'.

"A cursory glance at the wealth of paintings which now adorn the walls of the Drill-hall discloses three grand masterpieces of TITIAN and GUIDO, fully illustrative of the genius of the painters. A large number of Royal Academy pictures, representing some of the great masters in the modern school of painting, such as Millais, Gainsborough, Cooper, Goodall and Stansfield, and others by artists scarcely less famous, were sent by Mr. W. T. Lewis, of Mardy; Mr. G. T. Clark; MR. WILLIAM MENELAUS; Mr. F. W. Harris, of Treharris, and others interested in the Exhibition. It would, indeed, require more than a single visit to form a due appreciation of these Works alone. Water colour paintings are also in good force, and some exquisite etchings by Turner will well repay a close inspection. Nor should there be forgotten in connection with the pictures a fine series of portraits of the great ironmasters of Cyfarthfa, contributed by Mr. William Crawshay.

"Various studies by eminent sculptors, including the busts of

Henry Richard, M.P.,
Thomas Stephens,
Sir John Guest,
G. T. Clark and
'Gohebydd'

will also command special attention, the productions of William Davies and David Davies, as Merthyr men, being particularly calculated to arouse the interest and admiration of local visitors.

"Such works will perhaps gain most notice from persons of cultivated taste, but the exhibits coming under the head 'Curiosities' will meet the popular taste in many ways.

"Pre-eminent in the miscellaneous collection is the case of ivory carvings lent by the Premier, Mr. Gladstone; to which may be added a fine example of Swiss wood-carving by hand, lent by Mr. G. T. Clark. Messrs. Elkington's show of silver-plate, one of the most attractive samples of which is the enamelled dessert service, made for the notorious King Theebau, of Burmah; also a splendid suite of armour from the South Kensington authorities.

"The Japanese curiosities from Mrs. H. Martin, of Newcastle, and Mr. Newcombe of Brecon, must gain more than passing notice, as these cases make an attractive show, but there are two items among the curiosities to which attention should be directed, as they are not conspicuous and may chance to be overlooked. We refer to a pair of old Roman shoes, and a shovel of the same period, which are exhibited by Mr. W. T. Lewis, as having been found embedded in the mines at Llantrisant, which this would indicate, were once worked by the Romans.

"This sketch will sufffice to show that the Hall contains a collection of ob-

162

jects calculated to excite a deep interest among all classes, and to tend to cultivate the taste of the masses."

A week later, under the heading "A Private View", a detailed account of items
on display at the Merthyr Tydfil Art Exhibition appeared in the *South Wales
Weekly News* (29.5.1880). We have extracted paragraphs from this account,
which refer to items exhibited by William Menelaus.

"... and still more conspicuous, a life-size painting of St. Francis clinging to
the cross, by Stirzzi (from the collection of Mr. Menelaus, to whom it was presented by the great gun manufacturer Herr Krupp)."

"Great and unchallengeable as are the merits of these old Works of Art, the
eye turns with a sense of relief to the less sombre and more varied productions
of modern artists. The central attraction of this class on the north wall is 'The
Misty Mountain', which occupies a large share of the fourth panel. It is a bold
conception, elaborately portraying wild scenery of a style familiar to all who have
wandered amid the mountains of Scotland, and ranks as one of the grandest productions of Peter Graham. It was lent by Mr. Menelaus, who secured it for his
gallery at the substantial outlay of £1,000. On the opposite wall hangs a com-
panion picture, and contributed from the same gallery, affording further proof
of the genius of this artist. Its title 'Wind' refers to an atmospheric effect worthy of a Turner, for while gazing upon it we can scarce dispel the illusion that a
vapoury mist is driving before one, and fast enveloping the roaring torrent which
rolls impetuously down the hillside. Returning to the northern panels, we observe that Mr. Menelaus has also sent a notable study 'Joan of Arc' by Millais,
which forcibly represents the kneeling figure of the heroine, clad in armour, and
in the act of supplicating Divine grace to carry on her mission. Mr. Menelaus
owns, among other attractive works near at hand, 'The Cock Fight' by Hodgson,
and a charming pastoral cattle scene, illustrative of Cooper in his happiest mood,
which by the way, finds a match in a picture from the collection of Mr. W. T.
Lewis, of Mardy."

"In this area we again came across a valuable contribution from Mr. Menelaus,
'A Winter Retreat of Soldiers', which hangs low upon the wainscot, but should
not be lost sight of, as it is a characteristic work of Benassit and formerly belonged to the famous Mendel Collection."

" 'The Border Keep' by Walter Paton (another from the splendid collection
of Mr. Menelaus), in the details of which the artist appears at his best, and to
Mr. Menelaus also is due a characteristic landscape by Van Luppin."

"Turning to the water-colours, which cover nearly half the south wall, and a
portion of the west end, we may particularise 'The Convent Raven' (lent by Mr.

Menelaus), a scene strongly suggestive of the tale of the 'Jackdaw of Rheims' in the Ingoldsby Legends, in which a sedate-looking bird is keeping company with an old monk in the Cloisters; the artist is H. S. Marks, R.A."

"On the opposite side of the Hall is a beautifully proportioned statuette of a warrior, by J. H. Foley, R.A., owned by Mr. Menelaus."

Methyr's Reaction to Mr. Menelaus's Munificence to Cardiff, 1882

The news of Mr. Menelaus's proposed gift of valuable paintings to the town of Cardiff predictably caused consternation in Merthyr Tydfil.

A strong and balanced editorial appeared in the *Merthyr Express* for January 7th, 1882, this contains some eternal truths and is given in full. Perhaps the lesson has been learned, a parallel can be drawn with the advance erection of factories and offices, in the hope that firms will be found to tenant them.

"It will be no exaggeration to say that the brief announcement which appeared in the newspapers on Monday morning that Mr. Menelaus had signified his intention to present pictures of the value of £10,000 to the town of Cardiff, took away the breath of every person in Merthyr and Dowlais who read it. Here was another example of these unfortunate towns being passed over in favour of another place, with which, unquestionably, it would puzzle the most astute to discover anything approaching to an identity of interest between the munificent donor and the community to be benefited by his splendid gift. We have no right to question the motives by which Mr. Menelaus has been actuated in this matter.

"Doubtless the reasons which decided him in favour of Cardiff were satisfactory enough, for all that we cannot restrain the flood of regret, which is being poured forth on all sides, that this noble collection of paintings, seen and admired by thousands during the Merthyr Tydfil Art Exhibition, is destined to adorn another town than our own.

"It may be alleged, with a truth which none can deny, that the town of Merthyr does not possess a proper place for the suitable exhibition and preservation of such valuable treasures of art; and on the other hand it is a fact that the town of Cardiff is expending many thousands of pounds upon a magnificent building intended to be the home of a Free Library, School of Art and Design, and a Museum of Art.

"CARDIFF SET ABOUT TO PROVIDE FOR CONTINGENCIES WHICH WERE, TO ALL APPEARANCES, ONLY REMOTELY PROBABLE.

"The spacious room to be devoted to pictures was resolved upon before the owners had a single painting to hang upon its walls. The Hon. Member for the

Borough gave the first picture, Mr. Menelaus has now followed with many pictures, and these examples will influence other owners of similar works of art. It illustrates with striking effect the experience of our daily lives, that no provision for any good and useful purpose will ever be made, without being properly utilised.

"If the people of Merthyr had had the SPIRIT OF THE TIMES working within them, and courageously availed themselves of their powers to build a Free Library, not only would there have been no opposition from the great rate-payers, but it may be taken for granted that Merthyr, and not Cardiff, would have benefited by this great gift.

"Had the disposition to provide means of culture been made apparent beyond a doubt, even if the accommodation had not been in existence, it is most probable that the offer would have been made here (Merthyr) first; and the mere expression of a conditional intention to bestow such treasures, would have been sufficient to have stimulated the townspeople into the effort necessary for making proper provision for them.

"But this much is beyond the pale of disputation: if a community will not rise to an occasion and prove their desire to be helped, and their worthiness to receive help, no help will be forthcoming.

"The principle expressed in the Scriptural declaration, that to him that hath much more shall be added, and from him that hath nothing, even that which he hath shall be taken, contains an eternal truth which holds good for all time, and applies with equal force to communities and to individuals.

"If we lie supine upon our poverty, and put forth no hand in an effort to rise, no hand will be stretched out to give us the grip that will place us on our feet. God helps those who help themselves, is only expressing the same truth in another form. If we do nothing for ourselves, nothing will be done for us; but so long as we are content with the position which we now occupy, so long will those who can help us and would help us let us remain there undisturbed.

"Moreover, we furnish them with the most powerful and cogent reasons for doing nothing. If we complain that they do nothing for us, they turn round and say, what do you want us to do? Show us by some convincing proofs that you are anxious to march with the times, and to lift your heads up to the light, and we will listen to you, but you cannot expect us to provide unasked means of cultivating taste and a love of the beautiful in nature and art, institutions in which you evince no interest, it would be throwing pearls to swine. That is their answer, and there is no gainsaying it.

"If instead of rallying their forces to defeat every trifling suggestion for improving the town and its inhabitants, those townsfolk who preach from one text, and one only - don't spend any public money except what the law absolutely compels you to spend - would join hands and present the hearty spectacle of cordial unanimity, we should have an irresistible case with which to go to the wealthy residents and owners of property, and ask for their generous assistance in promoting a good cause.

"If we went with an unbroken front, showing unity of purpose, heart and will, our appeals would not be made in vain. But while our energies are expended on unprofitable differences and efforts to thwart each other's intentions, we pronounce our own condemnation, and deprive ourselves even of the right of remonstrance when we see the priceless treasures that might and would be in the heritage of Merthyr carried away from us to enrich others.

"Verily, we sell our birthright for a mess of pottage."

The Menelaus Bequest to Cardiff

William Menelaus was an avid collector of quality paintings. Prior to his death in 1882, he arranged to donate thirty-eight paintings to the town of Cardiff. Menelaus left the paintings to Lord Bute, Mr. George Thomas Clark (Dowlais), Mr. R. O. Jones and Mr. W. T. Lewis, in trust for the benefit of the town of Cardiff. The value of the paintings in 1882 was £10,000. See Borough of Cardiff Council, General Purposes Committee Minutes 365, 366, 387, dated the second of January, 1882.

The Twentieth Annual Report, 1881-82, Cardiff Free Library, Museum and Science and Arts Schools Committee, Borough of Cardiff, reported that the New Building for the Free Library, Museum and Schools for Science and Art (i.e., the portion of present-day The Hayes Library adjoining the cemetery) was formally opened by the Mayor of Cardiff, Mr. Alfred Thomas (later Lord Pontypridd), on the 31st of May, 1882, with pomp and ceremony, the procession comprised members of all the Corporate and Public Bodies and Trade and Benefit Societies in the town. The day was observed as a public holiday.

The Mayor gave a Conversazione in the evening, to upwards of seven hundred ladies and gentlemen, in celebration of the event, and was presented with a gold medal to mark the occasion.

The Twentieth Annual Report also mentioned that the late William Menelaus, Esq., of Dowlais, had generously offered to present a number of Works of Art to be placed in the Fine Art Gallery in connection with the New Building.

The Committee recorded the valuable services rendered by Mr. W. T. Lewis, Aberdare (later Lord Merthyr), in obtaining the Menelaus Collection, and thanked

Mr. Lewis for the MARBLE BUST, sculpted by Sir Thomas Brock, presented by him in memory of Mr. Menelaus. (See Minute 1098, Free Library and Museum Committee, 19.12.1881.)

Irrelevant to our present theme, but a fascinating reminder of little-known Cardiff Works of Art, recently cleaned, reference was also made to six sculptured panels, placed at the Trinity Street end of the Free Library building, which typify

THE INDUSTRIAL ARTS   Agriculture, Mechanics and Commerce (combined with figures of Literature and Philosophy)

and

THE FINE ARTS   Architecture, Music and Culture (combined with figures of Painting and Sculpture)

Executed in stone, in *alto-relievo*, these panels were produced by Mr. R. L. Boulton, sculptor, of Cheltenham, from drawings prepared by him from the Architect's sketches.

The 1881-82 Report also mentioned that the Cymmrodorion Society had presented to the Corporation the original model of the statue of RELIGION, by the Merthyr Tydfil-born sculptor Joseph Edwards; this was given to the Free Library.

The Twenty-First Annual Report, 1882-83, as above, referred to the arrival of the Menelaus Collection, the pictures had been placed in the Council Chamber until the Gallery was ready for their reception.

The Collection was then hung in the Municipal Art Gallery, formally opened on the twenty-third of October, 1883, by the Mayor of Cardiff, Gaius Augustine Stone, Esq.

This Report also mentioned that Mr. F. W. Harris had presented portraits of George The Third and Queen Charlotte, by Allan Ramsay.

The Twenty-Second Annual Report, 1883-84, mentioned that a remarkably life-like BUST in marble of William Menelaus had been received from William Thomas Lewis, Esq., J.P., of Aberdare. The BUST was placed on a pedestal and displayed in the centre of the Menelaus Collection.;

To afford additional protection to the valuable Pictures and Exhibits in the Museum during closing time, an IRON GATE was placed on the flight of stairs leading to the Museum.

A report in the *Merthyr Express* for 16.10.1897, page eight, column four, recorded the theft of a painting from the Menelaus Collection. This item has not been recovered to date (1994); it was a small porcelain panel, about eight inches square, painted in oils, by a leading artist, and was a copy of Murillo's "Peasant Boy". Its intrinsic value was about twelve pounds, it was one of a pair.

The theft of coins from Cardiff Free Library Museum was recorded in the *Western Mail* for the thirteenth of February, 1885, page two, column eight.

A booklet was printed, dated 31.5.1882, listing and commenting on the paintings in the Menelaus Collection. Written by Thomas Henry Thomas and Edwin Seward, a copy exists in Cardiff Central Library, W-4-329, 948. 2 (640) THO. Cardiff Central Library is no longer housed in The Hayes building and exists in a modern building nearby.

The Menelaus Collection is now part of and merged with the Art Collection at the National Museum of Wales, Cathays Park, Cardiff.

Death of William Menelaus, 1882

Menelaus suffered a serious illness in November, 1879. He was treated by Dr. Cresswell, who obtained the advice of Dr. Davies, Merthyr, Dr. Edwards, Cardiff and Dr. Andrew Clark, London. Menelaus recovered.

However, Menelaus died at Tenby on 30.3.1882 and was buried at Penderyn Churchyard, where his wife of a few months, Margaret Jennet, daughter of Jenkin Rhys, Llwydcoed, had been laid to rest in 1852.

Amongst those who attended the funeral were nephews, Letelle Darling, Charles Darling, brother-in-law Rees H. Rhys, J.P., Llwydcoed,

> Lord and Lady Aberdare,
> Mr. and Mrs. G. T. Clark,
> George Martin, Dowlais,
> William Jenkins, Consett,
> Edward Williams, Middlesborough,
> W. T. Lewis, Aberdare,
> Dr. P. R. Cresswell,
> William T. Crawshay.

A memorial plaque to William Menelaus was erected in Saint John's Parish Church, Dowlais.

A letter from one, Sandford Jones (*Merthyr Express*, 15.6.1912 p.12) mentioned that a portrait of William Menelaus, painted by Mr. Gillies Gair, was available. Sandford Jones had written to Mr. Justice Darling, a nephew of Menelaus, suggesting that he should purchase this painting and present it to Merthyr Corporation. Mr. Justice Darling was not aware that Menelaus had sat for a portrait and enquired if it had been painted from a photograph. The outcome is not known.

A Dowlais Library Minute, about February 1924, resolved that the thanks of the Committee be tendered to Mr. C. Darling, 81, Albert Hall Mansions, London, for a gift of a portrait of Mr. W. Menelaus, late manager of the Dowlais Works.

POEM. In Memoriam. W. Menelaus, Dowlais. Died March 30th, 1882

A solemn gloom
Has fallen sadly on us all,
And he, whose life was one endeavour
To follow Duty's constant call,
Has passed away from care for ever
To man's last home.

At Duty's call,
With punctual and prompt response,
He, without thought of self, obeyed,
He was admired and feared at once,
And by his friends on every side
Beloved of all.

Grave and severe,
by nature fitted to command
His dignity would never bend;
He ruled with firm and steady hand,
A master stern, but valued friend,
Just, but austere.

Skill merits fame!
Abilities of pre-eminence
Were his, and yet he ever sought
Not to attain pre-eminence,
But to assist the man of thought
To win a name.

He never tried
By vain parade to be renowned,
He rather chose obscurity;
Yet deeds speak out, with trumpet sound,
Of MENELAUS, for ages yet to be
Our boast and pride.

His life was passed
In mighty works that won success,
In unremitting toil and care
A life of noble usefulness;
And known, respected, far and near,
He died at last.

Reached is the goal,
The place of rest where cares are not,
And to man's sympathising Friend,
Who knows the hardships of our lot,
To His care, humbly, we commend
This great man's soul.

> E.C.R.
> *Merthyr Express* 8.4.1882 p.5.

Mrs. Rosalind Freeman, Art Department, National Museum of Wales, is thanked for providing photographs of two paintings from the Menelaus Collection,

N M W 21   Cattle in Landscape.   A. F. Bonheur.
N M W 35   The Challenge Refused.   J. E. Hodgson.

and also a photograph of a bust of Menelaus, sculpted by Sir Thomas Brock (N M W 1167).

The National Museum of Wales, Cathays Park, Cardiff, is thanked for permission to publish these photographs.

Early Schooldays

by GLANMOR WILLIAMS

A short time back, I had occasion to drive from the junction on the Heads of the Valleys Road down into Dowlais along Pant Road. It was dark, and I couldn't see too clearly, but enough to realize that major changes had taken place since I'd come down that way last. There were many new houses; and some familiar landmarks, like the old Caeracca Bridge, had disappeared. Then to my utter amazement and intense dismay, as I looked in the direction where my old school had been, my unbelieving eyes saw nothing. I realized with an awful shock that all the old school buildings had disappeared and the site had been cleared. I felt bereft! A whole slice of my past existence had been cut away without my even being aware of it. A sharp stab of *hiraeth* - nostalgia, for those of you who are unfamiliar with the Welsh word that is virtually untranslatable - went through me. My mind flashed back sixty or seventy years to the happy early schooldays I'd spent there, the teachers who'd set me on my way, and the boys and girls who'd been my classmates. In one sense, of course, it makes very little difference that the buildings have now gone, because the memories still remain with me, remarkably sharp and vivid after all this time. For seven years, between 1924 and 1931, from the age of four until eleven, next to my home that school had loomed largest in my life.

Looking back now, the first thing that strikes me is what a long way it was for a child, especially in the infants' school, to have to walk from Francis Street in Dowlais, where we lived, to Pant School. It was about a mile each way in the morning and at lunchtime, and again the same distance in the afternoon. Four miles every day was quite a stint; but we never seemed to think anything much of it when we were children, I suppose we belonged to an age which was accustomed to walking. None of our parents had cars; the nearest thing to private transport in our circle was a costermonger's horse and cart, and he had better things to do with his conveyance than take us to and from school in it. Public transport of a sort did exist in the shape of buses; but they were very few and far between and not at all convenient, even if we could have afforded the fares.

So we made our way along the main road to the school, unescorted except for some of the older children who obligingly kept an eye on us. Not that there was a great deal of traffic to take account of; an occasional van or car, and many more horses and carts. There was also the railway which crossed the road, along which heavy works engines puffed their laborious way, followed by their attendant retinue of coal trucks. The worst hazard - at least as far as I was concerned - was the regular processions of livestock that used to come galloping down the road on their way to the slaughterhouse. Their accompanying herdsman always seemed to be an unconscionable distance behind them, and his excitable, barking dogs were more calculated to drive the animals into a frenzy rather than to their destination. I sometimes felt as though I was facing a Wild West-type stampede of lively bullocks. Many a time I remember pressing myself against the wall so as to squeeze as far as I could out of the path of these fearsome beasts! In retrospect, I suspect that the wretched animals were more scared that I was.

Ordinarily, there were many things along the route to attract the attention of curious youngsters. As we approached the open country between the limits of Dowlais and the beginnings of Pant, we came first to a miscellaneous series of tin sheds, which housed a miscellany of animals and vehicles. Outstanding among them were Tommy Axhorn's splendid team of Belgian bays. These magnificent horses were the pride and joy of Tommy, our local undertaker. He loved exercising, washing, grooming, and generally titivating his handsome horses and his funeral conveyances. We used to view these performances with great interest, offering admiring, or sometimes critical, comments for Tommy's benefit. He was an unusually tolerant man, who would put up with the unsolicited observations of lively kids with infinite good humour. But when the bays, replete with funeral plumes, and the cabs were turned out in all their glory for a funeral, we could only stand in unabashed admiration.

A short way further on, the railway from the works crossed the road to arrive at the public weighing machine. There, I was fascinated by the massive shire horses, with their fine, intelligent heads, powerful hind quarters, and their shaggy fetlocks. As they drew their heavily-laden, old-fashioned carts, I always felt they had a look of infinite patience on their dignified, unmoving faces. Their names always interested me; for the most part, the nomenclature was pretty unimaginative: "Ben", "Stout", "Taff", with an occasional more exotic one, like

172

"Emperor" or "Champion" thrown in. With the closing down of the Dowlais Works in the late nineteen-twenties, all this activity came to an end.

Meantime, the ordinary passenger line continued up towards Pant, parallel with the road. It carried on to Pant Halt and eventually to the intriguingly named Pant Aerial Station. (I never did discover, now I come to think of it, where the "Aerial" came from.) This was a Great Western line, and just before it arrived at Pant Halt, it crossed over the LMS line which made its way on to Abergavenny. The LMS was graced with its own stop at Pantysgallog Halt. Even as a child, it struck me as very odd that a little place like Pant had no fewer than three stations. The LMS line was a source of great delight to us. The train used to emerge from a tunnel just below the school amid a great cloud of steam and belched its way furiously up the slight gradient, coming to an abrupt halt at Pantysgallog, as though exhausted after its manful efforts. Conversely, it used to leave the Halt in the opposite direction very stealthily and sidle down the gradient towards the tunnel surprisingly quietly, as if it had every intention of taking the tunnel unawares. We used to love standing behind the hedge alongside the line and observe its antics. Or, better still, stand on the bridge that crossed it and immerse ourselves in the clouds of steam that enveloped us like incense. But Pantysgallog is inseparably associated in my mind with memories of blissful summer picnics in Pontsarn and Vaynor, one stop down the line.

The other line that went up through Ponsticill towards the Beacons had similar associations, but this time with excursions to such havens of delight as Dolygaer, Torpantau, and Talybont. That Brecon and Merthyr line was the subject of endless scurrilous stories amongst us, on account of the leisurely pace at which the trains proceeded along it. One anecdote told of a guard trying to persuade a man picking blackberries near the line to board the train. "No thanks," demurred the reluctant customer, "I'd like to oblige you, but I'm in a hurry today." Another reported an exasperated passenger exploding with rage when he got to Merthyr. "If I'd been travelling a hundred years ago I'd have got here faster." "Ah, well," commented a phlegmatic porter, "you can't expect any better - it's the same engine."

Around the school were open fields, with a couple of farms within a stone's throw. They bore their ancient and attractive Welsh names. On the one side was Cwmrhydybedd ("The valley of the ford of the grave"). It was an appealing, if gloomy, name, and nobody seemed to know whose grave it was. The farmer there was a man called Eddie James, and he delivered our milk every morning. He looked every inch a farmer: about average height but very powerfully built, with a ruddy, weather-beaten face. I made a friend of him for life by persuading him to buy a raffle ticket, on the strength of which he won a remarkably fine gold watch. On the other side was a very old farm, which has now disappeared and even in those days was ringed with houses and a railway on three sides. Its name was "Caerhaca" ("The field of the rake"), though it was ordinarily spelt "Caeracca" and always pronounced "Cracker". The farmer, Siencyn Richards, was quite a character, and his son, Glyn, who was in school with me, was even more of a lad. Pant still preserved a number of the charming old Welsh names, which went back to a pre-industrial era. There was Pantysgallog("Hollow of the thistles"); yr Hafod ("summer dwelling"); Pantcadifor ("Hollow of Ifor's seat"); Garth ("enclosure"); Tai'r Efail ("House of the smithy"), and so on. The local authority had the wit to name some of the streets on their post-1918 housing estates with attractive Welsh names like Rhodfa ("Avenue") or Heol y Bryniau ("The road to the hills").

The existence of the farms in the immediate vicinity of the school was a reminder to us of the farming life and the agricultural seasons, although we were living in an essentially industrial town. Not that you could entirely escape the industrial influence, even on a farm. Cwmrhydybedd must have leased some of its fields to the Guest, Keen and Nettlefold's Company to enable it to graze its horses. On a post erected near the road stood a menacing notice, which read "Guest, Keen and Nettlefold's Ltd. Trespassers will be strictly prosecuted. By order of the Board." I can still feel that tremor of anxiety going through me as I read those threatening words. They conveyed an image to my childish mind of a group of stern-faced, elderly men, all with dark suits, wing-collars, and heavy gold watch-chains, sitting round a table. I seemed to see a trembling miscreant brought before them and being threatened with all sorts of dire punishments too awful to contemplate! If that notice was meant to terrify the unwary, it certainly succeeded in my case.

Of my earliest days in school I have only the haziest recollection. I remember my mother telling me much later that I didn't want her to come with me to school; I must have thought that would have been unbearably *infra dig*. I wanted to go along with the other children in case I should be regarded as a "mama's boy". That was all the greater a risk since I was an only child. I suppose there must have been some language difficulties, because, at that stage, I spoke mostly Welsh and my knowledge of English was distinctly sketchy. Hardly any of the rest of my companions spoke any Welsh, so communication may have been something of a problem. But I must have been able to make myself understood and grasp what was being said to me, because I don't remember any difficulties or misunderstandings, except on that memorable occasion when the girl next door, who was some years older than I was and had constituted herself my unofficial guardian, was trying to get me to look at the cows up on the hill, and what she came out with for "up on the hill" was "lan llofft" ("upstairs"). I confess that I was for a moment pretty puzzled. In the school itself, however, there were at least three of the teachers who would have been able to help me by speaking Welsh. They were all ladies, and all of them were very kind. There were the Miss Morgans - always distinguished as "Miss Morgan Fat" and "Miss Morgan Thin". The former was, indeed, a comfortably upholstered lady, very jolly and good-natured. I was a bit of a favourite with her, though I didn't altogether care for the way she rather enjoyed hugging me. The other Miss Morgan was much more sparely built and rather austere-looking, though I must say I always found her very kind. As if one pair of ladies with the same name were not enough, the other two on the staff were both called Jones. The one was "Miss Jones the Governess", who was the headmistress, and the other was Miss Winnie Jones, who was an extremely good pianist. They were all very well adapted to infants' school teaching and they created a lovely warm atmosphere in the school.

I can't truthfully pretend to remember much of what they taught me. I recall, of course, the solemn intoning of the tables - "twice one is two, twice two are four", and so on. I didn't like "sums" much and wasn't very good at them, nor am I still! But I do recall the joy of learning to read and what immense pleasure it gave me to be able to do so. I was a very avid reader from an early age. I remember better the wide range of games we used to play in the yard: "Touch", "Fox and Hounds", "Hide and Seek", "Highbacks" (i.e. leapfrog), and many others. What comes back to me more vividly than almost anything else is one of the favourite games we played in the open space that ran around all the school buildings. This we used as a kind of D.I.Y. running track. We would divide up into two teams, each captained by the two biggest and strongest boys - two heroes called Frank Jennings and Clifford Sims. Frank was my "captain" and I hero-worshipped him. The teams were roughly equal in attainments, and we would take it in turns, one from each team, to run around the yard in opposite directions, in a sort of glorified relay race. As I was one of the slowest runners, my turn always came near the end. That left me in a fever of anxiety, hoping that some of the stronger runners in my outfit would have built up enough of a lead to ensure that I wouldn't have the humiliation of ending up last. It didn't always work.

The great wide world outside didn't impinge very much on our innocent pursuits. What Thomas Gray wrote of the pupils of Eton College might equally well have been said of us:

175

The little victims play.
No sense have they of ills to come,
Nor care beyond today.

But even then, there were some events which created infinite excitement among us. One was Cardiff City's appearance in the Cup Final. I don't believe any of us knew very much about Cardiff City's footballing champions, but we were all passionately partisan in our support of them. The delight we experienced in their victory over The Arsenal was quite intoxicating. If, as was widely rumoured, the Welshman who kept goal for The Arsenal had deliberately let the ball into his net, then I'm afraid our biased opinion was, so much the better. Another sporting contest which aroused great concern was the heavyweight contest between Gene Tunney and Jack Dempsey. We knew even less about these two gladiators than about Cardiff, but we were deeply divided this time in our allegiance. Some were dedicated to Dempsey, others to Tunney. I was myself a Dempsey man and was deeply disconsolate when he lost. Another bitter disappointment to me was when the Welshman, Parry Jones, lost the world land speed record to Malcolm Campbell. I had two toy racing cars: one a model of "Babs" (Parry Jones) and the other of "Bluebird" (Campbell). When I "raced" them against each other, "Babs" invariably triumphed.

A very different event that we all knew about and discussed earnestly was the General Strike of 1926. There were all sorts of rumours flying around about soldiers being brought in, what their role and that of the police would be, and what sort of injuries they might inflict. In a working-class area, our sympathies were very much on the side of the strikers. My grandparents lived round the corner from us and I used to call in there on my way home from school. My grandfather had in his younger days been a collier, but had had to give up work underground because it affected his eyesight so badly. His reaction to the news about the soldiers interested me very much. "Oh!" he said in deeply resentful tones, "the government has always been doing that sort of thing." Then he went on to tell me in graphic terms the story of Dic Penderyn and the Merthyr Riots of 1831, and how soldiers had been sent to Merthyr by the government of the day "to shoot innocent people", as he put it. It was my first lesson in local social history; not exactly unbiased, perhaps, but it fired my imagination and I never forgot it. At that time I was my grandparents' only grandchild and I was greatly indulged, not to say spoiled, by them. It was my practice to call in on them briefly on my way home from school to see what they were having for dinner (it was years before the term "lunch" ever entered my vocabulary). Then I went on home to see what Mother had prepared, and if I didn't fancy it as much as what they were having in Mamgu's, back I would go to my original port of call and eat with them. My mother was a superb cook, but even so, there were some kinds of meals which appealed to me much less than others.

I adored both my grandparents and I loved spending time with them. My grandfather was a very good singer, and in his boyhood had been bosom friends with the celebrated Dowlais musician, Harry Evans. In later life, Harry was rather cross with Tadcu because he wouldn't take musical training more seriously. But he took it seriously enough to practise regularly at home, and there were few things I liked better than to listen to him rattle off some of his favourite arias. As a result, I acquired a reasonable working knowledge of many of the favourite baritone solos from operas and oratorio - "Total Eclipse", "It is enough", "Honour and Arms", "O ruddier than the cherry", as well as old Welsh favourites like "Merch y Cadben" ("The Captain's Daughter") . But the one I liked best of all was the "Torreador's Song" from *Carmen*. Not only the rousing and dramatic aria itself, but also the narrative of the opera as supplied by my grandfather. He was a highly intelligent man, who made a point of studying the words very carefully and, better still, of acquiring a knowledge of the story and the dramatic situation unfolded in the opera or the oratorio. I think the version he gave me of the amorous Carmen's affaires was suitably edited for a youthful listener, but I found the whole episode very gripping. Some fifty years later, my wife and I visited Seville. As we stood on the bank of the River Guadalquivir opposite the main entrance to the bull-ring, I gazed nostalgically on the charming little statue of Carmen that stands there. It took me back immediately to those occasions when I listened spellbound to my grandfather, as I was first being introduced to that young *femme fatale*'s tragic career being rehearsed for me by him all those years before.

My grandmother, like my grandfather, had a keen ear for music and a good voice, as indeed did my mother and all her family. It was they who, unbeknown, first planted in me a deep love for music, especially for the human voice, which I have treasured all my life. As I've got older, I've become more and more dependent on the joy and solace that music can bring. I was also fortunate that my grandparents, like my parents, had many books around the house; far more, I think, than were usual in many working-class homes at that time. I was an eager and voracious reader, and they encouraged me to be so. My father, particularly, enjoyed reading and he readily shared his love of it with me, though I have to admit that many of the books in which he delighted - weighty theological tomes - were not altogether to my taste. I much preferred it when he brought novels or travel books home from the library. One of the features of my grandparents' little private "lending library" was that they had a number of the classical novels of the last century on their shelves - works by Dickens, Scott, Thackeray, *John Halifax Gentleman*, *The Last Days of Pompeii*, and the like. I wouldn't want to suggest that I read these while I was in the infants' school, but I was certainly deeply into them from about the age of seven or eight onwards.

By that time I had moved up to the "big school." How well I remember the staff there; especially those who taught me, but also many of those who didn't. The headmaster then was J. Moseley Jones, a short, sturdily-built man, with twinkling eyes, a bald head, and a rosy-apple complexion. He was a delightful personality, who retained his youthful sense of mischief until his death at the age of ninety. He retired within two or three years of my coming into the school, and was succeeded by a man of very different type - George Brown, tall, strict, and rather austere and forbidding. Most of us found the contrast between him and Mr. Jones a bit painful, and we went in great awe of Mr. Brown. The first of my class-teachers was Richard ("Dick") Humphreys. He was a nice man in many respects, but he'd had a very bad time in the first world war and his temper could be a bit fragile. He and I normally got on very well, but one day, he blew his fuse and threw a book at a boy sitting in front of me. Wisely, the intended victim ducked, and the book struck me on the side of the face. I'm sure that Dick was more upset by the incident than I was, but my mother was understandably more put out than anyone. She always insisted for years afterwards that, whenever I was tired or unwell, the mark used to show up on my face. I think if she hadn't reminded me, I should probably have forgotten the incident long ago.

Among the other men on the staff, not one of whom actually taught me, were ?Edward Chapman, Goronwy Griffiths, and Goronwy Williams. Griffiths was a lively, athletic figure, and a keen tennis player. Williams was a shorter, stouter man, with a most genial Pickwickian smile. I always liked him very much, perhaps because he made a great fuss of me as one of the few who could speak Welsh to him. I was also good at reciting, and he liked getting me to perform for him. I was genuinely sorry to see him leave when he got promoted to a headship in another school.

There were two ladies who taught me: Miss Lilian Webb in Standard Two and Miss Gwladys Davies in Standards Three, Four and Five. So much emphasis used to be placed on the "scholarship" class in those days that it was the practice in Pant to provide greater continuity by having the same teacher to take the class through for two or three years. I could hardly have been more fortu-

178

nate in my teacher. She was in early middle age, with an air of calm, natural authority. There were never any discipline problems, nor any suggestion of the use of the cane. She had an instinctive gift for imparting knowledge in a thorough, but interesting, fashion. while she made sure that we were all thoroughly drilled in "sums" and "composition", both of which made up the staple fare of the scholarship examination, she obviously took a much broader and more humane view of what education was supposed to be concerned with. She interested us in all sorts of wider topics, and would, for example, encourage us to read Arthur Mee's *Children's Newspaper*. She was also very keen to get us to express ourselves effectively - orally and in writing. I remember, too, how she took us to the rare Shakespearean productions that came to the Temperance Hall in Merthyr on the odd occasion. I owe her an enormous debt, and I still hold her in the highest esteem and affection. The one thing that surprises me is that, although she spoke Welsh very well herself and regularly attended Gwernllwyn Welsh Independent Chapel, I don't recall her ever teaching us any Welsh. Admittedly, most of the children in the class knew little or no Welsh, and that may have convinced her that there was not much point in trying to do so. The other consideration may have been that it wouldn't have helped us at all in our preparation for the "scholarship" examination, and might even have served to distract our attention.

That "scholarship" loomed large in our lives, of course. But, on looking back now, I'm not at all sure that it dominated our existence to the extent critics of the old system have claimed it did. I still remember very vividly the day of the actual examination. Those of us who wanted to enter the "Castle" School had to go to Cyfarthfa Castle in Merthyr to sit the examination, and appropriate arrangements were made to transport us there in good time. The grandiose setting of that mock-medieval castle in which the Crawshays had once lorded it were rather offputting, with its tall, crenellated towers and its high ceilings. To make matters more scarifying, as the first part of the examination was proceeding during the morning, there was a violent thunderstorm, hardly calculated to concentrate the young aspirants' minds wonderfully on the serious academic business in hand. It certainly wasn't a very propitious ambience for me, because most of that session was taken up with arithmetic, which was at best not my forte.

We lunched in the school canteen, and I found myself sitting next to a senior prefect presiding at the head of the table. He was very amiable and he conversed freely with us in an effort to make us feel at home, I imagine. His name, I discovered, was Vivian Davies, and I think he must have been about eighteen years of age. With his fresh complexion, neatly-combed and brilliantined fair hair, and dressed in dashing plus fours, he seemed to me to be a veritable demi-god. I had always been under the impression that only the very smart and well-to-do wore clothes as modish as that! Imagine how much further his stock went up in our estimation when we learned that he played rugby and cricket for the school, represented them at athletics, and intended to go on to college. Odd how much detail one recalls from an encounter that could not have lasted more than about three-quarters of an hour.

Back in, then, to the afternoon session, when my spirits were raised notably by the requirements of the essay and the questions on general knowledge. I thought I might have made some amends for the less-than-brilliant mathematical performance of the morning. I emerged, feeling that, with a bit of luck, I might just scrape in somewhere in the lower half of the list of successful candidates. We now had to find our way home, no transport having been arranged for us. Two of my closest friends, Ron Evans and Arthur Kenvin, and I proceeded to catch a tram running from Cefn to Pontmorlais and there caught another tram up to Dowlais. It took us an age to complete that odyssey, and I began to have some worries about whether it would take as long as that to get home every day in the event of my eventually going to Cyfarthfa School.

In due course, the results of the fateful test were made known. To no one's surprise, my friend, Ron Evans, topped the list for the whole of the borough. He was an extraordinarily able and versatile boy, who was to go on to pursue a very distinguished academic career. Very much to my own surprise, I found that I'd come next on the list. I could only conclude that the essay and the general knowledge questions had compensated for what I knew perfectly well had been a distinctly indifferent showing on the "sums". Still, there it was; I was now set for the next stage in my educational pilgrimage. The cloud-capped towers of Cyfarthfa Castle beckoned.